The politics of
health in Europe

MANCHESTER
UNIVERSITY PRESS

European Policy Research Unit Series

Series Editors: *Simon Bulmer* and *Mick Moran*

The European Policy Research Unit Series aims to provide advanced textbooks and thematic studies of key public policy issues in Europe. They concentrate, in particular, on comparing patterns of national policy content, but pay due attention to the European Union dimension. The thematic studies are guided by the character of the policy issue under examination.

The European Policy Research Unit (EPRU) was set up in 1989 within the University of Manchester's Department of Government to promote research on European politics and public policy. The Series is part of EPRU's effort to facilitate intellectual exchange and substantive debate on the key policy issues confronting the European states and the European Union.

Titles in the series also include:

The governance of the Single European Market Kenneth Armstrong and Simon Bulmer

Immigration and European integration Andrew Geddes

Mass media and media policy in Western Europe Peter Humphreys

The regions and the new Europe ed. Martin Rhodes

The European Union and member states ed. Dietrich Rometsch and Wolfgang Wessels

Political economy of financial integration in Europe Jonathan Story and Ingo Walter

The politics of
health in Europe

Richard Freeman

Manchester University Press

Manchester and New York

distributed exclusively in the USA by St. Martin's Press

The right of Richard Freeman to be identified as the author of this work has been assserted by him in accordance with the Copyright, Designs and Patents Act 1988.

Published by Manchester University Press
Oxford Road, Manchester M13 9NR, UK
and Room 400, 175 Fifth Avenue, New York, NY 10010, USA
http://www.man.ac.uk/mup

Distributed exclusively in the USA by
St. Martin's Press, Inc., 175 Fifth Avenue, New York,
NY 10010, USA

Distributed exclusively in Canada by
UBC Press, University of British Columbia, 6344 Memorial Road,
Vancouver, BC, Canada V6T 1Z2

British Library Cataloguing-in-Publication Data
A catalogue record for this book is available from the British Library

Library of Congress Cataloging-in-Publication Data applied for

ISBN 0 7190 4213 5 *hardback*
     0 7190 4214 3 *paperback*

First published 2000

06 05 04 03 02 01 00   10 9 8 7 6 5 4 3 2 1

Typeset in Sabon
by Servis Filmsetting Ltd, Manchester
Printed in Great Britain
by Bookcraft (Bath) Ltd, Midsomer Norton

Contents

List of tables and boxes

Tables

Boxes

Preface

This is a book about health, politics and Europe.

Why health?

Health matters, more than it ever did. Simply, it has become one of the core concerns of contemporary western societies. For most of their members, and for most of the time, such societies have long since established the conditions under which basic needs – for the physical security of food and shelter – are met. Now, health is pursued in affluence and at leisure, both by individuals and by the societies to which they belong (the irony being that health seems to matter most to the most healthy societies). Concerns about health shape decisions about the food we eat, for example, and about how we spend our leisure time. Aerobics classes reflect our concern for physical fitness just as bovine spongiform encephalopathy (BSE) testifies to our anxieties about risks to health. The medical ethics of birth (abortion, genetic screening) and death (euthanasia) are frequent and recurrent news items. In soaps as much as in documentaries, our media indicate that we are as concerned with health, illness and medicine as with law, crime and policing.

The social significance of health correlates with its economic importance. In Europe at least, almost all governments guarantee almost all of the costs of acute medical care to almost all of their citizens. This means that one of the largest single components of government spending in advanced industrial countries, after transfers, is that devoted to health care. This kind of welfare spending has helped to fuel the development of service-based, post-industrial economies. Health care is labour intensive, making the health sector a key area of employment as well as consumption. In terms of production, medical technology and pharmaceuticals companies are vital elements of the changing economies of western countries.

Why politics?

Social and economic activity of this scale is inevitably political, too. This means several things. To describe them as political is to recognise that health issues are distributive issues, in which what is at stake is, in Lasswell's phrase, 'who gets what, when, how'. This 'what' – health and health care – is a highly prized and very expensive commodity, which means, in turn, that the distribution of health goods is likely to be subject to intense conflict. In turn, again, the resolution of such conflict is likely to be incomprehensible without reference to some concept of power, whether it be power to enforce compliance with a particular decision, to set a policy agenda, or to shape the less conscious perceptions and demands of social and economic actors in much more subtle ways. The corollary of all this, again almost inevitably, is that health politics in the twentieth century is characterised by the increasing involvement of the state. The right of access to health care has become a defining term of democratic citizenship. Across countries, the greatest proportion of health spending is derived from public sources. Health issues are processed by public bureaucracies in generally routinised if sometimes unpredictable ways.

It is this public aspect which determines the particular focus of this book. A framework for understanding the politics of health and health care is set out in chapter 1, and the increasing scope of state responsibility is described and discussed in chapter 2. The distinctive institutional configurations of the health care state in Europe are assessed in chapters 3 (national health services) and 4 (social insurance systems) in turn. These provide descriptive accounts of the way health systems are organised in different countries but also give some indication, in a political sense, of the ways they work.

That said, the book is necessarily eclectic in terms of the disciplines on which it draws. Writing about doctors and patients in different countries (chapters 6 and 7), for example, means taking up problems and issues in medical sociology. And because, since the late 1970s, it is the cost of health care which has concerned governments most, the book also reflects a widespread concern of health policy research with problems of health economics. Economics figures here, however, less in respect of the analysis of resource flows than in terms of broader, explanatory theorising. Chapter 5 shows how, to some extent, health care reform can be understood as path dependent, just as the decisions of economic actors can be seen as contingent on previous ones. In chapter 6, the relationship between the medical profession and the state is treated as one of countervailing powers in which, as Galbraith wrote of markets, power on one side creates opportunities and potential rewards for the other. In chapter 7, now following Hirschman, user behaviour is conceptualised as the expression of exit, voice and loyalty. Other chapters take up the more general, interdisciplinary idea of the system, first introduced in chapter 1; it is used to understand government attempts to reform health care (chapter 5) and redefine responsibilities for public health (chapter 8).

The book is explicitly comparative, and comparison is essential to the analyses it develops. Any study with more than one case can be described as comparative, although in politics 'comparison' is generally (and loosely) taken to mean cross-national study. In social science, this kind of work is by no means exclusive to politics, but is perhaps most fully developed there: it is the method which politics has made its own. This cross-national, comparative approach inclines the material to a secondary literature based in politics, just as the disciplinary framework which politics provides reinforces its comparative approach.

Conventionally, comparison is taken to have two essential goals, evaluation and explanation. Evaluation is the concern with what works. At least part of the logic of comparative work is that we can establish who does things best and then do likewise. Are tax-based health care systems cheaper and more effective than insurance-based ones, for example? If they are, though, does it necessarily follow that more expensive systems should – let alone could – be reformed? 'Lesson learning' is an essential part of the rationale of comparative inquiry, but lessons are in practice difficult to identify, and even more difficult to learn.

Explanation is the concern to work out why things happen as they do. One reading of comparative analysis is that it is the closest social science can get to experimentation and the methodological paradigms of 'real' (natural) science. All comparative research can be formulated as hypothesis testing. Universal access to health care might be the outcome of political pressure by organised labour, for example. Then take a set of countries where health care and labour have been organised in different ways, and see what connection there might be. At best, this makes for useful and exciting theory-building. At worst – often – too many other variables intervene. Different countries show different levels of economic development; some political systems are more responsive to reform pressure than others, and capital as well as labour is organised in different ways. At the same time, the general scope of comparison across countries cannot help but miss some of the detail of particular national experience. What this means in practice is that we should be wary of expecting too much from comparative analysis. Its value lies in its generation of mid-range theory, of the form which explains why A is more like B and less like C. Its real virtue, in doing this, is its prompting new reflection both on the meaning of specific circumstance and on the applicability of grander social theorising.

There is another, perhaps even prior purpose to comparative research, too, one which is probably more widely and more casually adopted, but because of that much less explicitly acknowledged and considered. This has to do with exploration. One of the first impulses to look at how they do things in other countries is simply because it's interesting. We like to know what they do there, it's interesting but different, interesting because different. And then we realise that, at some level, it's much the same. A central aim of this book is simply to explore the different ways in which different countries do similar things, to describe the pattern of difference-within-similarity that is health politics in Europe.

Why Europe?

The book is explicitly concerned with the liberal democracies (which are also advanced industrial economies) of western Europe. Its focus is European partly for the same reason that it is comparative, which is to avoid some of the limitations of single country studies. As a comparative work its perspective is different (which, as implied, is really only to say that it is limited in different ways).

The countries covered in detail here – Italy, Sweden and the UK, and France and Germany – constitute a purposive sample. As chapter 1 explains, the distinction between national health services and social insurance systems is not real, but an abstract formulation which makes a wealth of information more manageable. Choosing these countries makes sense not because they are somehow representative of general types but because, between them, they are indicative of particular sets of problems in the politics of health and health care.

The working assumption here is that the public provision of health care is embedded in a distinctively European politics. It is predicated on a highly developed economic capacity and highly sophisticated modes of social organisation. For this reason, the scope of most cross-national studies of the health sector is restricted to advanced industrial countries, simply for the sake of comparability. Health politics in the developing world, for example, betrays very different problems and concerns, which are managed in very different ways. But health care in Europe also embodies a particular set of expressly political assumptions about the state, its responsibilities and the rights of citizenship. To varying degrees, these hold in other developed nations, too, such as Australia, Canada, Japan and New Zealand. New Zealand has some claim to having established the first National Health Service, in 1938. Health care in the US, by contrast, though a much more public system than rhetoric often allows, is significantly less so than its European counterparts. Within Europe, too, there are exceptions to the pattern discussed in this book, Switzerland being perhaps the most significant. Nevertheless, the argument here is that the general, economic, social, cultural and political characteristics of west European countries are distinctive, if not necessarily or wholly exclusive to them. These countries tend to be among the world's biggest economies; they are among its oldest established liberal democracies; they afford its most extensive social rights. They are what are sometimes referred to as the 'mature' welfare states, which perhaps means only that they have struggled longest with the pains of growing up. Those struggles are the subject of this book.

Acknowledgements

My understanding of the comparative analysis of health policy and politics has been enriched by discussion with a network of researchers which met at the European Consortium for Political Research (ECPR) Joint Sessions of Workshops in Madrid in 1994 and Oslo in 1996. I have felt lucky to belong. Viola Burau, George France, Peter Garpenby, Fiona Mackay, Richard Parry, David Wilsford and Bruce Wood read and commented on different parts of the manuscript, offering invaluable judgement and making important corrections. It goes without saying that any remaining errors of fact and interpretation are my own.

Many of the earliest drafts of this book were first used in teaching in the universities of Edinburgh and Dundee. Students at both institutions saw and dutifully made sense of the worst of it, and the final product is better than it would have been without them.

I owe an enormous debt to my series editor, Michael Moran. Its intellectual measure is clear from the books and papers cited in the following pages. But it is a professional and not least personal one, too.

Manchester University Press has been extraordinarily patient. Richard Purslow commissioned the book; Nicola Viinikka is the last in a series of editors and assistants who have worked on it. I am grateful to all of them for their continuing commitment and support.

Material which first appeared in Ranade, W. (ed.) *Markets and Health Care. A comparative analysis*, Longman, 1998, is reproduced here by permission of Pearson Education Limited. Material which appeared in Clasen, J. (ed.) *Comparative Social Policy. Concepts, theories and methods*, 1999, is used by permission of Blackwell Publishers.

*Morag, Helen
and Christopher*

1

Health politics

This first chapter is about the concept of the health system. If a system can be described as a set of relationships between a set of things, then this chapter is about the things which together constitute the health sector in advanced industrial societies, and about the ways in which they interact. The purpose of the chapter is to establish an intellectual framework for the chapters which follow. Its material is drawn from medical sociology, health economics and political theory. To use a linguistic analogy, it is concerned with the grammar and vocabulary of health policy and politics. The chapter tries to convey both the complexity and the essential simplicity of the health political arena. It does so by addressing a series of simple questions: what is a health system?; what different sorts or types of health system exist?; how do they work?

Health care delivery: doctors, managers and patients

For present purposes, the health system can be disaggregated into subsystems of delivery, finance and regulation. These might be described as the functional processes of the health sector. At the centre of the delivery of health care are those qualified to practise medicine – doctors. The power of doctors or physicians consists in their control over patient care; this means, in turn, that they determine the use of resources in health care. They control admissions to hospital, levels of treatment and length of stay. They also create demand for capital costs, such as investment in new technology. Typically, by organising as a profession, doctors have sought to establish and maintain independent, collective control over the clinical or technical content of their work, and over the social and economic conditions under which it is carried out. That said, important divisions exist within medical professions in Europe, notably between hospital medicine and independent local practice. In the UK, the distinction between local practice and hospital medicine corresponds to a division between general practice and clinical specialisms. This is unusual; a common pattern in Europe (and North America) is for patients to consult specialists directly, in their own local practices.

If (because) the doctor is the central figure in health care, the hospital is the central location. Its changing role – and that of health care as such – is expressed in its architectural transition from church to warehouse to factory (Turner 1987). In the early modern era, care of the sick was often a special duty of certain holy orders. Later, the Poor Law institutions and asylums of the nineteenth century served to isolate and contain the sick. In the twentieth century, the hospital has had as much in common with the factory and the leisure centre as with any of its previous incarnations. It has been the stronghold of medical scientific expertise and professional power and the site of the most intensive use of resources, in terms of both labour and technology. In most European countries, some hospitals are operated by local or regional government, some by independent charitable foundations and some are run as businesses. The mix between sectors varies across countries.

Hospitals are subject to parallel structures of medical and managerial authority. The specific treatment decisions made by doctors in respect of individual patients are aggregated by administrators who maintain the resource flows within and between institutions. A degree of conflict between doctors and health care managers is endemic. As Björkman puts it, 'The primary decision-making struggle exists between physicians and administrators, a contest which effectively orders all other intergroup relations within the hospital ... physicians order relations through issuing medical orders, while administrators order relations by managing resources through a hierarchical chain of command' (Björkman 1989, p. 49). And just as hospital organisation might be described as a 'negotiated order' (Strauss *et al.* 1963, Turner 1987), so the health system as a whole can be said to represent a compromise between medical professional authority and rational public administration. The relationship between doctors and government is the subject of chapter 6 (below).

The doctor–manager dyad is cross-cut by that between doctor and patient. The therapeutic relationship is one conducted between individuals, in a peculiarly intimate yet rule-bound domain. The medical encounter is governed by rules of confidentiality and referral, certification and payment, in which power and authority are invested in the doctor rather than the patient. Where medical power is immediate and specific, that of the users of health care is indirect and remote. Some influence is won by virtue of the patient also being a taxpayer and voter. Users' political behaviour is examined more closely in chapter 7.

Health care finance: salaries and fees, taxes and contributions

Different ways of paying for health care necessarily involve different constellations of political and institutional actors, each with their own sets of interests to promote and defend. Financial flows in the health sector are important because they indicate lines of administrative and managerial responsibility: to this extent, money is a marker for power. Differences in the ways in which doctors are paid, for example, often express differences in professional status: hospital posts are usually salaried, while doctors in local practice usually derive their income from fee-for-service or capitation payments. The significance of this is that while fee-for-service payment tends to maximise doctors' earnings opportunities, salaried status implies that professionals are employees rather than independent contractors and that their work is potentially subject to organisational control. Similarly, hospitals may hold an annual global budget for the treatment and care they provide, and this may be set either prospectively or retrospectively, or they may receive what are known as *per diem* payments for each day a bed is filled by a patient. Different systems provide different incentives and different degrees of control to hospital managers (Gray 1993).

The simplest form of financial transaction in the health sector is one in which the patient pays the doctor directly for a service provided. In many countries, many patients pay small direct charges: for pharmaceuticals, for example, and sometimes for consultations. In almost all countries, however, almost all payment for health care is mediated by a third party. In most European countries, a proportion of the users of health services (usually a minority) has private insurance cover. In some countries, however, most services for most people are financed by government from revenue raised through general taxation, as in the UK. In others, such as Germany, the majority of users are compulsorily insured against health care costs (and against loss of earnings through sickness) under a social insurance scheme. Social insurance blends the major characteristics of each of the other two payment mechanisms: 'The very name *social insurance* reveals its dual nature: *social* denotes tax-like properties, while *insurance* embodies premium-like qualities' (Bodenheimer and Grumbach 1992, p. 447, emphasis in original).

The key distinction between social and private insurance is that membership of social insurance schemes tends to be compulsory where private insurance arrangements are voluntary. Private insurance premia tend to be risk-rated, meaning that payments are calculated to reflect the different levels of risk – related to age and sex, for example – of different individuals falling ill. Social insurance contributions reflect the collective risk of insured members, that is, the general liability of a fund. The important difference between funding health care by general taxation and by social insurance is that insurance contributions are usually both clearly identified and hypothecated, that is, specifically linked to health spending (Moran 1992). This has political costs as well as benefits: though social insurance payments are effectively 'pseudo-taxes' which enable governments to raise revenue for health care without being made accountable for health spending, they also make the cost of health care much more visible, creating political pressure as soon as they start to rise more quickly than wages.

Health care regulation: markets, hierarchies and networks

This serves to show that health systems are complicated, composed of a multiplicity of actors carrying out a variety of functions in a variety of ways. The relationships between them can be managed in different ways, too. The principal modes of coordinating or regulating health care systems are by competition, by command or central direction, and through organisational networks.[1]

In liberal capitalist countries, like those of western Europe, a large number of goods and services are allocated in markets. Relationships between producers, and between producers and consumers, are regulated or governed by price competition. The delivery and financing of health services, however, differs in important ways from the production and consumption of market goods. The supply and demand of health services are not directly regulated by price, since they are generally paid for by third parties such as governments and insurance funds. This means that both providers and users of health care (doctors and patients) are insulated from the immediate cost implications of their decisions. At the same time, demand for health services is controlled less by the claims of users than by the judgement of providers, that is, by the physicians who make decisions about treatment and referral (Björkman 1989, above). The informational asymmetry at the heart of medical care makes for the economic quirk of supplier induced demand: it is the doctor or service provider who, in most instances, decides which services the patient should receive. More generally, the demand for health care, which is an expression of the morbidity and mortality of individuals and populations, is itself essentially uncertain. Individuals cannot know whether or not they might become ill, when they might need treatment, or how much it might cost. Private health insurance represents one response to to this problem, but it generates secondary problems of moral hazard and adverse selection and there is no comparable mechanism for financing externalities (Le Grand, Propper and Robinson 1992).[2] It is for these reasons that the health sector is seen to exhibit signs of 'market failure'.

One response to market failure is to increase the role and responsibilities of the state (chapters 2 and 5, below). Taking health care facilities into public ownership makes it possible to control them directly, which usually entails a sophisticated form of administrative organisation or bureaucracy. The archetypal definition of bureaucracy is Weber's: he specifies a single, continuous organisation of functions, bound by rules and operating in a defined sphere of competence, in which a lower office is supervised by and answerable to a higher one (Weber, repr. Thompson *et al.* 1991). Effective administration of this kind is normally associated with a high degree of information gathering and strategic planning. However, the failings of the market are not necessarily corrected by the workings of the state. Bureaucracies are stable systems, but they also tend to be exclusive and inflexible. Public monopolies may promote equity in their application of standard rules and procedures, but they may have less incentive to seek or maintain productive efficiency than market enterprises, and may be less inclined to innovate. Professional monopolies may be self-serving, even while they guarantee certain standards of service to patients. Public subsidy for health care may resolve the issue of externalities (above), but it may also generate excess demand.

Sometimes, relationships between actors and institutions in the health sector may be regulated with little direct reference either to the market or to the state. The stability of systems is maintained by networks, sets of organisations connected to each other by more or less formalised relationships of mutual dependence. Here as in markets and hierarchies, however, the basis of decision-making may remain less than transparent to the users of health care (who are also, through their taxes and contributions, those who pay for it). In many countries, and for long periods of time, the health sector has remained an arena of private government.

Though the balance between state and market is struck in different countries in different ways, these underlying tensions mean that it remains a persistent source of health political conflict almost everywhere. What is at issue is the viability of different modes of coordination, in political as well as economic and functional terms. They may be taken separately, in their own right; more often, the point has been to find effective ways of combining them. This applies as much to relationships within organisations as between them. Private firms, including private hospitals, may be hierarchically or bureaucratically organised, just as much as public sector ones, and they have just as much need for planning. Similarly, governments may use market mechanisms to order the internal relations of what, at a general level, remain public services (chapter 5, below).

Different kinds of health system

Even in simplified form, the multiple variables presented here might seem to make for an almost exponential variety of arrangements for health care in different countries. Health care may be provided, financed and regulated (or governed) in different ways. It may be provided in hospitals or local practice, by specialists or by generalists; specialists may work in either location, while generalists, sometimes called family doctors, will usually work in local practice, either alone or in groups, or in multi-professional health centres. Different kinds of doctor will be paid in different ways. Hospitals may be owned by government or may operate for profit; many are non-profit making, independent foundations. Health care may be paid for out of general taxation or through insurance schemes, both public and private, while some spending can be attributed to 'out-of-pocket' payments by households. Finance and provision may be administered by different combinations of central, regional and local government, as well as parapublic, sector-specific agencies such as health authorities and sickness funds. Even if the therapeutic relationships at the heart of health care were relatively simple, the effect of detailed and difficult financial relationships in the health sector and the complex regulatory processes which accompany them would make for allocative systems of great complexity.

Health systems in Europe are indeed varied. Nevertheless, accounts of health policy and politics in Europe commonly refer to two principal types of health system: *national health services*, funded by general taxation, and *social insurance systems*, funded by payroll contributions. Tax-based finance tends to

imply universal coverage, the public ownership of health care facilities and a salaried medical profession. Insurance contributions, meanwhile, are paid into
funds organised by occupation or region. Funds contract with what is usually a
greater mixture of public and private providers of inpatient care, and with independent physicians paid according to the services they provide. Countries in the
centre of western Europe have social insurance systems (France, Germany and
Austria, and the Benelux countries), others have national health services
(Denmark, Sweden and the United Kingdom, Italy and Greece, Spain and
Portugal) (Weber 1990). That said, national health services were established
much later in southern Europe than in the UK and Scandinavia: in Italy in 1978,
in Portugal in 1979, in Greece in 1983 and in Spain in 1986. Here, it has been
argued that formally ambitious but underresourced social welfare programmes
amount to little more than an 'institutionalised promise' (Leibfried 1993, Parry
1995). In turn, recent studies of health policy in these countries suggest that they
represent a qualitatively different welfare politics, and that a 'third way' in southern Europe is becoming increasingly significant in comparative terms (Ferrera
1996a).

Classification of this kind is integral to comparative analysis, though it may
often remain implicit. It reflects a need to simplify the complex pattern of similarities and differences outlined above: classification, or descriptive modelling, is
a way of handling both commonality and variation without neglecting fundamental characteristics (Palme 1990). However, though the institutional landscape of health systems may look very different in different countries, they have
an essentially comparable geology. Different systems work in similar ways,
according to a common pattern, and they share common goals. Almost all
European countries seem to pursue a standard set of health policy objectives
including adequacy and equity in access, income protection, efficiency at both
macro and micro levels, a degree of freedom of choice for consumers and of
autonomy for providers (OECD 1992). In pursuing these aims, and whether they
are financed by taxation or by social insurance, nearly all countries guarantee
most of the costs of inpatient care to most of their citizens. This means, in turn,
that health systems are dominated by public spending, albeit to varying degrees,
and that most resources are concentrated on hospitals. Health care universalism
begins to break down as the focus of delivery moves away from the heartland of
the health system, the hospital, but it does so in most countries. Smaller proportions of populations are covered for smaller proportions of the costs of ambulatory care, medical goods and so on (Moran 1992).

Similarly, across countries health care is usually funded from a mixture of
sources, including taxation, national or social insurance, private insurance and
patient charges. Even the most strongly tax-based systems – Sweden is a good
example – have a significant insurance component, while mandated insurance
premiums are normally levied as payroll tax on employers and employees. The
point is not, after all, that there is any great distinction to be made between the
two principal methods of financing health care; rather, there is a wide range of

ways of raising public money to pay for health services. Fundamentally, the difference between tax-based and insurance-based systems is not as great as it is often made to seem. Taxation may be thought of as a form of compulsory insurance (Abel-Smith and Mossialos 1994), while insurance premiums are normally levied as a compulsory payroll tax on employers and employees. While different systems can sometimes be treated as though they represented different health care regimes they can also, at another level, be seen to represent little more than different forms of taxation. 'Taxes and premiums are not distinct entities; rather, a spectrum of financing methods exists with varying tax-like and premium-like features' (Bodenheimer and Grumbach 1992, p. 439).

This may imply that differences between countries in the organisation and financing of health provision simply do not matter very much (Fry 1991). Different systems exhibit a high degree of commonality, against which their specific organisational features are merely effects of the different political, economic and social structures of respective individual countries. But it also serves as a warning that health systems are not actually very systematic. Historically, they have been constituted in processes of often *post hoc* rationalisation by governments. The health system of any given country may be thought of as a number of systems – public and private, for example – superimposed one on the other, sometimes complementary, sometimes coexisting and sometimes competing. The parts do not necessarily cohere into a rational whole and it is important to be wary of introducing an artefactual rationalisation in the process of modelling. We look for order where there may be none, or at least less than we would like. What we refer to as 'systems' are really no more than packages or clusters of typical characteristics. Actual systems, of course, are only approximations to ideal types: no pure form exists, and all contemporary health systems are mixed. For this reason, it may be better to think of a range or spectrum of cases rather than discrete categories (cf., for example, Maxwell 1980). Furthermore, any simple description can only be a snapshot, while health systems have been in a considerable state of flux during the 1970s, 1980s and 1990s (chapters 3, 4 and 5, below).[3] Health systems are dynamic, continually adapting and readapting to the wider political, economic and social systems of which they are a part.

System, state and polity

The puzzle presented here is not one that needs to be resolved; it serves instead to point to the possibility of different approaches to comparing and contrasting health systems. When, around 1970, social and political scientists began to take an interest in the comparative analysis of health systems, their writing – perhaps inevitably – tended to be exploratory and descriptive (and sometimes also, uncertainly, evaluative) before establishing any analytic or explanatory purpose.[4] The field developed quickly during the 1980s as, in seeking better solutions to common problems of the health sector, governments and policy scientists began to look for understanding and insight from abroad. Research was preoccupied with the finance and organisation of health care, and in particular with the problem of cost control. This work was led by economists, and drew heavily on OECD data and publications. The categorisation of health systems according to their mechanisms of finance reflects this dominant interest in economic efficiency. As a result, comparative research in health policy and politics tends to have been concerned primarily with the internal administrative order of health systems – with different ways of regulating, financing and delivering medical care – at the expense of the relationship between the health system and its social, economic and political environment.

From an economic perspective, health policy appears a technical problem rather than a political one. More or less casually used, the notion of the *health system* tends to reinforce understandings of it in functional terms.[5] But the issue here is not that different modes of organisation make systems more or less expensive or efficient – though that is undoubtedly important – but that they have different political implications. One way of addressing these is by foregrounding the state. In this construction, the health system is coterminous with public (state) intervention: health policy problems are problems of and for the state. And because health problems are state problems, health systems may be understood as being embedded in those political processes of which the state forms a part.

Michael Moran defines the *health care state* as 'that part of any state concerned with regulating access to, financing, and organising the delivery of, health care to the population' (Moran 1992, p. 79). It has three aspects or 'faces' (Moran 1995a). It is of course a welfare state, concerned with patients' access to health services, with citizenship and with the appropriate extent of professional power. But it is also concerned with regulating and promoting industrial interests in pharmaceuticals and medical technology, and in some cases acts with regard to economic interests of its own. It may therefore be described as a capitalist industrial state. At the same time, it is a regulator of struggles between interest groups, both industrial and service-related. As a pluralist democratic state it institutionalises the distributive conflicts of health politics and policy making. 'To study the health care state,' therefore, 'we must examine it as the regulator of patient care conditions; as the participant in competition among producers of health care goods and services; and as the arena in which distributional conflicts occur' (Moran 1995a, p. 770). The provision of health care in advanced industrial societies, then, is not merely a functional system or even primarily an economic one, but is also and essentially a complicated political one.

But there are other dimensions of health politics perhaps not fully captured by the construct of the health care state. At the core of health systems are ultimately individualised relationships between doctor and patient and between doctor and manager, as the first part of this chapter tried to show. These relationships are marked by social divisions of class, race and gender, among others, by the activity of social movements and by the operation of social values. Power is exercised not only in and through the state, which means that, ultimately, the politics of health must be predicated on some concept of the social. In this vein, Daniel Fox thinks in terms of a *health polity*, which 'includes more people than providers and consumers of health services, more institutions than a health care delivery system. It is more than an aggregation of policies ... [it describes] the ways a community ... conceives of and organizes its response to health and illness' (Fox 1988, p. 316).[6] The attraction of this concept is that it allows for the social, yet retains a clear sense of the political. Health politics reflects the interests of state, market and community and the conflicts between them. At the heart of those conflicts, of course, remains the state; in the end it is the state which regulates conflict *per se*.

Understanding health politics

The categorical framework presented here so far points to a set of significant actors in health politics, both individual and collective, and to axes of intrinsic conflict. Conflict (and sometimes collaboration) occurs between doctors and patients, between those who provide and those who manage health services, between states and markets, between states and citizens, between those who raise health care finance and those who pay, between the sick and the well. These reveal the extent to which, in advanced industrial societies, issues of health, illness and health care are politicised. But how are these conflicts to be understood in any more systematic way? How do we understand the distribution and use of power in health systems? How far does the conceptual vocabulary of the health sector obey grammatical rules? If health politics can be likened to a game of multidimensional chess (Klein 1974),[7] what are the rules of this game? How can we make sense of the politics of health and health care?

Earlier in this chapter, health systems were described as distinctive bundles of medical, administrative and financial organisations. If institutional characteristics – these organisations and the more or less formal rules which link them – are the basis for distinguishing between different systems, then consequent theorising is also likely to be *institutionalist*. If institutional differences matter at the level of description, they will almost inevitably also matter at the level of explanation. Indeed, much recent comparative work emphasises the significance of political systems and institutions in shaping or defining the outcomes of pressure group activity.[8] This may be reinforced by arguments that the state itself has interests which it can advance and defend in struggles with groups. At the same time, however, we can only make sense of institutions in terms of their interaction with interests. The relationship between institutions and interests is an iterative one.

Given the position of doctors in the provision of health care, it is perhaps unsurprising that many analyses should begin (and sometimes end) with them. *Elite theory* – sometimes referred to as 'power group' explanations (Navarro 1989) – acknowledges the extent to which political power is unevenly distributed between interest groups, and that policy outcomes tend to be biased in favour of the most powerful or established interests – such as, here, medical professions. Perhaps the most widely used version of elite theory in health political research is Robert Alford's *structural interest theory* (Alford 1975). Structural interests, as Alford conceives them, are those served (or not served) by the way in which society is organised. They do not necessarily have to be organised into identifiable interest groups in order to find expression. Power is not shared equally between such interests; they may be described as dominant, challenging or repressed (Alford 1975). In health care, the dominant structural interest is that of the professions. While conflicts may occur within and between professional groups, the principle of professional monopoly and autonomy in the provision of health care continues to be protected. It has come to be challenged, nevertheless, by those concerned with the increasingly complex organisation and funding of health services. Members of this group include civil servants, hospital managers, insurance fund administrators and politicians. Meanwhile, the interests of health service users, that is of patients and the public, may be described as repressed (Alford 1975). Essentially, therefore, '[H]ealth care institutions,... must be understood in terms of a continuing struggle between major structural interests operating within the context of a market society – "professional monopolists" controlling the major health resources, "corporate rationalizers" challenging their power, and the community population seeking better health care via the actions of equal health advocates' (Alford 1975, p. xiv).

Groups' power may be established informally and de facto. Alternatively, the authority of specific groups in policy making may be formally licensed: such systems are referred to as *corporatist*. Corporate actors in the health sector may include unions and employers, as well as medical professions and health insurers. In different countries and in different ways, some of these not only seek to influence policy making, but are also charged by government with carrying it out (Cawson 1982). Schmitter's classic definition is of 'a system of interest representation in which the constituent units are organized into a limited number of singular, compulsory, noncompetitive, hierarchically ordered and functionally differentiated categories, recognised or licensed (if not created by) the state and granted a deliberate representational monopoly within their respective categories in exchange for observing certain controls on their selection of leaders and articulation of demands and supports' (Schmitter 1974). This involves states and groups in 'a structured relationship of mutual dependency' (Day and Klein 1992, note 7); chapter 6 (below) returns to this theme.

Pluralists conceive of the health sector in a different way, thinking of it simply as a multiplicity of interest groups competing for power. The implicit position of historical accounts of health policy making is often pluralist: narratives of negotiation and manoeuvring among ministers, civil servants and doctors' leaders are written as though they were unstructured competitions for influence, in which the state serves as a neutral arbiter of power. Pluralism appeals in its simplicity, and is sometimes seen, wrongly, as a default theory[9] Its strength lies in identifying the range and fragmentation of interests in the health sector:

health policy is shaped not only by payers and providers, but also by the industrial producers of health goods such as technical equipment and pharmaceuticals, by employers, by parties, and not least by the users of health care and the organisations and movements which represent them. Its weakness lies in its inability to address the consistent privileging of some interests over others.

Marxist accounts, by contrast, rest on the premise that health care is provided by households and by the state in the interests of capital. The class structure, individualist ideology and experience of alienation characteristic of capitalism are reproduced within health systems. The division of medical labour between doctors, nurses and ancillaries reflects the divisions of capitalist society along the lines of class, gender and race. Medicine reinforces individualist rather than social or structural explanations of health and disease, a process which in turn serves to buttress prevailing (capitalist) economic interests. Power and knowledge in health systems are seen to be held by medical professionals; individuals and groups are consequently disenfranchised, discouraged from taking control of the forces which determine their health. At the same time, the health sector represents a market for capitalist interests in medical technology and pharmaceuticals. The interdependence of government, military and the defence industry – the 'military–industrial complex' – is mirrored in the industrial penetration of the health sector, described in turn as the 'medical–industrial complex' (Ehrenreich and Ehrenreich 1971). The social and economic relations of advanced capitalist countries are manifest in their health care systems: 'The different types of funding and organization of health services are explained primarily by the degree to which ... differing class aims in the health sector ... have been achieved through the realization of class power relations' (Navarro 1989, p. 392).

Similar sorts of explanation can be based on gender, as well as on race. *Feminist* analyses show that medicine is one of the ways in which men assume power over women. This affects women both in terms of their status as health workers and in terms of their experience of health and illness. Medicine/patriarchy has extended its authority into such important areas of women's lives as sexuality and reproduction. Women's psychology, too, is frequently defined, through medicine, as unstable and abnormal. The medical division of labour, in which women become nurses and men become doctors, reflects patriarchal social relations. At the same time, racial divisions are impacted on those of gender and class. High proportions of manual grade employees – cleaning, catering and portering staff – come from marginalised ethnic and immigrant populations. Equally, these may be among the poorest and most disadvantaged sections of society, at once more susceptible to ill-health and less likely to gain access to health care. Since the end of the nineteenth century welfare provision has been a key aspect of nation-building, while access to health care has become a defining feature of citizenship. In the fields of genetics and reproduction in particular, and not only in Nazi Germany, modern medicine can be accused of pursuing racialised goals.

Central to these perspectives is the observation that health and social identity are connected in a fundamental, intimate way. Health and disease, like law, are ways of establishing community, of defining 'inside' and 'outside', of separating what is 'good' from what is 'bad'. Social divisions according to gender, ethnicity, sexuality and disability are reproduced in, and partly constructed by, systems of health care. That said, analyses of this kind are much more developed at the macro and micro levels than in the intermediate domain which cross-country comparison tends to occupy. They are the subject of exciting work in social theory and medical sociology, but remain as yet poorly defined in comparative research.

In many ways, health policy and politics might be read as quintessentially modern. The modern state is ambitious, confident and capable, its actions based on bodies of technocratic expertise such as engineering and law. Modern society is a mass society, reflecting in part its dominant modes of production and consumption, but also ideas about the parity of human beings. In all of this, health politics appears paradigmatic. Between the mid-nineteenth and mid-twentieth centuries, the provision and use of health care in Europe came to be based on medical professionalism and universal entitlement. The formation of the health care state was based in a politics of Left and Right, its consolidation in post-war consensus and economic growth. But by the end of the twentieth century, the sovereignty and capacity of the state, the status and value of scientific (including medical) knowledge and the nature and security of individual identity were each being called into question.

For all its promise, medicine seemed unable to counter contemporary threats to health such as heart disease, cancer and AIDS, as well as the common cold. Doctors themselves seemed distant, the profession exclusive and self-interested. There was a new interest in alternative or complementary therapies, often carried by new social movements. These, rather than established political parties, pressed the sectional claims of groups identified by gender, ethnicity and sexuality rather than class. As traditional solidarities broke down, the recognition of difference came to matter as much, if not more than the achievement of equality. The state itself was caught in what Daniel Bell has described as a mismatch of scale: it had become both 'too small for the big problems of life and too big for the small problems of life' (Bell 1987).[10] Contemporary political issues, including health issues, were at once more global and more local than the nation-state. The state began to reconfigure, and sometimes offload, the production and distribution of some of the goods and services it had relatively recently acquired, including transport, telecommunications and many welfare functions. At the same time, both public and private sector organisations had become increasingly complex, as evidenced by the proliferation of managerial tasks and posts. All of this makes for a very different, much more complicated and fragmented picture of the health political arena.

As with different conceptions of the health system, the point here is not to choose between different theoretical approaches. The purpose of this book is is not to look for any general, universally applicable understanding, but to develop specific analyses of diverse health political phenomena. In doing so, different chapters necessarily employ different analytic frames. There is no pursuit of any single explanation of health politics, not least because 'health politics' is no single thing. It is best to think of it as 'a complex of different if related arenas, with different if overlapping sets of actors' (Day and Klein 1992, p. 463). Different theories are applicable in different contexts, and are more or less powerful according to the problem to be explained.

Notes

1 For an introduction to ways of thinking about markets, hierarchies and networks, see Thompson *et al.* (1991).

2 '*Moral hazard* is the phenomenon that once a person is insured against an eventuality her actions may make it more likely to occur ... *Adverse selection* arises when insurance companies find it difficult to distinguish between good and bad risk individuals ... The consumption (or production) of a commodity is said to create an externality when a third party who is not involved in the decision to consume (or produce) it is none the less affected by it ... If the effect is adverse, it is described as an *external cost*; if it is beneficial, as an *external benefit*' (Le Grand, Propper and Robinson 1992, pp. 44 and 46, emphases in original). See Hsiao (1995) and Appleby (1998) for further introductions to market economics in health care.

3 Chapters 3 and 4 deal with national health services (Italy, Sweden and the UK) and social insurance systems (Germany and France) in turn. This is not because these countries' health systems constitute particular ideal types nor because it might establish which one is better than the other, but because it represents a way of raising a range of problems in the comparative analysis of health politics in western European countries.

4 In 1987, an extensive review of the field concluded that 'In general it can be said that the majority of the studies are descriptive. There is usually no clear model for analysis, even in those studies that in other respects could be classified as analytical. Models and theories are seldom dealt with' (Atteveld, Broeders and Lapré 1987, p. 108).

5 For a more strongly theorised account, see Field (1973). Chapters 5 and 8 (below) return to the idea of the health system as such, making more explicit use of it as an analytic tool.

6 Significantly, the idea is floated at the beginning of a discussion of the impact of AIDS on health policy in the US. It testifies to the problems of understanding political responses to a new health problem which broke the boundaries of many previous conceptions of the domain of health policy making and its dominant interests (chapter 8, below).

7 Cit. Heidenheimer (1979, p. 491).

8 For further discussion of institutionalism in comparative studies of health policy and politics, see Freeman (1999).

9 Interest in pluralism has recently been renewed; for (re)introductions, see Jordan (1990) and McLennan (1995).

10 A version of this paper was reprinted as 'The world in 2013', *New Statesman*, 18 December, 31–38, from which this reference is taken.

2

The health care state in Europe, 1880–1980

Introduction

By 1980, almost all European states guaranteed access to health care to almost all of their citizens. In 1880, none of them did. This chapter is concerned with the emergence and consolidation of the health care state, that agglomeration of public mechanisms for the finance, delivery and regulation of health care described in chapter 1. To be sure, state activity in each case had its precedents, in most cases reaching back much further than the previous century. In scope and intensity, however, these are far outweighed by the intervention which followed. It is the hundred-year period of increasing state involvement – what might be described as the *étatisation* of health and health care – which is addressed in this chapter, and which forms the background to the contemporary health politics explored in the ones which follow. The material is necessarily schematic: the aim is not to provide a comprehensive history, but to look for some simplicity in a topic of enormous complexity.

Its role is to substantiate two of the claims made at the beginning of this book. The first is that health care in Europe is now more public than private: a standard OECD typology describes 'public reimbursement', 'public contract' and public integrated' systems (Hurst and Poullier 1992). This kind of classification is discussed in chapter 1, and taken up again in chapters 3 and 4; what is significant here is that the 'public' epithet is common to each type. State intervention has become an intrinsic aspect of contemporary health care, and this chapter begins to show how and why.

Until the eighteenth century, however, European states were more preoccupied with their own existential need for security, broadly conceived: with defence and foreign affairs, and with law enforcement. The prime domestic concern was to raise sufficient tax revenue to finance those activities. The nineteenth century brought greater attention to economic development, including investment in transport and communications, and support for industry. In the twentieth century, social programmes such as health, education and social security have come to constitute the bulk of states' regulatory and administrative activity (Rose 1996). Across countries, these areas currently absorb the largest part of public spending, and form the largest area of public employment. The second claim, then, is that, owing to the relative size and complexity of the health sector, developments there exemplify and embody the projects and problems not only of the welfare state more generally, but indeed of the state as such. The central-ity of the state in health care is reflected in the centrality of health care to the functioning of the state.

The chapter begins by briefly describing developments in different countries. It then explores the introduction of compulsory health insurance in Europe, and the concomitant establishment of medical professional authority. It discusses the universalisation of access to health care, a process which was sometimes incre-mental and sometimes more radical but which was in each case more or less com-plete by the mid-1970s. It goes on to explain how, by then, the scope and ambition of health provision outstripped both the administrative or governing capacity of states and the resources which could be drawn from economies in relative decline. These tensions are expressed as the 'growth to limits' of the health care state in the period 1960–80; their resolution is left for later discussion, in chapter 5. For now, the key questions are these: why do states – almost all European states – come to support and then guarantee access to health care? Why do they do so in different ways? To borrow from Navarro (1989), why do some countries have health insurance systems and others have national health services? What is the effect of public intervention on the contours of health politics?

Patterns of development

The introduction of statutory health insurance is conventionally taken to mark the entry of the state into health care. It has a significant pre-history, however, in the regulation of institutional care, medical professional activity and public health (Kuhnle 1981). For centuries, religious orders had provided an embyronic form of hospital care. Some was also provided publicly, usually by local parish and municipal government.[1] Poor law arrangements which met the immediate needs of the destitute operated from the sixteenth to the eighteenth centuries, interrupted by a 'liberal break' in the nineteenth (Kuhnle 1981). European cities operated many more, much bigger public hospitals than their English counter-parts. Until the introduction of the New Poor Law in 1834, England was excep-tional in its emphasis on out-door, parish-based sick relief (Pelling and Harrison 1993).

The state was also increasingly involved in the accreditation or licensing of doctors, as signalled by the UK's Medical Act of 1858. But a Royal College of Physicians had been established by charter in London in 1518, and a College of Medicine in Stockholm in 1663 (Garpenby 1989). A division of medical trades originating in the continental city-states was reflected in Scotland, though less markedly in England, where it was more readily assumed that medicine was a free trade. Physicians were formally educated in the humanities as well as medi-cine; surgeons were also barbers, offering a range of personal services, including blood-letting and the treatment of sores as well as surgery, while apothecaries were traders and dealers in drugs and spices (Pelling and Harrison 1993). A system of salaried district physicians was established in Sweden as early as the eighteenth century, reflecting the inability of a rural economy to support private medicine as well as a powerful and highly developed public administration (Garpenby 1989). Absolutist rulers on the continent developed systems of medical policing, in which both preventive and curative activity attracted the interest of the state. Environmental health problems, especially those to do with sanitation, became a common concern of urbanising societies, as indicated by legislation in the UK in 1848 and 1875.

The legislative development of the health care state in France, Germany, Italy, Sweden and the United Kingdom from 1880 is summarised in table 2.1. Germany is viewed as the 'pioneer' in national health care (Leichter 1979), by virtue of its being the first country to introduce a public, compulsory system of health insurance for industrial workers in 1883. Myriad schemes were consolidated under one code in 1911. Though the scope of the system has periodically increased, it is remarkable for its organisational resilience. The administrative framework laid out by Bismarck, refounded in West Germany after the Second World War, remains clearly distinguishable in contemporary German health care. Frequent and radical regime change in twentieth-century Germany, from Wilhelmine Empire to Weimar Republic to Third Reich to Federal Republic, makes this fixity the more notable.

In France, a system of medical assistance established a right to medical care for the poor in 1893, and legislation to support and encourage social insurance provision by mutualist societies was introduced soon after, in 1898. Health insurance was made compulsory for all employees in 1930, and extended to farmers and the self-employed in the 1960s. Medical professional freedoms had been defined in the 1920s, forming something of a bulwark against the general, standard and compulsory aspects of the health insurance system as it evolved before and after the Second World War. Though a national fee schedule was imposed on doctors in 1960, a strong demarcation persists between a state controlled public hospital sector and the liberal professionalism which characterises ambulatory care.

Health care in the UK has been shaped by a series of milestone reforms, beginning with the New Poor Law of 1834. The health insurance system instituted in 1911 was a contributory scheme for working men. In 1946, it was replaced by the tax-funded and universalist National Health Service. Further reform brought some organisational consolidation in 1974, and more radical restructuring in 1991. This pattern of successive major changes seems to suggest a different kind of health politics, one in which government intervention is more confident and systematic.

Sweden is notable for its early provision of medical care by the state, combining salaried physicians in rural areas with municipal hospitals. County councils were formed in the 1860s, charged with operating somatic hospitals. Public subsidies helped to finance voluntary sickness funds from 1891, their membership increasing after 1931 once they were required to provide medical as well as cash benefits to their members. It was not until the mid-twentieth century that a universal national health insurance scheme was implemented in Sweden, in the mid-1950s. In 1960, the counties took charge of hospital-based outpatient care, accruing further responsibilities for District Medical Officers in 1963 and mental hospitals in 1967. Fee-for-service payments for hospital physicians were abolished in 1959 and all other private activity in public hospitals prohibited by the Seven Crowns Reform of 1970, which made hospital doctors fully salaried civil servants. County councils were made responsible for planning all health services in 1983.

Before the formation of the Italian National Health Service (*Servizio Sanitario Nazionale*, SSN) in 1978, health care in Italy was financed by a variety of social insurance schemes based on employment and administered by autonomous, quasi-governmental funds. A general scheme covering private sector employees was established in 1943, while other schemes for public employees, the self-employed and particular occupational groups were set up in the interwar period and during the 1950s and 1960s. The Italian health system then looked much like Germany's. The new SSN, modelled by contrast on the UK's NHS, replaced these diverse arangements with a unitary and universal scheme. The relative lateness of such fundamental reform begs important comparative questions about the different paths of welfare state development in northern and southern Europe (Ferrera 1989).

The introduction of statutory health insurance, 1880–1940

Health care finance became a collective issue before it became a public one. This has to do with interrelated processes of industrialisation and democratisation, both of which point to a deep connection between social insurance and industrial labour. By the middle of the nineteenth century the costs of ill health, in terms of lost earnings as much as of the cost of treatment and care, could not be met by individuals. More and more households were becoming dependent on wage labour: in such circumstances, absence from work through sickness represented an acute existential risk. Mutualist arrangements, including cooperatives and friendly societies, provided sickness and other benefits to their members, who were mostly working men in relatively stable factory employment (Hage, Hanneman and Gargan 1989). In contrast to industry, the agricultural and service sectors tended to be organised in family units, able to draw on the greater resources of large households and extended kinship networks while largely espousing a liberal ethos of independent self-sufficiency. The collective finance of social welfare represents a relatively greater burden to producers in these sectors, where the impact of taxes and contributions is more immediate than among large businesses, which are better able to pass on costs by raising prices. By the same token, the perceptible benefits are relatively smaller (Hage,

Table 2.1 The health care state in Europe, 1880–1980

	France	Germany	Italy	Sweden	United Kingdom
Before 1880			1865 communes obliged to provide medical care to poor	1864 county councils made responsible for hospital care	1834 Poor Law
1880		1883 sickness insurance	1886 state subsidies to voluntary sickness insurance funds		1886 non-paupers entitled to use Poor Law hospitals
1890	1893 medical assistance 1898 regulation of mutualist insurance			1891 health insurance	
1900	1901 categorical assistance for TB		Many mutual aid funds converted into company funds		
1910	1910 sickness insurance extended	1911 consolidation of insurance schemes under one code; extension of sickness insurance to domestic servants, agricultural and white collar workers			1911 health insurance
1920	1927 Medical Charter establishes principles of 'la médecine libérale'		1927 compulsory TB insurance scheme		
1930	1930 health insurance for employees made compulsory			1931 Sickness Funds Act establishes state subsidies to approved health insurance funds	

1940	1945 reform and generalisation of national health insurance		1943 many company schemes consolidated into National Institute for Health Insurance (INAM)	1946 National Health Insurance Act passed	1942 Beveridge Report 1946 National Health Service Act
1950		1951 employers and employees given equal representation in fund administration 1955 sickness funds and doctors' associations made public bodies 1955 income ceiling for compulsory health insurance raised	voluntary health funds proliferate after 1955	1955 NHI implemented 1958 regional system of specialist hospitals 1959 private beds and ffs payments for hospital physicians abolished	
1960	1960 national fee schedule for independent doctors 1961 health insurance covers farmers, and (1966) the self-employed	1969 continued payment of wages legislation	1968 hospital reform	1960 counties made responsible for hospital-based outpatient care. 1963 District Medical Officers and 1967 mental hospitals transferred to counties	1962 Hospital Plan
1970	1970 Hospital Act	1972 statutory health insurance covers farmers, and (1975) students 1976 income ceiling for compulsory health insurance raised	1974 sickness fund debts transferred to regional governments 1978 Servizio Sanitario Nazionale established	1970 Seven Crowns Reform 1971 retail pharmaceutical distribution nationalised 1983 counties responsible for all health service planning	1974 NHS reorganisation

Sources: Aggleton (1990); Ferrera (1989); Flora and Alber (1981); Garpenby (1989, 1995); Ito (1980); Jones (1985); Kervasdoué and Rodwin (1984); Kingdom (1996); Korpi (1995); Murswieck (1985); OECD (1992, 1994); Pierson (1991); Spence (1996); Thane (1982); Wilsford (1996).

Hanneman and Gargan 1989). In the political realm, industrialisation was broadly coincident with democratisation. The franchise was extended to all adult males in France in 1848, Germany in 1871, Sweden in 1909, Italy in 1913 and the UK in 1918 (Pierson 1991). Industrial workers began to organise politically in unions and parties: governments faced new forms of political pressure and new sets of demands.

Industrialisation, urbanisation and democratisation are contextual features of the development of health care states: they begin to explain why state-sponsored health insurance began to appear in Europe between 1850 and 1950, rather than before or after that, but they reveal little about *how*. They don't immediately explain why Britain, for example, the earliest and most advanced industrial country of the period, should be the last to regulate health insurance, nor why France, the first with universal male suffrage, should be one of the last to make it compulsory. What are the political mechanisms or processes which connect socio-economic development to social and public policy in different countries?

The first country to introduce publicly mandated health insurance, Germany, was then authoritarian, aristocratic and paternalist. The process by which it did so is described in box 2.1. Essentially, it can be understood as having been driven by the need to defend the legitimacy of the new, unified state, as well as its bureaucratic and entrepreneurial elites, against the claims of a rapidly mobilising industrial working class. In France, a little later, 'the reform movement was led by republican politicians in order to fulfill the fundamentally bourgeois objective of social peace' (Stone 1985, p. xi).

In comparative context, though there is a very general relationship between industrialisation and welfare state development, there seems to be an inverse relationship between social legislation and democratisation, in the sense of social demands, articulated by parties, being heard in a legislature with significant political authority. Where liberal democratic institutions develop early (as in the parliamentary governments of France and the UK), welfare state development appears relatively retarded (Flora and Alber 1981). Though their democratic aspect may have articulated a demand for some form of social policy, the liberalism of these countries discouraged intervention in the market. Autocratic and sometimes paternalist regimes (such as Germany and Sweden) had no such ideological preconception and, with little democratic legitimation or constraint, their governments faced militant labour movements. There was for them a powerful, if defensive motivation to institute welfare programmes; they also tended to have the necessary bureaucratic capacity to set up state-regulated welfare. '[T]iming is related to the way in which the state is organised. Authoritarian states worry about legitimacy and are early for this reason. Democratic states worry about consensus and are late for this reason' (Hage, Hanneman and Gargan 1989, p. 277).

Even then, in liberal democratic countries, it is liberal and conservative, reforming but avowedly non-socialist, governments which first make major commitments to social insurance. In France, it was the Radicals, republican,

Box 2.1: Foundation of the health care state: Germany

The German *Workers' Sickness Insurance Act* of 1883 provided access to medical services as well as income maintenance during illness and maternity and funeral benefits. All industrial wage earners were statutorily obliged to join. Workers paid two-thirds of their insurance premia and employers one-third; both parties were represented proportionately on sickness fund boards. Funds themselves contracted with physicians on the basis of capitation. The scheme incorporated many existing trade-based funds and set up additional district funds for those not otherwise covered.

The unification of Germany had been completed in 1871. An economic boom imediately followed in 1871–72, which accelerated a process of industrialisation and urbanisation already under way. There were 2 million factory workers in Germany in 1867, but 6 million by 1882. Socio-economic change made for changed and unsafe working conditions, and also for the loss of traditional forms of social protection. Social reform – the sickness insurance scheme was part of a package which included industrial accident insurance (1884) and pensions (1889) – was part of a dual 'carrot-and-stick' response to a rapid growth of political organisation among workers. Welfare benefits were matched by a raft of repressive anti-socialist legislation. They were more or less explicitly designed as a political bribe, offered to promote allegiance to a new political and economic order.

In context, the scheme was not a radical innovation. Prussia, the core of the new German state, had regulated medical fees as early as 1623. By the mid-nineteenth century, public insurance schemes had begun to be implemented in critical occupations such as mining, as well as other private and voluntary schemes. Some workers formed mutual aid schemes, and employers established others: in 1856 the steel manufacturer Krupp had introduced a compulsory health insurance for workers, who shared the premium with their employer. The general effect of the new legislation was to formalise and universalise previously piecemeal organisation and experience.

It required minimal levels of public administration or finance, and was the least contested of contemporary social reforms. Doctors, usually opposed to contracts and payment by capitation, had limited organisational strength before the *Hartmannbund* was formed in 1900. In any case, the legislation applied only to a small, impoverished section of the working population which represented a new client group for doctors' services rather than a change to the basis on which they were consulted by others. It made no new or significant demands on employers: some ran their own schemes already and so would be relieved of that responsibility; many shared a concern to defuse worker discontent and the new arrangements might even contribute to productivity. The principal source of opposition to the Act was from Social Democrats, to whom it represented a possible threat to workers' party allegiance, and who argued that it did not address their more basic needs such as income and housing, nor the causes of their ill-health.

Source: Leichter (1979, pp. 110–124).

anti-clerical but committed to the rights of property who advocated social reform at the turn of the century (Stone 1985). The insurance legislation of 1930 was first approved by a broad coalition government and then amended and introduced by a centre-right administration (Korpi 1995). It was Lloyd George's Liberal government which introduced health insurance in Britain in 1911. In Germany, it was a Christian Democratic government which refounded and extended the social insurance system in the 1950s. For these governments, the introduction of social insurance represented some expression of paternalist responsibility, if also a self-interested concern to mollify a potentially threatening working class. Importantly, too, social insurance was that form of welfare finance which fitted best with liberal precepts. Its independent finance and administration set limits to state intervention. It was based on desert as much as need, in that benefits were paid according to contributions, acting as a means of status protection rather than social redistribution. Income ceilings protected the right of the wealthier to pay more, as well as middle class virtues of independence and thrift; they also served to maintain a commercial sector in health care which was exploited by private practitioners. Social insurance interfered with the market distribution of employment and earnings much less than any alternative.

For similar reasons, the first statutory schemes tended to be resisted by Left parties and organised labour as instruments of social control. Their logic was conservative rather than socialist. At the same time, trade unions and social democratic parties tended to represent workers in work rather than out of work, and then those in more or less stable and continuous rather than casual or part-time employment. They were relatively better-off, many having made arrangements for themselves in company or cooperative schemes, often on their own terms. Statutory organisations represented a real threat – part of governments' calculation – to the way in which workers' own self-governing funds acted as bases of labour power. This is why, for example, Bismarck's initial intention to centralise the administration of the German scheme introduced in 1883 was specifically resisted by Social Democrats in the Reichstag (Rimlinger 1971, Hage, Hanneman and Gargan 1989).

Statutory health insurance and organised medicine
Professions and states are inextricably linked (chapter 6), and their combined effect on relations of power in health care at the end of the nineteenth and the beginning of the twentieth centuries should not be missed. What was happening was that the organisational strength of doctors was coming to outstrip that of patients, the insured users of the services they provided. In Germany, for example, doctors were forced to organise to counter the power of sickness funds, which were essentially patient-run bodies: they were governed by employers and employees, with majority representation in the hands of workers. A fund would appoint one or more doctors to treat its members, paying them by capitation. The *Hartmannbund*, the professional association of doctors in ambulatory care,

was founded in 1900, and its demands are revealing: for fee-for-service payment, and higher rates of remuneration; for free patient choice of doctor, and for limits to social insurance coverage (to protect private practice). By 1913, as again in 1923, the federal regulation of sickness insurance contracts was being negotiated by peak agreement between doctors and funds, represented equally.

This marked a stage in a long process of depoliticisation of sickness insurance. In England and Wales, the local committees which had administered the health insurance scheme since 1911 were simply abolished by the NHS Act in 1946. In Germany, the post-war refoundation of the compulsory scheme was part of the new corporatism expressed in the social market. In 1951 employer–employee representation in sickness fund administration was made equal, as it was later in France, where the centre-right Pompidou government also replaced elected representatives with appointees in 1967 (Korpi 1995).[2] In 1955, German sickness funds became public bodies, as did Doctors' Associations (Murswieck 1985). A constitutional court judgment in 1960 made the panel system illegal and established the right of independent physicians to practise where they wished. In this way, the independence of doctors from funds was institutionalised, and the process of incorporation of health care into the state complete. In Germany, the expansion of the system made territory a more significant unit of fund organisation than occupational group. In different ways, then, and often very slowly, broadening collective responsibility for the consequences of disease began to detach health finance from class and party politics.[3] In turn, the dominant axis of health politics became that between the state and a major interest group, the medical profession (chapter 6).

The universalisation of access to health care, 1940–1980

A common pattern in the long-term development of public health services has been for statutory agencies to begin by providing medical services to the destitute, as under the English Poor Law (Jones 1985). Next, these tend to be widened to particular categories such as low income workers, children and older people. This may be accompanied by a shift from assistance to insurance, that is, from the provision of minimum benefits financed directly from public (usually local) sources to entitlement to benefit in proportion to contributions paid. Then, in turn, policy coverage is extended upward and outward to the general population.

Across European countries, health care entitlements have been extended to increasing proportions of European populations in the post-war period (Moran 1992). The proportion of populations with entitlement to hospital care under a public scheme – what might be seen as the core entitlement in health care – was near universal by the early 1970s; this applies to ambulatory care, too. Such uniformity suggests that the expansion of health citizenship has been driven by forces operating across political cultures and institutional settings: the progressive industrialisation of European societies, and their concomitant urbanisation; democratisation, which has helped to realise the social rights of citizenship, in part by heightening elected governments' concern to promote and protect their own legitimacy; the expansion of the service sector in advanced industrial economies, which has affected patterns of both employment and consumption; demographic change, which has increased the proportion of the elderly in the population; developments in biotechnology, which have enhanced the capacity of medicine to do more for more people. Specifically, more health care was being provided by qualified doctors and more of it in hospitals, both factors making it increasingly expensive. For the middle classes, the relative benefits of insurance were much greater than they had been in the late nineteenth century, and the costs less. The strategy of increasing access to public schemes, in so far as it tended to have been advocated by left parties (below), was one which bourgeois and conservative parties found difficult to oppose. The universalist project in health has been broadly consensual (and, for the same reason, retrenchment has been hesitant and slight [chapter 5]).

Two routes to universalisation are distinguishable. The first was incremental, achieved by the piecemeal expansion of social insurance, as in France and Germany, and in Italy until the 1970s. The second was more radical, in which universal access was instituted at a stroke by creating national health services in the UK and, later, Italy. In Sweden, universalism was brought about by the national health insurance provision legislated for in 1946.

Extending social insurance
After the Social Security ordinance was passed in France in 1945, national health insurance was gradually extended over the next thirty years: farmers were included in 1961 and the self-employed, including artisans and professionals, in 1966 (Kervasdoué and Rodwin 1984, Korpi 1995). In Italy, occupational funds proliferated in an uncoordinated way during the 1950s, the recommendation of a parliamentary commission to extend public health insurance having been rejected by a centrist coalition government in 1948. Continuing leftist proposals for national social insurance schemes found little echo (Ferrera 1989). In Germany, greater numbers of people were brought into the statutory scheme by raising the income ceiling under which insurance coverage was compulsory, first in 1955 and then again in 1976, and by extending its scope to farmers in 1972 and students in 1975.

In these countries, health care systems were growing, but their organisational frameworks remained static and ill-defined. Institutional stasis is an effect of complexity (though complexity itself generates local tensions and more general structural problems: these are explored in chapters 3 to 5, below). The social insurance systems of post-war Europe brought together a diversity of insurers catering for different social and occupational groups with discrete interests; public, private and charitable providers, as well as local, regional and national governments. In different ways, all were subject to the demands of patients, both insured and uninsured, of unions and employers as well as doctors, and of the parties, organisations and coalitions which represented them. Complexity itself was an indicator of the relatively low involvement of the state.

Radical reform was unlikely to be introduced by governments which were highly unstable in France and Italy, highly decentralised in Germany, and which were presented with such intricate policy making environments. For each partial intervention had created, and then sustained, a particular structure of interest. Any given occupational fund, for example, serves the interests not only of a specific employment group, but also of the managers and office workers who operate it and of the hospitals and doctors who provide the care for which it pays. In turn, each has an interest in the continued existence of the system within which the fund works. Universalist, rationalising reform tended to be resisted by existing funds, by employers (who risked paying more for more compulsory employee members of public schemes), by the medical profession, and by bourgeois parties. And the longer such a system had been established, the less likely it was to be radically reformed. As Leichter writes of Germany, 'The development of health care policy in the Federal Republic ... since 1945 is testimony to the resiliency, some might say obduracy, of preexisting public policy' (Leichter 1979, p. 137). If this is so, that is, if the development of health systems might be expected to be incremental, the significance of radical reform is all the greater. The institution of national health services, and even of universal national health insurance, is an exceptional event which needs to be explained.

Creating national health services

Universalist legislation is passed in particular circumstances. The first, contextual one, is that of the patent failure of existing arrangements. In England, by the time the National Health Service Act was passed in 1946, voluntary hospitals were scarcely viable in financial terms; many were dumping patients to municipal hospitals. In turn, health care was then absorbing something like 50 per cent of local government budgets (Hage, Hanneman and Gargan 1989). In Italy, by the 1960s, hospital care was deteriorating in quality in the face of increased demand; hospitals were still formally charitable institutions, though dominated by rigid medical professional hierarchies (Ferrera 1989). Reform in 1968 served to increase hospital costs quickly and substantially: the SSN reform of 1978 was triggered by the debt crisis of existing insurance funds (OECD 1994, Spence 1996).

A second factor was the contingent strength of pro-reform, invariably Left parties. In Sweden and the UK in 1946, and in Italy in 1978, Left parties were unusually strong while inter-party conflict, at least on health policy, was relatively low. Social Democratic parties extended and universalised the partial systems introduced by liberal and conservative governments a generation or more previously. It was a Labour government which established the NHS in Britain. Social Democrat governments in Sweden passed compulsory sickness insurance legislation in 1947, took private medicine out of hospitals in 1970, and consolidated health care provision at county level in the 1980s. In Italy, the 1978 SSN legislation in part reflected the first participation of communists in government.[4] Similarly, in Germany, it was the Federal Republic's first Social Democrat government which improved sick pay arrangements for blue-collar workers in

1969.[5] Across countries, since 1930, the extension of sick pay entitlements has been closely associated with participation of Left parties in government (Korpi 1989).

A third factor was the balance of power between states and doctors, which was in large part a function of their respective organisation. In both the UK and Italy, doctors were divided among themselves while facing a more cohesive opposition (Honigsbaum 1979, Ferrera 1989). The strength or relative autonomy of the executive mattered much in Britain and Sweden. In both countries, once policy was formulated in government, it was unlikely to be vetoed in legislative or electoral arenas. In France, by contrast, the chronic instability of government majorities left parliament as the principal locus of decision making. There, it was much easier to mobilise conservative influence. The point is that veto groups – such as the medical profession – do not work to the same effect everywhere: not only are they better organised in some countries than in others, but different political systems offer them different opportunities to influence the policy process (Immergut 1990 and 1992, and see chapter 6, below).

The health care state, 1960–1980

On average, sickness insurance schemes covered less than 50 per cent of the working populations of European countries in 1930; by 1980, this figure was almost 80 per cent (Korpi 1995). In most countries, the effect of state-supported health insurance was to unleash demand for health care, which was met by increased supply, especially in the hospital sector. The hospital encapsulated the spirit of the age. It marked the burgeoning faith in science and technology held by societies beginning to be fascinated by television, dependent on refrigerators and excited by space flight. At the same time it appeared classless, safe and respectable, in a way in which institutional care rarely had before. Across Europe, post-war social progress was to be symbolised by a new hospital in every town (Anderson 1972).[6] In Britain, the institution of the NHS had involved the nationalisation of hospital care at the same time. In health care as in the utilities, coal and steel production, transport and communications, key sectors of the post-war economy were to be dominated by public services. The Hospital Plan of 1962 established national norms for local provision, envisaging the building of 90 new hospitals and the remodelling of more than 100 others (Klein 1989). The French Hospital Act of 1970, similarly, instituted a system of health planning which standardised bed ratios between regions, its effect being to add more than 50 000 beds to the system as a whole (Kervasdoué and Rodwin 1984). For the first part of the twentieth century, health facilities in Sweden had been the fragmented responsibility of local, regional and central governments (Garpenby 1995). Now, hospital services were expanded and gradually unified under the county councils. A parliamentary commission reported on the regional expansion and distribution of specialist facilities in 1958 (Serner 1980). The counties gained new responsibilities for hospital-based outpatient care in 1960 and for mental hospitals in 1967. The

Italian hospital sector was reformed in 1968. As elsewhere, a Hospital Financing Act in Germany in 1972 established a system of regional hospital planning, also providing for joint federal–regional capital finance and regulating operating costs, which were to be met through the insurance system (Altenstetter 1989).

One version of the development of the health care state would see the universalisation of access to health care by the 1970s as a near-perfect expression of the state in high modernity. Science and technology, professional judgement and bureaucratic reason were combined to provide sophisticated and effective health care to whole populations, as a right of citizenship, equally and comprehensively (at least, almost all citizens, and more equally and comprehensively than ever before). Among and above this, the state itself appeared hegemonic. Soon, it could be argued that 'the state defines the rules of the game and is also the principal actor. The state finances – directly or indirectly – a large part of the cost of health care. It also shapes policy in several critical domains: medical manpower and biomedical research, the purchase of equipment, the development of innovations, and the construction and modernisation of hospitals' (Kervasdoué, Kimberly and Rodwin 1984, p. xix).

However, the increased scope and cost of publicly guaranteed health care in Europe has been barely matched by the executive authority of governments. In France and Germany, governments have struggled to establish authority over independent, decentralised providers. Where the functional integration of ambulatory and hospital care progressed furthest, in Sweden, it did so only very slowly. The same kind of administrative separation was rationalised by the reform of the UK NHS in 1974, but not overcome. Even national health services did not become administrative monoliths. The establishment of ministries of health serves as a useful qualitative indicator of the slowly developing regulatory capacity of governments, and indeed of the halting construction of health care as a substantive and routinised field of public policy making (box 2.2).[7]

Until the 1980s, across countries, health care regulation was restricted for the most part to matters of finance, concerned with ways of paying for treatment and investment in health facilities. It was not otherwise concerned with delivery or with the kind of decision-making about the nature of care which remained the preserve of doctors. The trick was pulled of turning the vexed question of 'who gets what, when and how' over to the medical profession: political problems – the problems which had formed the substance of health political development for the preceding century – were converted into clinical problems (Klein 1989, p. 86). This mattered little in periods of economic growth and service expansion, but came to matter a great deal when resource allocation became much more difficult.

Growth to limits[8]

The growth of health care systems is driven by an internal dynamic of what has come to seem like permanent, limitless expansion. Developments in biotechnology feed supply and demographic change feeds demand, the two operating

Box 2.2: State capacity in the health sector

Health often occupies a relatively low position in ministerial hierarchies (Walt 1994). It is not always a cabinet post, and the health portfolio is often combined with others. Ministerial power tends to be greater in national health systems, where care is delivered in publicly owned facilities and financed largely through general taxation, though it is also predicated on the degree of centralisation of responsibilities, as differences between the UK and Sweden and between France and Germany reveal.

A Ministry of Health was first formed in the UK in 1919 (Wilding 1967). Apart from a brief period after the foundation of the NHS in 1948, it was not until the creation of the Department of Health and Social Security (DHSS) in 1968 that it was directly represented in cabinet; health and social security briefs were not separated until 1988. Health policy responsibility in Sweden is shared between central and local government. At the centre, it lay with the Ministry of Social Affairs until 1947, and then with the Home Office until 1963, when it was returned to Social Affairs. Planning and supervisory functions are the responsibility of a central government agency, the National Board of Health and Welfare, which was formed by amalgamating the previously separate National Boards of Health and Social Welfare in 1968 although, in the course of the 1970s and 1980s, increasing responsibility has come to rest with the county councils (Garpenby 1989). A Ministry of Health was established in Italy in 1958, though responsibility for hospitals was not transferred from the Ministry of the Interior until 1968. Even by 1978, it was seen to be barely adequate to the task of running of the new SSN (Ferrera 1989, France 1996a, Spence 1996).

Health policy responsibilities in social insurance systems tend to be dispersed among different combinations of Health, Finance, Labour and Social Affairs ministries. In France, the ministry with the health portfolio tends to assume different competences (and different names) under different governments (Pomey and Poullier 1997). In Germany, a Federal Ministry of Health was formed in 1961 by separating out functions previously held by the Ministry of the Interior, though constitutional provisions allowed it little room to claim administrative territory from other federal ministries or from regional states. It accreted new Youth and Family portfolios in 1969, and Women's Affairs in 1989, though key responsibility for sickness insurance remained part of the social security brief at Labour until the post-unification government was formed in early 1991. What had become a super-ministry of minor portfolios was then disaggregated, leaving a Federal Health Ministry for the first time holding comprehensive regulatory responsibility for the health sector.

together as medicine treats a population it has helped to grow old. In medicine, unlike other industries, the introduction of new equipment does not save money by reducing unit costs, but tends to increase the scope of, and so demand for, health care. It is not usually labour-saving, but likely to require additional investment in specialist personnel (Field 1973). This peculiar combination of demand and supply features in the health sector leads to a relentless increase in its size and complexity – and cost. In the end, inevitably, health systems came to rub against the boundaries of the economically possible. The period of expansion through the 1950s and 1960s into the 1970s had been coincident with – dependent upon – more general and sustained economic growth unparalleled in western industrial societies. The welfare state, as Klein put it, was 'the residual beneficiary of the Growth State' (Klein 1980a, p. 29). But with economic downturn in Europe and North America – triggered by OPEC oil price rises following the Arab–Israeli war in 1973, and increasingly apparent by 1975–76 – internal service expansion now met an opposing dynamic, that of external financial constraint. In the period before the 'oil shock' (1960–73), the average growth of GNP across OECD countries was 4.9 per cent; in the period after (1973–81), it fell by half, to 2.4 per cent (Bruno and Sachs 1985).[9] With recession, distributional issues quickly became acute.

For a long time, liberal democratic and industrial capitalist states had been trying to do two things. One was to promote economic growth; the other was to guarantee their citizens acceptable levels of social protection. For much of the time, too, the two projects had seemed mutually reinforcing: economic prosperity provided a surplus to be spent on welfare, and social investment supported continued economic growth. Economic policy and social policy went hand in hand, supported by widespread political consensus about the relatively expansive role of the public sector in each field. Now, what had been complementary suddenly seemed contradictory.[10] Welfare seemed less affordable, and social spending was detracting from economic investment. The consensus which had underwritten expansion evaporated. Conflicts of interest emerged between those who paid for welfare (employers and employees) and those who used it, between those in the labour market and those outside it. Within the health sector, the implicit contract between governments and doctors began to break down. The users of services began to lose confidence in both.

By the middle of the twentieth century, if not long before, health care in Europe had become 'political', in the sense that it was now a field in which the state was an increasingly important actor and which was now an inevitable and continuing concern of public policy.[11] Until the 1970s, however, while the share of public finance in health spending increased, the health sector remained an arena of more or less 'private government', one in which key decisions protected the exercise of professional technical autonomy. Health care was sponsored by the state but not governed by it: most systems operated without budgets. Even where, as in the NHS, a global budget was fixed by central government, this simply reflected the resource requirement indicated by the cumulative activity of

---

Box 2.3: The health care state: critiques

In the 1960s and 1970s, health policy and politics began to be suffused by a growing perception of crisis in the health care state. At bottom, this was a crisis of authority or legitimacy, posed by a number of separate intellectual critiques of both medicine and government, though it was soon to be exacerbated by a perceived crisis of resources. For an introduction to critiques of medicine see Allsop (1984), and of the welfare state George and Wilding (1976, 1984).

The most significant improvements to the health of populations were attributable to economic and social development, not to medicine (McKeown 1965, 1979). Later, it became clear that levels of health care spending made little impact on differences in mortality between social classes (Blaxter 1983) or between countries (Mackenbach 1991). For its part, the medical profession had subjected few of its procedures to appropriate evaluation (Cochrane 1971).

At the same time, sociologists began to deconstruct the dominance of the medical profession (Freidson 1970). The implication of medicine in social control began to be explored from marxist, feminist and structuralist points of view (Zola 1972; and chapter 1, above). Even more radically, it could be argued that it was medicine itself which made people ill (Illich 1976). Apart from the side-effects of medical care ('clinical iatrogenesis'), the damage done by medicine took social and structural forms: health services created a social dependence on medicine, serving both to reinforce a social order which made people sick and to undermine their personal autonomy.

These were congruent with neo-liberal and other critiques of contemporary government. For liberals, whose seminal texts were those of Hayek (1944, 1960) and Friedman (1962), the welfare state by promoting social 'rights' fostered unreasonable expectations, by interfering in markets was wasteful and inefficient, and by constraining individual freedoms was simply tyrannous. To others, government had become overloaded with tasks and responsibilities which it was incapable of meeting (King 1975). In so far as the function of the state was to support capitalist forms of accumulation, legitimating them through the public provision of welfare, the gap between government revenues and expenditures constituted a fiscal crisis (O'Connor 1973). The legitimation crisis was at least in part derived from the insufficiently participatory nature of western democracy (Habermas 1975 [1973]), an argument invigorated by the activism of new social movements among women and ethnic minorities.

---

doctors. The post-war period was one of enormous growth, both in the range and sophistication of health services provided, and in the categories and proportions of populations they served. The health care state had grown big, but it remained paradoxically weak. Its government represented at best a compromise between professional authority and public administration (cf. Heidenheimer 1980, Klein 1989), supported by a general societal consensus over the rightness of the systems which resulted from it.

Health and health policy then became 'political' in a different way, in the sense of being an object of contention. Contemporary critiques of medicine and government are summarised in box 2.3. Essentially, what was at issue was where to set the limits to growth, where – and how – to set the boundaries of the health care state. How much of its finance was to continue to be raised publicly, and how much privately, from service users? How much was to continue to be allocated by hierarchies of planners and administrators, and how much by competitive, market-like arrangements? How much centrally and how much regionally? How far was doctors' freedom of decision-making to be circumscribed? The resolution of each – let alone all – of these questions would require that the state assume greater authority in the regulation of health care than it had ever done hitherto.

The first phase of development of the health care state in Europe, which lasted roughly a hundred years (from 1880 to 1980), was about establishing and then universalising a public (state) presence in health care. A second phase, beginning around 1975, has been concerned with establishing new mechanisms of governmental control; it forms the subject of chapter 5, below. Before then, the book turns to more detailed exploration of health politics in different countries.

Notes

1 Barry and Jones (1991) reveal the close and complex relationship between charity and the state in early modern health care.
2 This was reversed by Mitterrand's Socialist government, which took power in 1981.
3 For critical accounts of this process, see Deppe (1987) and Widgery (1988). Donald Light pulls no punches in writing about the German case: 'One might say that the history of the German health-care system is the history of the profession and the state crushing grass-roots organizations of mutual aid' (Light 1986, p. 579).
4 For an account of the programmatic positions taken by different Italian political parties in the 1960s and 1970s, see Miguel (1977). For a closer reading of PCI involvement, see Robb (1986).
5 Employers were now obliged to continue to pay wages for the first six weeks' sick leave, so matching civil service and salaried labour arrangements, and removing what had been a class-based division in insurance entitlements.
6 Cit. Garpenby (1995).
7 For a review of the functional responsibilities of health ministries in Europe, see Abel-Smith *et al.* (1995, pp. 68–71).
8 The phrase is taken from a classic study: Flora (1986).
9 Cit. Pierson (1991).
10 Neo-liberal and neo-Marxist readings of what was widely perceived to be a 'crisis' of the welfare state were remarkably congruent. For discussion of the crisis literature, see Moran (1988).
11 These paragraphs draw on Starr and Immergut's conception of the changing boundaries of health politics (Starr and Immergut 1987, cf. also Flora and Heidenheimer 1981).

3

National health services: Italy, Sweden and the UK

Introduction

National health services are characterised by a high degree of state intervention: for the most part, health services are publicly financed and delivered by public employees in facilities which are publicly owned. The UK's National Health Service, established in 1948 by a reforming Labour government, continues to serve as a prototype of this kind of health system. Similarly, but more generally, Sweden is regularly taken as a model of a Social Democratic welfare state. Italy's *Servizio Sanitario Nazionale* (SSN) was the first national health service to be established in mainland Europe south of Britain and Scandinavia, part of a wave of universalist reform which also carried to Spain, Portugal and Greece (Ferrera 1995). Those of the UK and Italy are both relatively large systems, each covering populations of 57–8 million; Sweden is by a long way the smallest country in this study, with a population of less than 9 million.

The simple idea of the national health service belies its perhaps unexpected complexity. These systems were not purist conceptions realised without compromise, but represent instead administrative frameworks which were superimposed on pre-existing interests and the relationships between them. And they continue to operate in complicated institutional, political and economic environments. There are two key aspects to this complexity: first, in Italy, Sweden and the UK, public systems have always coexisted to a greater or lesser extent with private means of funding and providing health care. The national health services described here dominate their respective health sectors, but they are not monopolies. Second, the public sectors of these as of other economies have recently been subject to profound change. National health services are in a state of transition from a centralised, bureaucratic model based on hierarchy and rational planning to one which gives greater regulatory scope to locally managed markets.

This chapter shows the extent to which health systems of a similar kind are cast in slightly different ways in different national contexts. Its purpose is to uncover the ways in which, in a political sense, a national health service 'works'. It begins by comparing and contrasting the organisation, delivery and finance of health care in Italy, Sweden and the UK. In doing so, it shows how questions of finance are closely related to questions of equity. It then assesses one of the most salient problems of the national health service 'mission', that of the relationship between public and private, and the different ways it has been resolved. It goes on to show how different organisational forms give governments different degrees of control over the development of health systems. Outline introductions to different systems are given in boxes 3.1, 3.2 and 3.3.

Organisation, delivery and finance

In the UK and Italy, responsibilities for the provision of health care are invested in health authorities, distinct and distinctive public bodies which operate at both regional and local levels in the UK, and at local level in Italy. UK Health Authorities and, above them, Regional Offices form an administrative hierarchy of their own, separate from elected local government and subordinated to central government.[1] In Italy, local health bodies (ASLs) are formally agencies of regional governments. In Sweden, organisational responsibility for health care is held by county councils as part, albeit the dominant one, of their more general functions. The counties vary in size, with populations of between 60 000 and 1 700 000; some are currently amalgamating. English Health Authorities typically serve populations of approximately 300 000 while Italian localities are somewhat smaller, averaging 250 000. Health care accounts for two-thirds of regional government spending in Italy, and for three-quarters of county council spending in Sweden. This makes it the largest sector of decentralised government in Italy and, beside the social welfare services provided by municipalities, one of the largest in Sweden.

In all three countries, new distinctions have been drawn between administrative functions which were previously conflated. In the UK, following reform implemented in 1991, health authorities were reconstructed as purchasers of the health services required by their populations. Facilities such as hospitals, which were formerly directly owned and managed by these public bodies, became independent providers of health care (NHS trusts), for which they contract with commissioning purchasers. The change is known, self-evidently, as the 'purchaser–provider split'. Since 1992, similarly, some larger Italian hospitals have been made organisationally autonomous and given independent budgetary responsibilities, becoming something like UK trusts. This was meant simply as a process of devolved management rather than a way of introducing competition between providers for purchaser contracts (Bevan, France and Taroni 1992), although in many cases it has served in practice to encourage competitive behaviour. In Sweden, hospitals are still directly owned and run by the counties, though up to half of all councils had established organisationally separate purchasing bodies by 1994 (Garpenby 1995).

Patients in Sweden are assigned a doctor working in a local health centre. They may also consult specialists directly, in hospital outpatient departments,

Box 3.1: The organisation of health care in Italy

Overview   The Italian National Health Service (*Servizio Sanitario Nazionale, SSN*) is a product of legislation passed in 1978. It is financed through a combination of taxation and social insurance and is characterised by extensive local and regional autonomy and mixed forms of service delivery.

Service delivery   Responsibility for the provision of health care rests with 228 local health authorities (*Aziende Sanitarie Locali, ASLs*). Most beds (77 per cent) are in SSN hospitals, but a significant proportion of ambulatory specialist and diagnostic care is provided in non-SSN facilities.

Doctors in public hospitals are salaried. Many doctors in private hospitals have part-time contracts, allowing them to work independently. GPs are independent contractors to ASLs, earning income from capitation and additional service payments; most have comparatively few patients and many also work privately.

As in the UK, patients register with a GP and have access to hospital specialisms only by GP referral. There is a charge for pharmaceutical prescriptions, known as the *ticket*, which also applies to diagnostic testing and specialist consultations. Ten per cent of the population has private health insurance.

Finance   Global health spending was 7.7 per cent GDP in 1995, of which almost 70 per cent came from public sources. Until 1998, health care was financed in roughly equal proportions by general taxation and by statutory insurance contributions from employers, employees and the self-employed. Insurance-based funding has now been replaced by IRAP (*Imposta Regionale sull' Attività Produttiva*), a tax paid by firms and the self-employed. For now (and as before) this is supplemented by a state subsidy, which is calculated on the basis of a fixed per capita sum uniform for all regions, multiplied by the number of residents in a given region and less its insurance revenues.

Governance   The 20 regional governments have virtually complete responsibility for health care administration. They may spend more than they receive from the IRAP and the central allocation, but must finance it themselves. Central government is responsible for drafting the National Health Plan, which specifies goals and priorities for the health service, as well as uniform levels of provision. Lines of accountability are uncertain: regional health ministers are ultimately responsible to their own regional councils rather than the Ministry of Health. The ASLs are controlled by general managers appointed by the regions, and enjoy significant organisational autonomy. Their institutional precursors, the USLs (*Unità Sanitaria Locale*), were run by committees nominated by local authorities, making for a high degree of penetration of local health politics by parties.

Reform projects   A 'reform of the (1978) reform' process was initiated in 1992. Essentially, it embraced a dual strategy of the regionalisation of health financing and the introduction of managed competition at local level. Some larger hospitals have been made managerially independent.

Key sources: Ferrera (1995), France (1996a and 1996b), OECD (1994), Spence (1996).

Box 3.2: The organisation of health care in Sweden

Overview This is a public sector, tax-based system, characterised by a high degree of decentralisation.

Service delivery The county councils are responsible for the provision of health services to their populations; central and district hospitals and other health facilities are owned and run by them. Highly specialised services are organised on a regional basis, as is medical education. Primary care is provided in local health centres staffed usually by GPs but sometimes also by specialists.

Doctors are salaried, public sector employees. Eight per cent of physicians work full-time in private practice, paid through the national insurance system according to a fee-for-service schedule.

Until 1993 patients everywhere were assigned to doctors in public health centres according to where they lived, though recent reform initiatives have increased freedom of choice in some areas. They pay standard copayments for all consultations, prescriptions and inpatient stays. It has been normal for patients to consult hospital doctors in outpatient departments without referral, though county councils in some parts of the country are now introducing barriers to their doing so. A small private insurance sector covers less than 1 per cent of the population, typically senior executives whose cover is paid by their employers, or the self-employed.

Finance Total health spending amounted to 8.5 per cent of GDP in 1995, of which 83 per cent was derived from public sources. In 1992, 75 per cent of public health care costs were met by county council tax finance, 12 per cent from central government grants, 10 per cent from other sources and 3 per cent from patient charges.

Governance Health policy is led by county councils: 80 per cent of their activity is focused on health care. The councils' primary responsibilities make the Federation of County Councils a major player at national level. General legislative responsibility rests with central government (the Ministry of Health and Social Affairs), advised by a National Board of Health and Welfare, which also monitors and coordinates new initiatives.

Reform projects These are necessarily diverse, reflecting the various initiatives of different counties. Market-oriented reform was encouraged by the liberal-conservative coalition which replaced Sweden's longstanding centre-left, Social Democratic government between 1991 and 1994. Common patterns included the separation of purchase from provision; the allocation of funds to local districts on a capitation basis; hospital financing according to the volume of services provided and the development of a family doctor scheme. More recent trends are toward collaboration and hospital merger. The current amalgamation of some counties is likely to impact on the structure of health care provision.

Key sources: Brunsdon and May (1995), Garpenby (1995), Håkansson and Nordling (1997), Jones (1996), OECD (1994), Saltman (1998).

Box 3.3: The organisation of health care in the United Kingdom

Overview   The UK's is the prototype National Health Service: tax financed and publicly managed, now combining a high degree of central authority with local managerial responsibility.

Service delivery   Administrative responsibility for the provision of health care in England and Wales lies with Health Authorities (HAs), in Scotland with Health Boards and in Northern Ireland with Health and Social Services Boards. Health Authorities and Boards act as commissioners (planners and purchasers) of health services for the populations they serve, placing contracts with providers. Almost all providers of hospital and community services are now independent NHS trusts. In primary care, many larger practices have been able to use budgets awarded to them to purchase diagnostic and non-urgent (elective) treatment services from providers.

Hospital doctors are salaried, but may hold part-time contracts with the NHS and also work privately. Basic salaries may be supplemented by merit awards. General practitioners (GPs) are self-employed; their earnings are derived from a combination of capitation payments, fees and practice allowances.

Patients register with a GP. They have direct access to Accident and Emergency departments in hospitals, though access to specialists is indirect, by GP referral. There are charges for prescriptions, for dental checks and for ophthalmic testing. In 1994, 12 per cent of the population held private health insurance cover.

Finance   UK health spending in 1995 constituted 6.9 per cent GDP, of which 85 per cent came from public sources. Some 82 per cent of NHS funding came from general taxation, 13 per cent from National Insurance contributions and 3 per cent from patient copayments.

Governance   Central government (through the Department of Health, DoH) holds general policy responsibility for the NHS. It is also directly responsible for fixing a global budget for health services, which is determined in cabinet; for revenue raising through taxation and national insurance, as well as for allocating health budgets to regions. In England, eight Regional Offices of the NHS Executive in turn allocate resources to approximately 100 Health Authorities, which remain responsible for the delivery of care. Health Authorities, like provider trusts, are appointive rather than elective bodies. The health service in Scotland is responsible to the new Scottish parliament.

Reform projects   Drawing on the general principles expressed in the white paper *Working for Patients* (1989), the *NHS and Community Care Act* (1990) introduced what became known as the 'purchaser–provider split' or 'internal market' in health care. The organisational structure of the NHS continued to evolve as purchasers, both health authorities and GPs, merged in different ways to form more effective purchasing consortia. A white paper issued by the new Labour government in December 1997 outlined plans to develop what it calls 'integrated care'. Health Authorities will become responsible for Health Improvement Programmes, involving the assessment of local health need and the strategic planning of health care. Primary Care Groups made up of all GPs and community nurses will gradually assume responsibility for the direct commissioning of health services, drawing up long-term service agreements with NHS trusts.

Key sources: Baggott (1994), Culyer and Meads (1992), Ham (1997a), Hatcher (1997), Levitt, Wall and Appleby (1995), Mohan (1995), Ranade (1998a).

though more barriers are being introduced to their doing so. In Italy and the UK, patients must first consult the general practitioner (GP) with whom they are registered; it is the GP who refers the patient to hospital as appropriate. Primary care is thus a prominent feature of national health services; its significance lies in the role assigned to the GP as gatekeeper to more specialist (and expensive) care. GP activity is normally restricted to diagnosis, basic treatment and referral, including pharmaceutical prescription and sick note certification, while the hospital remains the locus of high technology treatment, specialist care and clinical research. In the UK, this has been described as essentially a demarcation of professional activity in which the consultant took the hospital and the GP took the patient (Klein 1989).

In all three countries, access to health care is a right of residence or citizenship. It is not based, as in social insurance systems, on an individual's contribution record: perhaps the defining characteristic of the national health service is the abolition of the individual basis of health funding. That said, the difference between the two kinds of system remains relative rather than absolute. Even in these national health services, the socialisation of the costs of health care is incomplete. Health finance is not derived entirely from general taxation – only in Denmark is this the case – but from a mixture of general taxation, social insurance and patient copayment. Before changes made in 1998, for example, Italy's social insurance scheme (paid mostly by employers) provided half of all public health finance. But this did not make Italy a social insurance system: 'social insurance' here refers to money raised by centrally administered national insurance schemes; it has little in common with the principles of the continental, Bismarckian model, (see chapter 4, below). The insurer is the state, not one of a set of independent funds. Nevertheless, the structure of Italian social insurance contributions has meant that the burden of health finance has been shared unequally between different occupational groups. The relative contribution of high-income private employees, for example, used to be greater than that of the self-employed, testing high earners' political tolerance of what was and is in principle a universalist system (Ferrera 1995).[2]

By the same token, the proportion of health funding derived from user contributions is highest in Italy, where copayment is known as the *ticket*. Introduced as a means of containing pharmaceutical demand, it was revised and extended a number of times during the 1980s (see Ferrera 1995). Prescription charges were introduced in the UK for similar reasons in 1952, soon after the NHS was formed. Charges are more wide-ranging in Sweden, where standard copayments are levied for each consultation (covering diagnostic testing, certification and referral to a specialist) and for inpatient hospital care as well as for prescriptions, though there is a limit to the amount any individual patient can be required to pay in the course of a year. All three countries operate means-tested exemption systems, which mitigate some of the negative effects of copayment on equity.

In the UK, Health Authorities are allocated money according to the size of their populations, though the total is adjusted to reflect age and mortality indicators. An earlier system of weighting developed by the Resource Allocation Working Party (RAWP) in 1975–76, which this supersedes, was designed to overcome the geographical maldistribution of services across the country. Many of the private and charitable health facilities for which the NHS assumed responsibility in 1948 had been located where wealthy metropolitan populations existed to support them. The RAWP mechanism was an attempt redistribute resources according to proxy measures of need, adjusting a previous pattern set by philanthropy and the market.[3] In a similar way, Swedish central government equalisation grants compensate for differences in the tax base of different county councils, and amount to 15 per cent of health care costs (Brunsdon and May 1995).

Public and private

The symbolic achievement of national health services is the socialisation (the public funding and delivery) of health care. This is not unique to these countries or to these systems; as the next chapter shows, the social insurance systems of France and Germany achieve comparable goals in contrasting ways. The national health services represent a particular form of the socialisation of health care in which extensive responsibilities are assumed by the state. The National Health Service in the UK may be understood as a nationalisation of health services, in the manner of the railways or the coal industry. It took place at a similar time, and for similar reasons. In an economic and ideological context deeply affected by war, a struggling sector made up of local government, charitable and private providers was taken over by a state confident in its capacity to manage key national resources. Not least because of its timing, the nationalisation of health care went much further in the UK than in Italy, though it came to be most extensively developed in Sweden.

And if the socialisation of health care is not unique, nor is it complete. Each country retains a system of patient copayment. And in each country, too, a small proportion of acute beds are still provided privately: 16 per cent in Italy, 7 per cent in the UK and 5 per cent in Sweden (France 1991, Hatcher 1997, Håkansson and Nordling 1997). Though the reorganisation of 1974 represented the high water mark of nationalisation in the UK, subsequent attempts to withdraw pay beds from NHS facilities provoked a bitter dispute with the doctors between 1974 and 1976, and were dropped with the change of government in 1979.[4] Though private beds in public hospitals were abolished in Sweden in 1960, and the effect of the Seven Crowns Reform of 1970 was to make both ambulatory and hospital physicians salaried employees, up to 5 per cent of doctors continue to practise outside the public system (Brunsdon and May 1995). In Italy, meanwhile, unlike in the UK, a number of providers of health care remained outside the SSN when it was created.[5] In many places, Italian localities have always been dependent on contracting with independent institutions and agencies for the provision of hospital and ambulatory care. The plurality of providers, newly (re)introduced in the UK and to some extent in Sweden, was built into the SSN (Bevan, France and Taroni 1992). Indeed, if the purchase of private sector services by the SSN were added to that by private patients, it could be argued that in 1991 35–40 per cent of all health finance was spent in the private sector (France 1996b).

The relationship between public and private in health care tends to be understood as a question either of ethics or of economics. The continued existence of private medicine, the implication that under certain circumstances access to health care remains related to the ability to pay, threatens the principles according to which national health services were developed: is the level of iniquity which results from the coexistence of private and public health care tolerable? A different kind of argument asks not whether the market is ethically appropriate, but whether it is economically efficient. Does the private sector guarantee or undermine public sector performance?[6] Both questions are compelling, but both miss the political dynamic inherent in the relationship between the two.

In all three countries medical professional freedom to practise privately is legally guaranteed, though it is perhaps most circumscribed in Sweden and most extensive in Italy. Ambulatory care doctors in both Italy and the UK have retained their status as private, independent contractors to the public health service instead of becoming its salaried employees. This is largely due to intense medical lobbying of successive reform discussions. Doctors' interests lie in maintaining their professional autonomy and in maximising their earnings: just as Aneurin Bevan is said to have 'stuffed the consultants mouths with gold' to ensure their participation in the prospective National Health Service legislated for in 1946, so 'It seems unrealistic to imagine healthcare in Italy without a significant private practice in which doctors earn large fees' (Bevan, France and Taroni 1992, p. 23). Ironically, one of the conditions of establishment of national health services seems to be that the nationalisation of health care remains incomplete.

In the UK, private health care is used by patients principally for elective surgery, that is, for acute but non-emergency hospital care. Some 12 per cent of the population is insured with private (mostly non-profit making) third-party payers. Individuals insured privately are concentrated in outer metropolitan areas and among professional and managerial socio-economic groups; half of those insured have their premia paid either wholly or partly by their employers as part of an employment package. In Sweden, the equivalent figure is less than 1 per cent; in Italy it is about 10 per cent. In all three countries, interestingly, health care can be delivered in public facilities but paid for privately, and it can also be delivered privately but paid for publicly. What is referred to as the private sector is often only semi-private, mediated by contractual relationships with the public sector. As a whole it remains small, and the private finance of private provision even smaller (France 1991). Few patients rely on it wholly.

Though its scope for expansion appears limited, the private sector has never completely disappeared. In countries with national health services, it fulfils important functions, almost to the extent that it can be seen as an integral part of public provision. Private facilities provide additional care to those who wish to pay for it, as well as a significant source of earnings for some doctors. The tolerance of private health care buys the tolerance of public health care by particularly influential groups of both users and providers – the wealthy patient and the hospital specialist. The private sector offers a political as much as a technical safety-valve for public services under pressure (Klein 1989). The relationship between public and private was an important aspect of the politics of foundation of national health services in Italy, Sweden and the UK, and became important again in the politics of retrenchment during the 1980s (chapter 5, below).

Governance: the organisational integration of national health services

The relationship between public and private, then, embraces not only that between state and market but also the tension between political control and professional autonomy. The workings of national health services raise 'questions of public control and accountability in circumstances where private decisions often determine public payments' (France 1991, p. 63). This public–private nexus is further complicated by the relationship between centre and locality. While tax-based public finance is centralised, health care is necessarily delivered in different localities. And local differences are potentially problematic for the universalist health care state. The boundaries between public and private, state and market, core and periphery represent the limits of the integration by the state of the various parts or functions of the health sector into a coherent whole. They suggest a way of describing the patterns of governance of national health services.

Different parts of the health sector can be more or less fully integrated into the state; the systems in which that process has been carried further than others are known as national health services (chapter 1). This process of integration reflects both the capacity of states and the authority of governments: the formation of national health services is predicated on a political victory of central government over professional, private and local interests. Its continued executive authority, in turn, is at least in part an effect of the institutions it designs. Where health services are most integrated, it can be argued, government decision-making is least constrained.

Institutional integration can be conceptualised along three axes: executive, central and public.[7] *Executive* integration refers to the power of national government, both in its own right and in relation to the judiciary and the legislature. A parliamentary government formed from a single party with an effective working majority in its legislature may be taken to be more powerful than one whose freedom of action is limited by a president, by its coalition partners or by opposition parties. *Central* integration means the extent to which policy making authority is concentrated at national rather than regional or local levels, though the freedom allowed by the centre to the periphery may vary over time.[8]

Integration of these kinds both creates and reflects the contextual assumption that a given policy field (in this case health) is normatively subject to government intervention, that is, that it is a public issue and one which is appropriately regulated by the state rather than by the market or by associations. This can be termed *public* integration; the integration of government is more or less significant only according to the extent of government authority over private interests such as doctors, hospitals and insurers, or indeed to the extent of the incorporation of those interests into something which is recognisably a public service.

Before 1991, and arguably still, the NHS in the UK exhibited a high level of organisational integration. In terms of the public dimension, almost all health care financed by the NHS was provided in its own facilities by its own personnel (France 1996a). While the status of the GP as an independent contractor means that public integration is formally incomplete, the virtual monopsony power of the NHS (the NHS is the sole purchaser of GP services, and lays down detailed contractual obligations on them) has made for effective integration. This is paralleled in NHS administration: health authorities in the UK are single-purpose, non-elected administrative bodies. They are field administrations of the centre, and have little relationship with local government. Health government in the UK is centrally integrated, and national government in the UK is invariably formed from a single party: between 1979 and 1997 the Conservative Party governed continuously and alone, advancing a distinct and confident ideological position. In combination, institutional and political factors gave central government a dominant authority in health policy making.

Sweden also displays a high degree of executive and public integration, but is strongly decentralised. Its government is drawn from a unicameral parliament, in which a Social Democratic hegemony established in the 1930s has faltered only briefly recently, between 1991 and 1994. There is little room for the market in either the finance or delivery of health care. In comparative perspective, perhaps the most notable feature of the Swedish system is its decentralisation: Sweden's is a kind of federal, rather than a national health service. Administrative control of the health sector is exerted through the ordinary structures of local government. County councils hold greater autonomy in respect of local health policy making in Sweden than do health authorities in the UK: their independence from the centre is much clearer, and their authority over medicine much greater, derived from their legitimacy as elected bodies (Ham 1988). In turn, this has made the Federation of County Councils the key player in national health policy development, though it has begun to lose cohesion in the 1990s (Garpenby 1995). Central government in Sweden retains framework responsibilities, though the control mechanisms available to it are very blunt. The Social Democrats withheld grant finance to councils on a number of occasions in the 1980s, and the conservative-liberal Bildt government froze taxes for the period 1991–93 (Garpenby 1995).

The integration of health care in Italy is much less clear. Since 1978, the SSN has remained dependent on contracts with private providers in order to deliver comprehensive levels of care (above). In the executive realm, Italian governments have tended to be short-lived coalitions, remaining relatively weak vis-à-vis the legislature and the judiciary. And while health ministerial capacity at the centre is seriously underdeveloped (France 1996a), integration is further compromised by confused relationships between centre and locality.[9] Interestingly, and in contrast to the UK, the creation of the SSN was intended as an act of administrative decentralisation (OECD 1994). The three-tier organisation of the Italian health service bears no more than partial similarity to the field administration of the NHS. In the UK, the Department of Health retains ultimate responsibility for managing as well as for financing health services. In Italy, although until recently the funding mechanism was centralised, management was devolved to regions and localities. This made for a separation of interests which was ultimately dysfunctional. While central government's interest lay in economic efficiency, regional governments – as elected bodies with constitutionally prescribed powers – were more concerned to meet their legal responsibilities to provide health care to their populations, and to maintain their organisational sovereignty independent of the centre (France 1996a).

The problem for the centre was how to control local spending. As long as regions did not have to finance USL[10] deficits, their efforts were best invested in lobbying central government for more funding, or blaming it for underfunding, rather than in monitoring and managing USL activity (France 1996b). There was considerable political benefit to be gained from capturing resources from the centre, but none from assuming responsibility for the ways in which they were used. When the SSN was formed, it was unclear whether the USL, the local body with exclusive administrative responsibility for health care provision, was accountable to regional or central government. USLs had been left to exploit, rather than resolve, the discrepancy between the financial reponsibility of the centre and the political responsibility of the region. Furthermore, they were controlled by local political nominees rather than by administrators prepared to take a lead from the centre (France 1996a).

The SSN was a major component of a large arena of sub-government *(sottog-overno)* in which, in Italy, the distribution of appointments and other favours was controlled by the parties. For a long time, health care was a political resource exploited by the *partitocrazia* (Ferrera 1996b): the incremental extension of insurance coverage to new occupations in the 1950s had created new administrative organisations and drawn new client groups to the Christian Democrats (DC) and Socialists (PSI); it also allowed them opportunities to extend privileges to providers, notably GPs working for insurance fund members,[11] as well as to find administrative posts for party supporters; it created opportunities, too, for the corrupt use of insurance fund reserves. What amounted to a structural mismanagement led to a debt crisis in health insurance in the 1970s, which was written off with the health reform of 1978. Yet the Management Committees of the new USLs remained political appointments: the 'spoils' system *(lottizzazione)* continued to seriously undermine the efficiency and probity of the SSN throughout the 1980s (Ferrera 1996b).

Health reform in 1992 settled the fight between the centre and the regions for control of the USLs in favour of the regions, but combined it with responsibility for meeting any shortfalls in funding (France 1996b). Meanwhile, cutbacks, ceilings and extended copayments meant that, as political patrons, the parties had less and less to offer their clients. In a climate of retrenchment, the SSN had become a political burden rather than a resource. From 1992 to 1993 an anticorruption backlash began to transform Italian party politics, and the effect of the simultaneous introduction of general managers to the USLs, appointed on a contractual basis with performance-linked remuneration, was to further reduce the party governance of the health system. As a result of these tortuous and contextual political processes, the relationship between core and periphery in Italian health politics appears to have more in common with the Swedish model than with the UK.

Integration and control

But what difference do varying degrees of integration make for the operation of health systems? One way of exploring this question is by examining patterns of health spending, both among national health services and in comparison with social insurance systems. Perhaps the key health policy problem for governments of advanced industrial countries in the 1980s and 1990s has been to control health spending (chapters 2, above and 5, below). Are some health care systems more expensive than others, and does more integration make for more control?

In general terms, there is a positive relationship between national wealth and health spending. The richer a country, the greater the proportion of its GDP it will spend on health care (Newhouse 1977, Hitiris and Posnett 1992). Within Europe, however, countries with similar levels of GDP – France and the UK, for example – spend different amounts on health care (Gray 1993; appendix 1). These differences can't be explained by varying measures of the possible demand for health care, such as the age structure of particular populations; they seem instead to be related to differences in its supply. And what are described here as

Table 3.1 The elasticity of health spending, 1960–1990[a]

	1960–70	1970–80	1980–90
France	1.31	1.20	1.19
Germany	1.32	1.44	1.11
Italy	1.48	1.07	1.16
Sweden	1.54	1.22	0.87
United Kingdom	1.23	1.15	0.96

Note: [a]Elasticity of growth of total expenditure on health to growth of total domestic expenditure.
Source: OECD (1993, table 1).

national health services tend to absorb lower proportions of national wealth than do social insurance systems. While France and Germany spend roughly 10 per cent of their GDP on health care, Italy and Sweden spend between 7.5 per cent and 8.5 per cent, and the UK less than that (appendix 1).[12] As a proportion of all health spending, public expenditure on health is higher in Sweden and the UK than France and Germany, though it is significantly lower in Italy. This follows from the descriptive accounts of different systems in this chapter and the next. As a proportion of GDP, however, health spending in all three national health services is significantly lower than in the social insurance systems (appendix 1).

Of itself, however, this says little about the impact of government. Information about the development of health spending over time (table 3.1) says more. In general, the elasticity of health spending in relation to GDP across countries was much greater before 1975 than after (Schieber and Poullier 1990 and chapter 2, above). In Europe, real health spending grew 70 per cent faster than GDP from 1960 to 1975, but only 30 per cent faster in the period immediately after that (Culyer 1990). Simply, and predictably, health spending grew more quickly in the period of the long boom from the mid-1950s to the early 1970s than in the period of economic austerity which followed. Yet, again, there are differences between different kinds of health system. As table 3.1 shows, the elasticity of health spending fell more dramatically in national health services than in social insurance systems. In the period 1960–70, the growth of health spending outstripped total domestic spending furthest in Italy and Sweden and least in the UK, with France and Germany showing a comparable rate in between. By 1980–90, health spending appeared most controlled in Sweden, with that of Italy falling to the levels of France and Germany. It is arguable that this reflects the consolidation of public health services in Sweden through major reform in 1970 and 1983, and the introduction of the SSN in Italy in 1978 (chapter 2, above). Meanwhile the elasticity of health spending in the UK has remained consistently lower than that of France and Germany.

The implication is that public funding makes for public control. What is important about the public element in health financing is that it is the product of an explicit policy decision: 'The public element in the finance of health care is special in that decisions about spending are quintessentially political' (Culyer 1990, p. 34). Since its foundation, NHS spending has been the outcome of an annual cabinet decision. The further implication is not that different health systems are more or less expensive in themselves, but that different ways of financing health care provide greater or lesser opportunity to control health spending. Sweden was the only country actually to reduce its proportionate health spending before 1985, by a strategy of central and local government cost containment. Essentially, it is the single payer who is best able to counteract the ability of providers (doctors and hospitals) to increase their income by increasing the supply of services and the fees charged for them. And if public funding makes for public control, greater degrees of public funding might be expected to make for greater degrees of public control. This is because it is organisational integration which both increases relative levels of public funding and which makes control effective. Public spending as a proportion of total health spending is lower in Italy than in Sweden or the UK (appendix 1, and above); this is partly why Italy shows a greater elasticity of health spending than its comparators (table 3.1).

A slightly different story needs to be told for the period 1985–95 (appendices 2 and 3). Health spending in Germany was controlled much more radically and quickly than in France, where it has continued to rise; the reasons for both will become clearer in chapter 4, below. Health spending in Sweden has continued to contract under pressure from continued economic difficulty, as the foregoing analysis would predict. In the UK, health spending has risen again, partly in anticipation of major reform and partly as a consequence of it. A perception of crisis in 1987–88 brought some emergency funding, which was supplemented in order to ease the passage of projected radical reform in 1990–91, with further increases following from the costs of expanded management functions. But these fluctuations were the effect of government control, not an escape from it: the general thesis relating integration to control is sustained.

In Italy, health spending rose rapidly in the late 1980s. This follows from the low level of integration of the Italian health service, in relation to its comparators. In Italy, the regions have normally overspent the budgets allocated to them for health care, claiming that central allocations made on the basis of macro-economic criteria were insufficient to meet the health care needs of the populations they serve. Total funding levels were effectively determined by a process of intergovernmental bargaining. What was happening was this: 'An initial appropriation is granted by central government for a given fiscal year; deficits begin to emerge during the same fiscal year; regions and [USLs] predict dire consequences for the capacity of the [SSN] to provide adequate care; central government concedes supplementary funding during the fiscal year or covers the deficits of the [USLs] after that fiscal year has closed, at times considerably long afterwards' (France 1991, p. 70). In the period 1990 to 1995, public spending on health as a proportion of GDP contracted significantly, partly as a result of reform, and partly reflecting the Italian government's commitment to containing its public sector deficit in order to meet the Maastricht criteria for membership of the European Monetary Union (EMU).

All of this is not to claim that national health services are necessarily any more successful than other kinds of health system. Indeed, the political control of health finance may itself constitute a problem, if its consequence is that services are starved of funds. This is an argument which has been raised vigorously in all three countries (Ham, Robinson and Benzeval 1990). Although countries with lower levels of health spending are not necessarily those with lower levels of health, the seeming cost effectiveness of their services holds only as long as it is based on measures of mortality and morbidity. The perception of the success or efficiency of national health services would no longer be justified if broader measures of quality such as waiting times and patient satisfaction were taken into account (Pfaff 1990); inefficiency can be expressed as poor quality as well as oversupply. Of itself, cost containment is not necessarily a virtue (Culyer 1990).

In each of these countries, for example, patients may have to wait for treatment, notably for specialist outpatient consultation and diagnostic testing, and then for subsequent non-urgent surgery. In the UK and Sweden, waiting lists rose in the latter part of the 1980s, becoming the specific object of regulation in the 1990s. The UK government published a Patient's Charter in 1991, implemented in 1992, which clarified the rights of NHS users and set standards for the reduction of waiting times. While the number of people waiting very long times (more than a year) has been reduced, the number of those waiting shorter periods has continued to increase, to more than 1 million (Ranade 1998a). NHS waiting lists tend to become an electoral issue, attracting targeted spending and ministerial intervention to reduce them in 1992 and 1997. In Sweden, the Federation of County Councils and the national government published a guarantee, effective from January 1992, covering diagnostic tests and defining a set of disease categories to be treated within a specified time (three months) (OECD 1994). In Italy, patients waiting more than four days for outpatient care may use a contracted hospital outside the SSN or outside their locality and even, for highly specialised care, outside the country (Bevan, France and Taroni 1992, France 1997). Authorisation to use alternative local services tends to be readily given, though that for care abroad has become increasingly tightly controlled. Across countries, the acknowledgement of the waiting list problem may be as significant as the means of addressing it. But in so far as the problem is characteristic of national health services, an effect of the political control which is able to restrict resource inputs for health care, the solution, similarly, tends to be a form of local managerial intervention, led by central fiat (cf. Ham 1997a).

All forms of health finance have associated problems. Social insurance systems, as the next chapter will show, have been confronted with rising costs. By the end of the 1980s, tax funding seemed no longer able to generate resources for health care at a level sufficient to satisfy demand. Though it may have been the NHS's great achievement to 'universalise the adequate' (Klein 1989, p. 147), times had changed. The adequate was no longer enough. In all three countries, established solutions to the problem of the relationship between state and market in health care were beginning to fail. The substance and process of subsequent reform is discussed in chapter 5. For now, the important question is what impact those changes have made on what we have defined as one of the key characteristics of national health services, their organisational integration.

Reform

In Sweden, the Social Democratic government was replaced by a conservative-liberal coalition in September 1991, which set up a reform commission to investigate the finance and organisation of health care, also addressing questions of rationing and priority setting. Its brief implicitly questioned county council responsibilities, though the councils successfully resisted the government's family doctor and private practitioner schemes of 1993–94. Inter-party wrangling between Conservatives at the centre and Social Democrats in the counties was resolved by a Social Democrat election victory in the autumn of 1994. For their part, counties continue to experiment with the purchaser–provider split and with GP fundholding.

The health care market constructed in the UK by NHS reform in 1991 is an internal one. Quasi-public providers (hospital trusts and GP fundholders) have continued to meet public responsibilities with public money. Current changes, creating Primary Care Groups, seem likely to improve their cohesion, while the capacity for strategic planning on the part of Health Authorities has been increased. Meanwhile, reform has strengthened rather than undermined the central integration of the NHS: the governing bodies of trusts are appointive rather than elective, and are chaired by central government nominees. The power of the centre is being enhanced by the establishment of National Service Frameworks, a National Institute for Clinical Excellence and a Commission for Health Improvement. In general, the autonomy of local management tends to be promoted only in so far as it conforms with central objectives (France 1996b).

The management of health care competition is much weaker in Italy than in UK. Reform there has created markets in which accredited public and private providers treat patients according to tariffs set by the regions. Regions and localities, constrained by the principle of patient freedom of choice of provider, often have little control over which services patients use, and to what extent. Central grants are allocated to regions on a weighted capitation basis, with overspends to be financed by the regions, who are now given powers to raise health care revenue in addition to their responsibilities for spending. Regions have been entitled to increase both contribution rates and copayments, within certain limits (France 1996b).

The organisational structure of national health services – their institutional integration – has clearly been affected by recent reform: indeed, that was the point of much of it. For the most part, however, it is difficult to see that it has been undermined. In the UK, it is the public axis which has been subject to most change: more systematic than in Sweden and, relative to its previous position, more radical than in Italy. But it has been reconstructed rather than reduced or removed. Similarly, increased local autonomy has been more than matched by the assumption of executive authority on the part of central government.[13] In Sweden, by contrast, it was the lack of central integration which obstructed the executive attempt to weaken public integration. The Italian SSN, meanwhile, seems both less public and less central: of all three countries, it is Italy which has come closest to the disaggregation of the health care state (Ferrera 1995, France 1996b).

This pattern, too, is explicable in terms of the preceding analysis. Increased integration makes for (and is made by) increased authority. But the concentration of authority also concentrates accountability (Pierson 1994). While higher levels of authority make it easier for government to formulate and implement health care reform, its concomitant accountability makes it unable or unwilling to cut back services valued by their populations. This helps to explain why the effects of reform on the users of health care, though significant, seem to be less radical in Sweden and the UK, the more integrated of the systems described here. 'Whereas the concentration of political authority clearly has a positive effect on social policy expansion, its impact on retrenchment appears to be more mixed' (Pierson 1994, p. 38).

In turn, it explains why reforms across the three countries have left the broad structures of health care funding unchanged. In part, this reflects a recognition on the part of governments that centrally funded, tax-based systems are effective in controlling costs. But in part, too, it is an effect of the continued political legitimacy of national health services. In Sweden, equity, tax finance and an element of planning continue to be seen as non-negotiable by reform commissions. In the UK, even a radical conservative government bent on marketisation was forced to declare that the NHS was 'safe with us'. In Italy, even if there was no longer anything for parties to gain from expanding service provision, there was at least something to be had from opposing the retrenchment strategies of opponents, in a kind of 'reverse auction' (Ferrera 1996b). Nevertheless, concern at the residualisation of the national health services – what Ferrera has elsewhere described as 'the conditioning of universalism' (Ferrera 1995) – remains. Where the use of market mechanisms in the distribution of health care is increased or extended, the commitment to equity is to some degree undermined. Reform in these systems has promoted allocative efficiency over social justice. Is it still right to talk of the health systems of Italy, Sweden and the UK as 'National Health Services'? What does that mean now?

In the UK, there is a familiar mantra that health services should be 'universal, comprehensive and free at point of use'. The NHS is of enormous symbolic value, representing the summit of Britain's welfare achievement. But, as this chapter has shown, it does not make the UK exceptional. Other countries have national health services, too. Nor, in this respect, are national health services very different from social insurance systems: universal access to health care is guaranteed just as well in other European countries (chapter 2, above, and chapters 4 and 7, below). In all three countries discussed here, the concept of national health care – of universal access to health care guaranteed by the state and financed from the public purse – remains more or less intact. But the real status of the idea of a health service, as opposed to a health system, is less clear. 'The NHS' is to some extent a rhetorical construction: to talk of it in these terms, as a single thing, is to lend a highly complex structure a monolithic appearance. In a similar way, Italy's SSN has been described as an 'institutionalised promise', though that also reflects its character as a very mixed form of NHS. Common reference to 'Swedish health services', by contrast, seems to acknowledge a greater regional plurality.

National health services, especially in Sweden and the UK, are currently preoccupied with working out the relationships between various institutional parts and their functions. The shell or superstructure of each system remains, but the rules have changed. In that sense, national health *services* were only ever administrative fictions. And now, new discourses of purchasers, providers and contracts, of commissioning and service agreements have taken their place, for which the word *system* seems better suited. Appropriately, too, these imply a transition from a paternalist, professional ethos, to a technocratic, managerial one.

At bottom, it may be the establishment of something definable as the public sector in health care which creates a problem of boundaries between public and private. And it may be those systems committed to equity which continue to view inequality as problematic. Similarly, it is the attempt to establish a bureaucratic hierarchy which invents problems of coordination. In social insurance systems, all of these distinctions are of much less ideological and political significance. In national health services, however, they represent problems which are forever reconstructed. It is those systems most driven by principles of equality and rationality which are most likely to be undermined by the failure to realise them.

Notes

1 Before Regional Health Authorities (RHAs) were replaced by the Regional Offices in 1995, the basic administrative unit in the NHS was known as the District Health Authority (DHA).

2 For more detailed discussion of equity issues in Italy, including comparison with the UK, see France (1996a, 1996b).

3 For an account of the 'territorial politics' of the NHS, see Mohan (1998).

4 For a detailed account of this episode, see Klein (1989, pp. 117–124).

5 These included ecclesiastical hospitals and both public and private university and research hospitals, as well as for-profit institutions. All but the last of these are administered independently but to all intents and purposes are considered to be SSN hospitals.

6   For specific discussion of the Italian case, see France (1991).
7   This schema draws heavily on Pierson (1994) and France (1996b). Pierson's horizontal and vertical integration, currently influential in new institutionalist analyses of social policy, are described here as executive and central integration respectively. Drawing on Pierson, but also on a different literature in neoinstitutional economics, France discusses the internalisation of the suppliers of services by those who finance them. This is also described as vertical integration. For the sake of clarity, these three significantly distinct features of institutional organisation have been separated and renamed.
8   See Ham (1988, pp. 395–397) for comparison of Britain and Sweden in this respect.
9   Robb (1986) shows how the difficulties of implementing SSN legislation were related to structural features of Italian society, including its ideological polarisation, the dominance of parties, its clientelism and the division between north and south.
10 *Unità Sanitaria Locale*, as ASLs were formerly known.
11 Many GPs acted as electoral advisers to their patients, especially in the south.
12 Until fairly recently, Sweden was thought to be a high spender on health care. There were various explanations for this, based on its relative economic prosperity (simply, Sweden had the money to spend) and on service and demographic factors (health provision was biased toward hospital-based care and the proportion of older people in the population was high). The underlying explanation is probably an artefactual one: the high figures usually reported for Sweden included social care budgets. Mental health budgets were reallocated to education and social security in 1985, while responsibility for residential care was transferred to municipal government level in 1992 (OECD 1994, Saltman 1998). The figure for total health spending used here is that given by OECD (1998); Saltman (1998) gives a lower figure for 1995 of 7.4 per cent of GDP.
13 For more elaboration, see Paton (1993, 1997) and Freeman (1998a).

4

Social insurance systems: France and Germany

Introduction

Health care in France and Germany is financed in large part independently of government, through systems of social insurance, and delivered by a mixture of public and private providers. In historical perspective, Germany is notable for its early development of the state-regulated provision of health care (chapter 2). More significantly now, it serves as a policy model: it is the prime example of what has been described as the 'public contract' pattern of the finance and provision of health care, that model on which other European systems are currently seen to be converging (OECD 1992, Hurst and Poullier 1992).[1] Germany's is also the largest system in Europe, covering more than 80 million people and, relative to GDP, the most expensive. The French system is smaller, approximately the same size as those of the UK and Italy in terms of the number of people it covers, but still significantly more expensive than any of the three national health services described in the previous chapter. Because of the way they are organised and the costs they incur, the French and German systems raise new questions about the government of health care.

As the last chapter showed, national health systems, while nominally simple, are in practice much more complex. Social insurance systems, by contrast, immediately seem highly complicated: a multiplicity of payers is mirrored by a multiplicity of providers, and the independence of both from government leaves their public/private status unclear. Yet their operation is perhaps simpler than it sometimes appears. This chapter begins by describing the organisation and delivery, finance and regulation of medical care in France and Germany. In order to capture the essence of this kind of system, as the previous chapter did in relation to national health services, it combines material from the two countries into a single discussion. As before, too, outline introductions to different systems are presented in boxes 4.1 and 4.2. The second part of the chapter then explores analytic questions about the nature of health politics in social insurance systems. It shows that here, too, problems of organisation, finance and regulatory authority in health care are virtually inextricable.

Box 4.1: The organisation of health care in France

Overview   This is a complex, universal but limited compulsory insurance system allowing for high degrees of freedom for both patient and doctor.

Service delivery   The CNAMTS (*Caisse nationale d'assurance maladie des travailleurs salariés*) covers 80 per cent of the population through a system of 16 regional and 133 local funds. Some 14 other, separate funds operating at national level cover specific occupational groups such as agricultural workers, merchant seamen and others. Statutory coverage is effectively universal (99 per cent). Benefits include income replacement as well as the costs of consultation and treatment. Two-thirds of individual insurance contributions are paid by employers, one-third by employees (in 1996, 12.8 per cent and 6.8 per cent of gross salary respectively). Health insurance payments cover approximately 70 per cent of ambulatory care costs and are made as reimbursements of consultation fees. Nine out of ten patients have supplementary insurance, provided either through *mutuelles* or private insurers, to cover copayment (known as the *ticket modérateur*).

  Two-thirds of beds are located in public hospitals, the rest in the private sector (which includes both for-profit and nonprofit institutions). Doctors in public hospitals are salaried civil servants, those in ambulatory care self-employed, independent practitioners. Half of all hospital doctors also work in ambulatory care. Ambulatory care doctors may be either generalists or specialists. Fee levels are negotiated by national agreement with sickness funds. Almost all doctors contract with the compulsory system, but up to a third depart from the negotiated fee schedule in favour of extra billing. Patients may choose and change their doctor as they wish, and may consult a specialist directly.

Finance   Health spending amounted to 9.9 per cent of GDP in 1995, public spending representing 81 per cent of the total. Social insurance accounted for 68.2 per cent of health spending and supplementary insurance for 10.2 per cent (7.5 per cent and 2.7 per cent through non-profit and for-profit schemes respectively); 3.8 per cent came from other public sources (central and local government) and 12.5 per cent from out-of-pocket payments by service users.

Governance   Regulatory authority for health care finance and coverage rests with the central government Ministries of Finance and Social Affairs and Health. Contribution rates, fee schedules and pharmaceutical prices are fixed by them. Regional and Departmental Bureaux of Health and Social Affairs coordinate the regional planning of medical equipment and local service delivery. The CNAMTS is responsible for the general development of sickness insurance; regional funds coordinate capital development, while local funds are responsible for the registration of members, for collecting contributions and the reimbursement of claims. The *caisses* are quasi-autonomous, subject to management boards representing employers and unions. Local hospitals tend to be well protected by local politicians: French mayors are often also parliamentary deputies with national influence.

Reform projects Public hospitals were given greater managerial autonomy in 1991. Clinical guidelines for the appropriate use of services, transferable patient records, and targets for growth in private practice fees and prescriptions were introduced in 1993. The *Plan Juppé* approved in 1996 proposed that the social security budget be fixed annually and in advance by parliament (rather than *ad hoc* by the insurance funds), and that higher levels of reimbursement be awarded to patients acceding to the gatekeeping functions of GPs; increased the sickness insurance contributions made by pensioners and the unemployed; introduced financial penalties for private practitioners who exceed spending targets and defined stricter accreditation procedures for hospitals.

Key sources: OECD (1992, 1998), Chambaud (1993), Letourmy (1995), Wilsford (1996), Kervasdoué *et al.* (1997), Palier (1997), Pomey and Poullier (1997).

Box 4.2: The organisation of health care in Germany

Overview This is the archetypal social insurance system, combining elements of solidarity with independence from government. Health care in Germany is financed by independent institutions and delivered by a mixed set of providers within a highly regulated framework.

Service delivery The compulsory insurance system (*Gesetzliche Kranken-versicherung*, GKV) is composed of a large number of independent sickness funds, which are of two kinds: regular funds (*RVO* – or *Reichsversicherungsord-nungskassen*), mandated by social insurance legislation, and substitute funds (*Ersatzkassen*). Regular funds include local or district sickness funds, company or factory funds and others catering for specific occupational groups such as miners, farmers and seamen. These cover 60 per cent of the population, including both blue and white collar workers. Substitute funds, which are former mutual aid schemes and usually have a nationwide organisation, cater for a further 28 per cent of the population, mainly white collar employees. Six per cent of statutory fund members have supplementary private insurance. Only high earners are allowed to rely on private insurance arrangements, which are usually non-profit schemes. Insurance contributions are financed in equal shares by employers and employees; benefits cover treatment as well as income maintenance.

Patients have direct access to doctors working in local practice, of whom more are specialists (60 per cent) than generalists (40 per cent). Patients are free to choose (and change) their doctor, though they must stay with one doctor during any one accounting period (three months). Until 1996, doctors' practice earnings were derived from a fee-for-service system, while being ultimately constrained by global budgeting; this has now been replaced by payment according to capitation and type of doctor. Most hospital doctors are salaried employees. Hospitals are owned and run by regional and local authorities (51 per cent of beds), by nonprofit organisations (35 per cent of beds) and some are run as businesses (14 per cent of beds).

Finance   Total health spending in 1995 amounted to 10.4 per cent of GDP. Social insurance payments made up 68.2 per cent of health care finance, while federal, state and local government funding accounted for a further 10 per cent, private insurance (including both patient reimbursement and payments to providers) for 6.6 per cent and user charges for 10.8 per cent.

Governance   Power to mandate procedural changes to the system lies with the legislature, responsibility for administration and implementation with the funds and doctors associations. National guidelines are implemented through regional agreements between states, funds, doctors and hospital providers. An assumption of corporatist self-government is sometimes betrayed by institutional fragmentation and, increasingly, by central regulation.

Reform projects   Recent reform has been conducted in three stages. In 1989, a *Health Care Reform Act* tied increases in sickness fund expenditure to increases in salaries and wages and introduced reference prices for drugs. In 1993, the *Structural Reform of Health Care* restricted the growth of health spending to the growth of sickness fund revenues; relaxed the former strict demarcation of hospital and ambulatory care; fixed doctor to population ratios; required that any over-spend of newly fixed drug budgets be repaid by doctors' associations and the pharmaceutical industry; changed hospital finance to payment by diagnosis rather than bed-day; introduced risk-pooling between sickness funds to improve equity; introduced freedom of movement between different kinds of fund as well as bringing some increase in cost-sharing. In 1997, further cost-containment and reorganisation legislation reduced sickness insurance contributions by 0.4 per cent and linked future increases to increased copayment, drew a distinction between basic and optional benefits and introduced a special levy for hospital maintenance.

Key sources: OECD (1992, 1998), Moran (1994), Schulenburg (1994), Altenstetter (1997), Greiner and Schulenburg (1997), Schwartz and Busse (1997), Freeman (1998b), Kamke (1998).

A crucial question of definition needs to be clarified first. What is meant by the term 'social insurance'? 'Social' and 'insurance' denote the two fundamental dimensions of health systems in turn, and each of them has both an organisational and an ideological basis. The idea of the social reflects their public, collective, compulsory aspect; that of insurance a more private, individual, voluntaristic one. Social insurance is publicly mandated, though paid for and provided by independent institutions. The obligation to be insured against health risks rests on the individual, though contribution rates are set at levels to cover the collective risks of those insured with a given fund. Members are entitled to health care on the basis of need, but receive income benefits proportionate to the value of the contributions they have made. In turn, the synthetic term 'social insurance' indicates that the system is a combination of these two, very different ways of organising health care. The individualism of the insurance principle is encased in a collectivism which guarantees universal access and makes for a degree of equity in burden sharing.[2] Inevitably, perhaps, this combination is not always as neat as the formulation suggests. It is the peculiar interface between individual and collective, public and private, state and market which is at the root of much of the difficulty of understanding these systems, as well as of the continuing complexity of their administration.

Organisation and delivery

In both Germany and France, sickness insurance benefits cover the costs of medical treatment (ambulatory and hospital care) as well as providing income replacement (sick pay).[3] The French national funds (*Caisses Nationales*) cover the whole population for the greater part of its health care needs; German statutory health insurance (*Gesetzliche Krankenversicherung*) covers the greater part of the population for all its needs. The *caisses* cover 99 per cent of the French population for health costs, less a substantial copayment for ambulatory consultations. For these, 87 per cent of the population has supplementary insurance through cooperative *mutuelles* and private insurers. In Germany, over 99 per cent of the population is insured against health risks, 88 per cent in the statutory scheme. Individuals are only exempt from statutory cover if their income is above a given ceiling, which is to say that only high earners are allowed to rely on private insurance arrangements, which are usually non-profit schemes. Some 75 per cent of the population is compulsorily insured in the statutory scheme while a smaller number (12–13 per cent) are voluntary members choosing to be insured in the GKV rather than privately (OECD 1992). Six per cent of GKV members have supplementary private cover (Greiner and Schulenburg 1997).

In both countries, most people join the undifferentiated general schemes, the local sickness funds (*Allgemeine Ortskrankenkassen, AOK*) in Germany and the local *caisses primaires* of the CNAMTS in France. In both countries, too, however, there also exists a set of independent occupational funds, which are counted as part of the public schemes. In part, these are the remnants of history, testifying to the workplace origins of social insurance, whether organised and financed by workers, employers or both. But they are indicators also of the continuing significance of the relationship between social rights and paid labour.[4] Meanwhile, the combination of segmented organisation and local administration makes for large numbers of funds in each case. There are almost 150 public funds in France and over 750 in Germany.[5] In both systems each fund, moreover, is a self-governing unit, with a management board composed of representatives of employers and trade unions (who represent fund members).

Two-thirds of hospital beds in France and half in Germany are located in the public sector. Other facilities are run by both for-profit and non-profit agencies. This range of providers means that the German hospital sector in particular is characterised by a large number of hospitals with low average bed capacity, while the ratio of beds to population is higher than in most other European countries. Hospital operating costs are met by sickness fund payments in both countries, and capital costs by regional and local governments. A system of global prospective budgeting for public hospitals in France was introduced in 1984–85. Until 1996, German hospitals were paid by sickness funds for each day a bed was filled (known as the *per diem* rate); case and procedure fees are now fixed centrally, with departmental day rates being left to local negotiation between providers and funds (Busse and Schwartz 1995). Private hospitals in both Germany and France are paid by bed-days. Capital development of hospitals is planned regionally, by state *(Land)* governments in Germany and by regional bureaux of health and social affairs in France. In France, patients may consult a hospital physician directly, without referral. German patients may consult a specialist directly, too, though that specialist will be in independent local practice. Access to hospital is by referral from a local practitioner; hospitals in Germany provide very little out-patient care.

Public hospitals in both France and Germany, as well as municipal medical centres in France, are staffed by salaried doctors. Other doctors work independently in local practice, and include both generalists and specialists. There are roughly half of each in France, though there are more specialists in local practice in Germany (60 per cent of the total) than generalists (40 per cent) (OECD 1992). Most work in solo rather than group practices.

Ambulatory care doctors in France are paid on a fee-for-service basis. The fee schedule is fixed by central government in negotiation with the doctors and sickness funds. Almost all doctors contract with the statutory insurance system, but up to one-quarter depart from the standard fee schedule in favour of extra billing (referred to as 'sector 2'). Patients are reimbursed by statutory insurers according to the national fee schedule, even when they choose to consult doctors who depart from it. Patients who do so must pay for the difference themselves, though they may have non-statutory insurance cover to help them. In order to treat patients under the statutory sickness insurance scheme in Germany, an independent doctor in local practice must also be a member of the relevant regional Association of Sickness Fund Doctors (*Kassenärztliche Vereinigung*). Associations are legally entrusted with ensuring the availability of services and have some obligation to inspect practice; their key task is to engage in collective bargaining over fee levels with insurance funds, and to administer payments to individual practitioners. Since 1997, doctors have been paid according to the category of physician to which they belong and the number of cases they treat each quarter (Kamke 1998).[6]

The way doctors are paid has important implications for how systems work. Indeed, health systems as such may represent not much more than elaborate ways of paying the doctor. Both French and German payment systems combine clinical freedom with patient choice, points of principle expressed in the traditional adherence of professional organisations to fee-for-service payment. In France, the national fee schedule has come to impinge on this to some extent (though sector 2 provision preserves a greater freedom of pricing for some doctors) as have collective contracts between physicans' associations and sickness funds in Germany.

Where income levels are more or less fixed *a priori* by capitation the material interest, if any, lies in treating less rather than more; the general practitioner in the UK, for example, has little economic incentive to treat, prescribe or refer. But where only the value of procedures is fixed by national or regional agreements, as is still the case in France and was so until very recently in Germany, doctors respond by writing more prescriptions and carrying out more diagnostic tests. This behaviour seems to be encouraged, moreover, by patient demand. The relatively high degrees of freedom allowed to both patient and doctor in social insurance systems seem to correlate with high levels of consumer satisfaction (see chapter 7). Patients like to choose their doctor, and like to consult doctors who seem concerned to satisfy them. And if patients not only expect to leave every consultation with a prescription but can also readily consult a different practitioner when their expectations are not met, then the physician who does not respond risks losing custom. Providers compete to meet demand by supplying more, better quality services; high numbers of consultations, procedures and prescriptions in turn fuel overall costs.[7]

For the most part, health service prices in both systems are regulated by government, usually in negotiation with payers (sickness insurance funds) and providers (doctors and hospitals). But because health care is paid for by third parties (insurers), fixed prices in practice fail to regulate either the production or the consumption of health care (chapter 1, above). In turn, this means that those systems which, historically, emphasise micro-level efficiency (OECD 1992), have come to risk macro-level unsustainability. In both France and Germany, the dominant discourse in health policy making for the last two decades has been the control of health spending. The contrast with the UK NHS, for example, is clear. There, where central control of health service finance amounts to effective control of the volume of service production, the perceived problem is that of underfunding. In social insurance systems, where governments have no such control, it is overspending.

Finance

Social insurance systems absorb larger amounts of GDP than national health services, and slightly lower proportions of their funding are derived from public sources (chapter 3, above, and appendix 1, below). In 1995, France spent 9.9 per cent of its GDP on health care, and Germany 10.4 per cent. In Germany, sickness insurance contributions are financed in equal shares by employers and employees; in France, employers pay approximately two-thirds and employees one-third of the gross contribution. In 1996, contributions averaged 19.6 per cent of total salary in France and 13.5 per cent in Germany (Palier 1997, Kamke 1998).

Statutory payments made by insurers to providers make up nearly 70 per cent of health spending in Germany; government funding, which comes from federal, regional and local sources and includes some payments to providers and investment capital a further 10 per cent; user charges account for 11 per cent and private insurance (both patient reimbursement and payments to providers) 7 per cent. French social insurance accounts for slightly more than 70 per cent of all health spending; supplementary insurance provided by the *mutuelles* and for-profit insurers for a further 10 per cent, copayments for 12.5 per cent and other public funding for 4 per cent (OECD 1998). It is important to note, however, that higher levels of personal spending and lower levels of public spending in France and Germany than in Sweden and the UK, for example, are neither so high or so low as to make these 'private' systems. Insurance contributions are deducted from wages, effectively constituting a form of payroll taxation.

The ways in which health care is paid for have a significant bearing on questions of equity. Contribution rates in France are fixed by the government for the *Caisses Nationales*, though there is some variation among non-CNAMTS occupational schemes. The high level of copayment required in ambulatory care tends to make health finance regressive, and this probably matters more than differences in contribution rates. Because rates in Germany are fixed by individual funds in order to cover the collective costs of their members, relatively low earners paying in to local funds with higher burdens of risk among their memberships inevitably pay higher rates of sickness insurance than others: in 1993, contributions ranged from 8.5 per cent to 16.8 per cent of gross wages (Greiner and Schulenburg 1997).[8] Unification made the problem of the differential risk burden between funds more acute, given the higher levels of morbidity and mortality combined with (and related to) lower incomes among the population of the former East Germany. A system of cross-subsidisation between funds to compensate for low revenues and high burdens (simply calculated according to the age and sex structure of fund memberships) was introduced in 1994.

Government

In France and Germany, as elsewhere, governments define the scope of health care entitlements, both in terms of the categories and proportions of their populations which are guaranteed access to publicly mandated health care, and in terms of the range and amount of benefits they receive. Yet the effective power of governments to control the operation of health care systems is circumscribed, in different countries in different ways.

In France, central government determines the scope and coverage of the insurance system, fixes contribution rates, sets fee schedules, controls budgets as well as salary and employment levels in public hospitals, and regulates pharmaceutical prices. Centralised, hierarchical planning is most clearly expressed in responsibilities for capital development in the hospital sector. Decisions about the location and distribution of major facilities are made by the centre on the basis of Regional Health Organisation Plans, which recently replaced what was known as the 'health map' (*carte sanitaire*) (Letourmy 1995). These are administered by regional and departmental bureaux. But far more of these control mechanisms are available to central government in respect of hospital than ambulatory care. Health care reflects a French policy style of public sector *dirigisme*, but only in part.

Government power in Germany is diffused across federal, regional and local tiers. The federal government is reponsible for health policy in general and for health legislation and jurisdiction, including professional and pharmaceutical regulation, medical research and contagious diseases legislation as well as the statutory sickness insurance system. Regional state governments approve federal legislation (in the parliamentary second chamber, the *Bundesrat*), supervise negotiations between physicians' associations and sickness funds; take responsibility for hospital planning and investment as well as for managing state-owned hospitals, and regulate medical education, which brings indirect control of the supply of doctors through manipulating the enrolment of medical students. In some states, public (environmental) health is devolved to the municipalities. A standing Conference of Ministers of Health of the regional states holds a further informal coordinating function.

Meanwhile, there are common tensions between core and periphery in both countries. Central state interests tend to lie in containing health spending; business and labour together exert downward pressure on labour costs such as statutory insurance contributions. Local and regional states (and local and regional politicians), however, with no responsibility for health finance, have a much stronger interest in expanding delivery, in new services, new building and investment, and the new employment each of these brings (Godt 1996). In the UK, by contrast, services are planned and delivered not by the local state but by agencies of the centre. It is not that this tension between core and periphery does not arise, but the possibilities of its being articulated are much more limited.

The problem of control is compounded by the relative weakness of central government agencies (chapter 2). The French health ministry has a small budget, and low prestige in what is a highly competitive, technocratic civil service (Godt 1996, Pomey and Poullier 1997). In Germany, similarly, health issues were formerly the responsibility of a relatively small department of health at the Federal Ministry of Youth, Family Affairs, Women and Health; these were taken over by a separate Ministry of Health formed in 1990, which also took responsibility for sickness insurance regulation, previously part of the social insurance remit of the Ministry of Labour and Social Affairs. But these remain specifically regulatory responsibilities; crucially, the federal government has no capacity of its own to implement policy but is dependent on other intermediary and subnational agencies' doing so (Alber 1991).

It is in the nature of social insurance systems that they exhibit lower levels of institutional integration than national health services (chapter 3). Central integration is at best partial, as described above. Executive integration is highly contingent, and a key part of the stories which unfold later in this chapter and the next. Public integration is limited by the corporatist, relatively autonomous structure and institutions of social insurance. In France, this means the CNAM 'technostructure' which effectively monitors and regulates the terms and conditions of contact between doctors and patients (Pomey and Poullier 1997). In Germany, the key player at national level is the Federal Committee of Physicians and Sickness Funds (Altenstetter 1997). Health politics in France and Germany – perhaps anywhere in the advanced industrial world – can be explicated in terms of the relationships between the state and organised interests.

States and interests

Social insurance systems are clearly not public systems in the way that national health services are, but nor can they be said to be 'private'. Finance and delivery are organisationally separate but publicly mandated: these are public systems with prices, not private systems with elements of public regulation. The space left by the state is not filled by a market. In so far as the public–private distinction has been reified in the national health services, it has been blurred in social insurance systems.

Some of the key actors in health policy in both countries here would themselves define these arrangements as 'free' systems. The idea of 'state medicine' is a spectre frequently raised against government initiatives in health policy debates in Germany, and not only by liberals and medical professionals. Conversely, the idea of *la médecine libérale* is a cultural banner of real significance in France. First expounded in the late 1920s, it proclaims freedom of choice of physician on the part of the patient, freedom of prescription or practice on the part of the physician, and assumes that payment is made directly by patient to doctor according to services provided. These are still the key organisational principles on which ambulatory care is based.

The concept of the free health system belies the ambiguity and tension in the relationships between the state and social actors in France and Germany. It is the stand-off between 'liberal medicine' and socialised health care (OECD 1992) which leaves the French health sector in particular perhaps the most complicated, least systematic of all European health systems. It is also the key to explaining why the system should be relatively expensive: the combination of a professional commitment to providing sophisticated health care to individuals and a public commitment to extending access to the whole population is almost inevitably a 'costly union' (Rodwin 1981).[9] In this context, the interesting questions are about how and why freedoms are asserted and protected, how and why they are compromised and withdrawn.

Since the late 1970s, there has been a general attempt in both France and Germany to link the overall development of health spending to the overall growth of GDP. This is normally expressed as a concern to stabilise insurance contribution rates, which in both countries have risen steadily. In France, this has been done in part through the ordinary mechanisms of regulation and bargaining described above. But these have been supplemented, even supplanted by what are known as ministerial *Plans*, which are essentially rescue programmes designed to stabilise welfare budgets (Palier 1997). Given that a *Plan* has been introduced on average once every eighteen months since 1975, these extraordinary measures need to be seen as an intrinsic aspect of the regulatory system (Letourmy 1995). Germany's Health Insurance Cost Containment Act of 1977 introduced the principle of an income-oriented expenditure policy, developed in further legislation in 1982 and 1983 and complemented by hospital reform during 1982–86. More fundamental ('structural') reform was attempted in 1989, 1993 and 1997.[10] In both countries, then, legislative activity over a twenty-year period constitutes what may be described as a routinisation of regulatory change.

How should this persistent activity be understood? At bottom, if the health sector can be thought of as 'an arena of struggle over the distribution of burdens and benefits' (Moran 1990), it shows simply how the intensity of that struggle increases in periods of financial constraint. But it does not mean that these systems are permanently on the verge of breakdown. It testifies to a contained instability, which says much about the political strength of the different political actors in social insurance systems, and about the relationships between them.

The instability or fluidity of health politics in France and Germany is derived from four associated factors. They are all essentially institutional. First, the sheer number of actors in the health care arena makes for decision-making processes of inordinate or unusual complexity. The 'free' systems necessarily function in conditions of systematic organisational uncertainty. In comparison with national health services, social insurance systems are complicated by the addition of an essential new actor, the insurance funds. These are not a single institution but a set of organisations, fragmented as much as segmented, competing as much as complementary. Second, the funds, the institutional linchpins of the system, have an uncertain legal and political status. They are semi-public, required by government to carry out certain functions but organisationally separate from it. Their gradual depoliticisation (chapter 2) has left a power vacuum at their centre. Third, because social insurance represents a much more straightforward institutionalisation of the health interests of capital and labour respectively, the boundaries between the health system and other spheres of economic and public policy are much more porous than are those of the UK or Sweden, for example. And fourth, the positioning of the state in the social insurance system is as uncertain as that of its mandated agencies, the funds. The state sets and operates the regulatory framework of the health sector, but it also has interests at stake; it is both legislator and actor. This means that opposing sides in health policy conflicts, providers and payers, taxpayers and patients, centre and locality are playing a game which the referee also needs to win, or at least avoid losing. At the same time, health ministerial capacities in both France and Germany are notably underdeveloped (above). The low level of integration characteristic of social insurance systems means that what might otherwise be routine policy decisions assume the status of legislative intervention. For all these reasons, health politics in this kind of system inevitably appears more labile than in national health services. There is no hegemonic role accorded to the state, but neither is there one for the market. Nor is there much evidence that systemic instability is genuinely critical. How is the political and economic order of social insurance systems established and maintained?

The production and distribution of health and medical services in Germany is ordered not by price but by negotiation.[11] Payments to providers are set in the course of negotiations with payers; they are not the result of marketplace activity. Negotiations take place at regional level between groups of sickness funds and physicians' associations, within what has been described as a 'highly formalized' relationship (Hurst 1991). Other negotiations take place at local level between funds and hospitals, reflecting what amounts to a bilateral monopoly (Hurst 1991, OECD 1992). A more general 'concertation' of negotiations is achieved in different ways (Henke 1986, Döhler 1991, Schulenburg 1992). Principal among these is a process of Concerted Action established under the terms of the 1977 Cost Containment Act (Henke 1986). The Concerted Action committee constitutes a national arena in which policy development is discussed by representatives of the major players involved in the finance, delivery and regulation of health care, including pharmaceutical companies as well as doctors' organisations, hospitals, sickness funds and governments.

The French funds, the *caisses*, are quasi-autonomous, managed by boards of union and employer representatives. But for their part, trade unions in France are weak and divided, unable to constitute themselves as a 'social partner' with leading responsibility for the social insurance system in the manner of their German counterparts. As a result, the difficult decisions regarding contributions and benefits have come to be taken by government (Palier 1997). Similarly, any positive influence the medical profession might exert on policy making is undermined by what has been termed its 'hyperfractionalism' (Wilsford 1996 and chapter 6, below). Thus it is the government which regulates and fixes both revenue and expenditure (contribution rates, fee schedules and pharmaceutical prices, for example) in the health insurance system (Godt 1996). Key responsibilities fall to the state almost by default. German decision making, by contrast, takes place within a stable, structured framework of negotiation which even the government finds it difficult to break. When reform does take place, it is significant that, in both countries, it is made possible by particular political conjunctures (chapter 5, below).

Pluralism, corporatism and the health care state

The social insurance system is a particular configuration of the health care state in Europe. Its key characteristics are the way interests are organised; this both reflects and determines the role and capacity of the state in health care in these countries. Health politics in France and Germany can only be understood in terms of the relationship of organised interests to each other and to the state.

In general, relationships between states and groups can be described as more or less organised or structured. An unstructured, pluralist conception would assert that 'most of the actions of government can be explained … as the result of struggles among groups of individuals with differing interests and varying resources of influence' (Dahl 1961, p. 5).[12] This is an understanding of politics centred on the organisation of interests and groups in society, rather than on the state. It assumes the existence of a number of groups or interests; its significance lies in its not assuming that any one group is necessarily pre-eminent, or dominant. In such a context, the process of policy bargaining is essentially unstable. But according to a more structured, corporatist conception of interest groups politics 'there are a few groups, each in a specially privileged relationship with the state … the groups have a dual role: both articulating demands on behalf of members and controlling members on behalf of government' (Jordan 1990, p. 296). This means that some interest groups – and some policy conflicts – are essentially more significant than others. The relationships between them, and between them and the state, may be formalised into regular negotiations.

The German health sector displays a kind of institutionalised collective bargaining (Döhler 1991) characteristic of corporatism. This is a layered or multi-dimensional corporatism: the sickness funds express an institutionalised relationship between capital and labour, and carry out tasks mandated by the state; in doing so, they negotiate with the physicians associations, which are also mandated bodies; the funds and associations, with a looser amalgam of hospital providers, together share responsibility for the finance and delivery of medical care. In this way, health policy negotiation is steered by intermediary groups and associations rather than by a public bureaucracy or by the market (Alber 1991). The German health system is a negotiated order, in which networks are more prominent than markets or hierarchies. The role of government is to write and rewrite the ground rules of negotiation, allocating and reallocating responsibilities to other agencies, defining functions, tasks and relationships and setting their ultimate financial constraints (chapter 5, below). Essentially, it acts as the 'architect of associational order' (Döhler 1991, 1995).

The French model, similarly, 'does not give the State the role of a dominant economic agent, but rather a role as the guarantor of the area for negotiation' (Letourmy 1995, p. 317). As in Germany, the formal role of government is not to make policy, but to rewrite the framework within which health policy negotiations are conducted. The problem is that the state is allocated supervisory or tutelary privileges over a set of actors which are individually weak and collectively tend to conflict rather than consensus. This leaves effective health policy responsibility uncertain. Where German governments can rely on mature and established corporate actors, the disordered pluralism of the health sector in France constitutes an effective veto on policy development. Its key features remain well protected, but the system as a whole is unable to adapt or respond to deepening crisis. In this context, one of the most significant elements of the *Plan Juppé* was to clarify health policy responsibilities, giving the government greater control of social security spending as well as subjecting the welfare budget to parliamentary approval (Kervasdoué *et al*. 1997, Palier 1997).

Since the late 1970s the health care state in Europe has been put under the combined and sustained pressures of technical development and cost constraint (chapter 2). In France and Germany, Europe's leading social insurance systems, this has induced a phase of increased, intensified health political negotiation. This is what the routinisation of reform in these systems really represents. At the same time, there is little evidence to suggest that the intensification of political bargaining has served to consolidate a corporatist organisation of the health sector. Both governments and organised interests in France and Germany are more or less continually concerned with the construction and reconstruction of reform coalitions. This manoeuvring makes for a fragmentation of health polit-ical interests while, in turn, the increasing pluralism of the health sector both allows and requires a reassertion of state authority. This restructuring of the health care state is described and discussed in the next chapter.

Notes

1   The public contract model is characterised by 'sickness funds, financed by compul-sory, income-related contributions, which contract directly with independent provid-ers for services supplied free of charge to patients' (Hurst and Poullier 1992, p. 179, OECD 1992, p. 137). See chapter 5, below.

2   Claus Offe describes social insurance as 'collective private property' (Offe 1990, cit. Clasen 1997, p. 68).

3   In both French (*assurance maladie*) and German (*Krankenversicherung*), health insu-rance is referred to as sickness insurance. Income maintenance is usually excluded from comparative health expenditure figures.

4   Employment status can be the basis of significant privilege: German civil servants are covered by a non-contributory scheme financed directly by government.

5   Recent change in Germany – unification and health sector reform – makes the number of sickness funds difficult to specify. Until 1990, a figure of 1100 was usually given for West Germany. Some 200 funds were created in the East when the insurance system was instituted there, making 1300 in all. Reform in 1993 was projected to reduce the number of local sickness funds from 270 to 20–30, through amalgama-tion (Abel-Smith and Mossialos 1994). Kamke (1998) notes 754 statutory funds, which is a 1996 figure from the Federal Ministry of Labour and Social Affairs.

6   Until 1996, medical procedures were allocated a point value on a nationally agreed rating scale. The monetary value of points was then fixed by negotiation between doctors' associations and groups of funds at regional state level, and varied between states accordingly. If the collective fees charged by physicians in any one state exceeded the total amount contracted between the funds and the physicians' associ-ation, the association would reduce the point value.

7   For a long time, German doctors have been subject to collective price agreements negotiated by their associations (above). While recent changes have sought to limit their service volume, too (Kamke 1998), it remains significant that capitation is not linked to registration as it is in the UK. The logic seems to be to maintain pressure

on the physician to satisfy the patient, which must be done by improving the quality rather than volume of services provided.

8   For more detailed discussion of this issue, see Wysong and Abel (1990).

9   Compare other commentators' headline summaries: 'negotiated waste' (Letourmy 1995), 'inconsistent regulation' (Kervasdoué *et al.* 1997), 'policy conundrum' (Pomey and Poullier 1997).

10 For a review of the latter, see Kamke (1998); more schematic, with a longer time-frame, is Altenstetter (1997).

11 The system has established 'comprehensive insurance coverage and freedom of choice but no free market on prices. Prices for medical services are set by negotiated fee schedules, *per diem* rates or other statutory pricing rules' (Schulenburg 1992, p. 716).

12 Cit. Jordan (1990, p. 289).

5

Reform and restructuring

Introduction

Beginning at the end of the 1970s, what has been described as an 'epidemic' of reform (Klein 1993a, 1995) swept the health systems of western Europe. Across countries, change has been both extensive and intensive since then, as well as extraordinarily persistent, and this chapter reviews its substance and significance in turn.[1] Legislative and administrative changes in France, Germany, Italy, Sweden and the UK in the period since 1980 are summarised in table 5.1. Immediately clear from the table is that what is referred to as 'reform' is no single thing, nor even necessarily any coherent package of measures. What is at issue here is the unprecedented intensification of the rate and complexity of change which has taken place in health care organisation in advanced industrial societies.

Chapter 2 (above) was about the extension of state involvement in health care, while chapters 3 and 4 set out in more detail the ways in which different systems work. This chapter returns to a common problematic, describing how the universalisation of the health care state was quickly followed by seemingly universal reform. Reform constituted a thoroughgoing re-examination and reconstruction of public authority in the health sector: it represents a continuing process of organisational stocktaking. The chapter sets out to explain why it took place, and why it took the form it did. It emphasises the importance of understanding the economic and political conditions under which systems operate. Reorganisation, it argues, was forced on governments by economic constraint, the result of economic downturn in the mid- to late 1970s. In the 1980s, governments were predominantly concerned with cost containment and macro-efficiency, that is, with controlling resource flows into health care and marking its boundaries with the wider economy. In the 1990s, attention has necessarily shifted to questions of micro-efficiency, that is, with the internal order of health systems (cf. Ham 1997b, Saltman 1998). The story is not one of the retreat of the state, but about the reconfiguring of its involvement in health care in order that its presence might be sustained.

Table 5.1 The reform of health care

France

1981   • 'sector 2' provision allows some doctors to charge fees above negotiated national schedule

1983   • negative list of drugs not reimbursable by statutory insurers introduced
       • patient copayment for hospitalisation introduced

1984   • global prospective budgeting for public sector hospitals

1986   • copayments for hospital stays and pharmaceuticals extended

1989   • national agency for health technology assessment established

1991   *Hospital Reform Act*
       • introduces regional planning of hospital care and medical technology
       • extends managerial autonomy of public hospitals and requires private hospitals to agree volume of service with insurance funds

1991   • employee social security contributions raised by 0.9%

1992   • indicative levels of spending agreed with doctors

1993   • closure of surplus hospital beds announced
       • introduction of clinical guidelines for medical practice
       • proportion of doctors' fees normally paid by patient raised from 25% to 30%, patient share of cost of necessary drugs similarly raised from 30% to 35%, that of comfort drugs from 60% to 65%

1994   • annual targets to be agreed between government and pharmaceutical industry for drug spending

1996   *Plan Juppé announces*
       • setting of social security budget annually and in advance by parliament
       • higher reimbursement for patients acceding to gatekeeping functions of GPs
       • financial penalties for private practitioners who exceed spending targets
       • stricter accreditation procedures for hospitals

Germany

1977   *Health Insurance Cost Containment Act*
       • introduces principle of income-oriented expenditure policy
       • creates Concerted Action forum for interested parties in health sector
       • re-introduces prospective budgets for payments from sickness funds to doctors' associations
       • strengthens medical audit
       • introduces risk-sharing across funds in respect of retired members
       • raises pharmaceutical copayments and requires family members with income above certain level to pay separate insurance premium

1981–82   *Supplementary Cost Containment Acts*
       • introduce patient copayments on medical aids and appliances and transport to hospital, extending them for drugs, physiotherapy and glasses

1982   *Hospital Cost Containment Act*
       • extends domain of concerted action to hospital care
       • requires that *per diem* rates for inpatient stays be negotiated between hospitals and sickness funds
       • involves sickness funds in regional states' hospital planning

Table 5.1 (*cont.*)

1983–84	*Amended Budget Acts*
	• introduce copayments for hospital care and extend them for drugs
1985	*Hospital Financing Act*
	• shifts mixed federal and regional state financing of hospital building to regional states
1986	*Federal Hospital Payment Regulation*
	• introduces prospective global budgets for hospital operating costs, to be negotiated between hospitals and sickness funds
1986	*Need Planning Act*
	• restricts registration of new doctors in some specialisms in some areas
1989	*Health Care Reform Act*
	• mandates that sickness fund expenditure increase no faster than wages
	• extends medical audit and quality assurance
	• introduces reference prices for non-patent drugs and other medical goods
	• extends copayments for hospital stays and patient transport
1993	*The Structural Reform of Health Care Act*
	• physician fees fixed at 1991 levels, tied to fund revenues until 1995; fee-for-service replaced by capitation and 'service complex' payments
	• introduction hospital payment by diagnosis rather than bed-day
	• regional drug budgets fixed; indicative drug budgets for individual practitioners introduced; reference pricing extended
	• risk-adjustment subsidies between funds
	• free movement between funds for insured members
1997	*Cost Containment Act*
	• reduces sickness insurance contributions by 0.4%
	First Reorganisation Act
	• mandates increase in copayments for any increase in contributions
	Second Reorganisation Act
	• copayment rates linked to development of wages and salaries
	• special flat-rate contribution for hospital maintenance levied to 1999
	• distinction made between basic and optional health care benefits
	• pilot projects in contracting between funds and doctors' associations

Italy

From 1978	• routinised revision of copayment regulations, including increased liability for prescription costs, extension to diagnostic procedures such as pathological tests and X-rays and experiments with application to specialist consultations, spa treatment and hospital stays; parallel amendments to exemption criteria introduced, using age and health risk rather than income
1983	• recruitment to SSN frozen
1984	• population ratios for major items of medical equipment fixed
1992–93	• after central allocation by capitation, all additional spending to be resourced by regions through taxation or charges
	• health districts made autonomous 'public enterprises', run by general managers rather than local committee, and their numbers reduced from 650 to 200–300

Table 5.1 *(cont.)*

• larger specialist hospitals become independent 'public hospital agencies'
• experiments with contracting to begin 1995
• SSN employees prohibited from holding either other salaried positions or other contractual relationships with SSN

1998 • insurance component of health care funding replaced by regional tax

Sweden

1983 *Health Care Act*
• makes county councils responsible for planning all health services

1985 *Dagmar Reform*
• converts funding of ambulatory care from retrospective, fee-for-service payment from national insurance system to prospective system based on capitation and administered exclusively by county councils

1988 • central government freeze on local taxation for 1990–92, later extended to 1993; bed closures and staffing cuts follow

1990–91 • Dagmar 50 project studies ways of improving productivity and performance in hospitals

1991 *Crossroads: future options for Swedish health care*
• Federation of County Councils report covers structure, organisation and finance of health care; developments at county level include: separation of purchase from provision; allocation of funds to local health districts on capitation basis; financing hospitals according to volume of services provided; internal market regulated by county councils

1991 • a government-funded waiting list initiative guarantees treatment for certain conditions within three months

1992 • Bildt government appoints Committee on Funding and Organisation of Health Services and Medical Care (HSU 2000), to report 1994; its brief to consider county council, primary care-led and compulsory insurance models for reform
• Family Doctor Scheme proposed
• responsiblity for social care transferred to municipalities

United Kingdom

1980 *Health Services Act*
• makes health authority cash limits legally binding
• weakens regulation of developing private sector by abolishing Health Services Board and reserving powers to Secretary of State

1981 • tax relief for employees' private health insurance

1982 • Rayner scrutinies of NHS efficiency introduced

1983 • performance indicators for health authorities introduced
• compulsory competitive tendering for ancillary services
• following *NHS Management Inquiry,* general management introduced 1984–86

1986 • introduction of *Resource Management Initiative* in hospitals, devolving budgetary responsibility to clinical directorates

1988 *Health and Medicines Act*
• introduces charges for eye tests and dental checks

Table 5.1 (*cont.*)

1990	*NHS and Community Care Act*
	• separates purchase from provision in health care, providing for managerially autonomous hospitals (NHS trusts), and allocating independent budgets to GPs to purchase non-acute hospital care for their patients; local authority social services departments are made lead agencies in social care
1997	Government white paper *The New NHS. Modern. Dependable* announces that
	• Health Authorities will become responsible for Health Improvement Programmes, involving the assessment of local health need and the strategic planning of health care
	• Primary Care Groups made up of all GPs and community nurses will gradually assume responsibility for the direct commissioning of health services, drawing up long-term service agreements with NHS trusts

Sources: Abel-Smith and Mossialos (1994), Bach (1993), Baggott (1994), Brunsdon and May (1995), Chambaud (1993), Ferrera (1995), Garpenby (1995), Kamke (1998), Glennerster and Matsaganis (1994), Mohan (1995), OECD (1992, 1994), Ranade (1998a), Schneider (1991), Schulenburg (1992, 1994), Wilsford (1996).

The fiscal imperative

Health care in Europe was becoming increasingly expensive. By 1975, in France, Germany and Sweden, public spending on health absorbed more than twice the proportion of GDP it had in 1960: in Italy, health spending had grown by more than two-thirds and in the UK by more than half (appendix 3).[2] Because the labour costs and tax rates needed to finance high levels of welfare spending make countries unattractive for economic investment, this continued rise in health spending constituted a 'fiscal imperative' for reform throughout the 1980s (Wilsford 1995). In the 1990s, it was exacerbated by further recession and the pressure placed on public budgets by governments keen to meet the Maastricht criteria for European monetary integration.

It was in this context that governments set out to control the volume of resources consumed by the health sector. Their strategies for doing so included setting limits to whole budgets or to some of their component parts, and reducing employment and capital investment. In 1977, for example, the German government introduced the principle of an income-oriented expenditure policy for the health insurance system, reinforcing it in 1989. In the UK, government had always been able to control the total amount of NHS spending by fixing its annual budget in advance; in 1980, cash limits were made legally binding on health authorities. Between 1990 and 1993, central government in Sweden imposed a freeze on local taxation, the bulk of which is used to fund health care. In Italy, as a result of a raft of changes made in 1992–93, health spending not met by central allocations was to be financed by regional governments. France moved to set a social security budget in 1996.

Prospective budgets for ambulatory care were introduced in Germany in 1977 and in Sweden in 1985. In Germany, physician fees were tied to the development of sickness fund revenues between 1991 and 1995. Prospective budgeting was introduced in the hospital sector in France in 1984 and in Germany in 1986. In France and Germany likewise, governments have sought to negotiate global drug spending with the pharmaceutical industry. Reference pricing was introduced in Germany in 1989 and a total pharmaceutical budget fixed prospectively in 1993. Ambulatory care doctors have been given indicative drug budgets, both in Germany and in the UK.

Personnel cuts were imposed on Regional and District Health Authorities in the UK in 1983, while the Italian government blocked further recruitment to the SSN in the same year. In both countries, too, new restrictions were placed on the additional earnings of doctors working in the public sector. Germany restricted the registration of new doctors in 1986 and introduced doctor to patient ratios in 1993. In France, physician access to sector 2 was frozen temporarily in 1990. Meanwhile, the growth of capital spending on major items of medical equipment was checked by introducing regional planning arrangements in Italy in 1984. Existing arrangements in France were extended to cover the use as well as acquisition of such technology in 1991. The UK closed hospital beds in the mid-late 1980s, and there were similar closures in France and Sweden in the early to mid-1990s.

These changes were about limiting – governments have almost never been able to reduce them – the volume of financial flows into health care. Attempts to raise more revenue for health care or to reduce the scope of entitlements have been the exception not the rule, even though the reason health systems had become more expensive was because more people had come to use more services more often: most of the growth in health spending was to be explained by rising rates of health care utilisation (Culyer 1990, Pfaff 1990, Schieber and Poullier 1990). Access to publicly funded health care had become effectively universal, while advances in medicine meant that a greater range of treatments was possible. Chronic illness, which is less easily or readily treated than acute illness, was more prevalent than before. A more informed public had learned to express greater demand for services, coupled with higher expectations of quality and privacy. At the same time, services themselves had become more expensive because they involved more sophisticated equipment and more specialised staff (Gray 1993).

But if systems had grown to limits (chapter 2, above), reform had limits, too. Remember that the health systems of western Europe are embedded in specific social, political and economic systems. The health care state has three faces: it is not simply a 'welfare state', but also a 'capitalist industrial state' and a 'pluralist democratic state' (Moran 1995a): 'Health care systems help shape capitalist economies and are shaped by those economies; they help shape democratic politics, and are shaped by democracy' (Moran 1998, p. 21). The economic orthodoxy of the 1980s was that economic performance was being inhibited by the ever-increasing 'social wage' – that proportion of earnings absorbed by taxes

and contributions to finance welfare. To spend more on health care would pro-
gressively reduce the capacity of the economy to fund it at all. Meanwhile, the
increased use of health services, while the principal explanation of rising costs,
testified to the increasing importance of access to health care in people's lives.
Retrenchment of any kind was likely to be highly contested, and governments
would risk much by embarking on it. In this way, the pluralist democratic face of
the health care state mitigated against the significant curtailment of benefits, and
its capitalist industrial face against much additional revenue raising.[3]

The partial exception to this is copayments or user charges, which have been
raised and extended in most countries, often more than once. They have been
most used in Italy,[4] where there has also been ultimately muted discussion of
allowing individual and group opt-outs from public provision. Copayments were
increased in conjunction with other legislation in Germany in 1981–82, 1983–84,
1989 and 1993, while a small additional health insurance contribution was levied
for hospital maintenance between 1997 and 1999. In France, charges were raised
in 1986 and 1993, and in the UK most notably in 1989, when they were introduced for eye tests and dental checks (though NHS prescription charges have
been raised at other times, too). The expansion of sector 2 provision in France
by definition brings with it extra billing. However, copayments tend to be applied
only to what might be termed medical peripherals, such as food and accommodation costs in hospitals, prescription drugs, dentistry and ophthalmics, and
they are invariably paralleled by elaborate exemption arrangements. No country
moved to reduce basic entitlements in this period, and core funding arrangements in tax-based and social insurance systems have remained unchanged
(Ranade 1998b, Saltman and Figueras 1998). Health care is still very much a
public affair.

Management, quality and competition

For key contextual reasons, therefore, the fiscal imperative has come to be be
focussed on the providers and administrators of health care rather than those
who use and/or pay for it. In general terms, too, macro-level cost containment
measures have been effective. Global budget growth is no longer a serious
problem in European health care systems. However, a significant indirect effect
of limiting resources without reducing output may be to drive down quality. It is
because of this that cost containment has everywhere been accompanied by
administrative changes designed to affect individual and organisational decision
making about the allocation and use of resources (OECD 1992). Direct control
of spending has been complemented by increasing the managerial functions of
both payers and providers, by making quality norms and standards more
explicit, and by introducing elements of competition. Most countries have also
sought to direct activity away from hospitals.

General management was introduced into the NHS in the mid-1980s, and is
now a feature of Italian districts (ASLs) and hospitals as well as the public hos-

pital sector in France. In the UK, hospital doctors were allocated budgetary responsibility for clinical directorates in 1986. In 1989, German sickness funds were given a new freedom to terminate contracts with inefficient hospital providers. In 1990–91, the Dagmar 50 project in Sweden studied ways of improving productivity and performance in hospitals. The introduction of the internal market into the NHS from 1991 enhanced the managerial responsibilities of health authorities, and effectively invented those of GP fundholders and hospital trusts.

Governments have also used changes in methods of funding to manipulate patterns of health care provision. Fee-for-service payment of doctors in ambulatory care was replaced by a capitation system in Sweden in 1985. Similar changes were made in Germany in 1993 where, at the same time, hospitals began to be paid by diagnosis rather than for each day a bed was filled. More specifically, physicians' prescribing practice can be constrained by listing drugs not covered by respective public schemes (a negative list) or, alternatively and more effectively, drawing up a limited list comprising only those drugs which are (a positive list). A negative list was introduced in France in 1983, and a limited list announced in the UK in 1984. In Germany, similar schemes have been proposed but not so far implemented. Meanwhile, medical audit was strengthened in Germany in 1977 and again in 1989, and introduced in the UK after 1990. Clinical guidelines were introduced in France in 1993, and hospital accreditation procedures tightened in 1996. Performance indicators were established for UK health authorities in 1983, and waiting list initiatives set up there in 1989 and in Sweden in 1991.

Competition is a key feature of new health policy environments. It features much more strongly in health policy debate and change in national health services than insurance systems – perhaps necessarily, since the separation of purchase from provision is characteristic of social insurance systems almost by definition (Moran 1994). Hospital ancillary services were made subject to compulsory competitive tendering in the UK in 1983. With the introduction of the internal market, providers of medical care such as the new hospital trusts also came to compete for Health Authority contracts. This pattern is echoed in some Swedish counties. In Italy, competition among providers for patients is much less regularised (chapter 3, above). In Germany, it was made possible for individuals to move between different kinds of sickness fund in search of lower premia and improved benefits. The strategy underlying these changes is better described as 'public competition' than marketisation. These bounded markets – in so far as they are markets at all – are very different to those which the introduction of highly integrated national health services was intended to replace. In the wake of reform, competition takes place among public providers for contracts held by public bodies and financed by public money. The managerial functions associated with contracting (information-gathering, planning, professional regulation) are starkly counterposed to naif conceptions of the market.

Medical care is expensive, and hospital care its most expensive component. The financial and organisational reform of health care in Europe has been accompanied by strategies of dehospitalisation and demedicalisation, both explicit and implicit. In different countries, various incentives work to reduce the length of inpatient hospital stays, and to encourage the relocation of patients (and budgets) to social care facilities. German hospitals, for example, have been allowed to provide outpatient care, while minor surgical procedures are now also provided by doctors in local practice, both in Germany and in the UK. Meanwhile, responsibilities for social care have been separated from health care more clearly than before, and accorded to local authorities in the UK in 1991 and to Swedish municipalities in 1992. Germany introduced a social care insurance scheme in 1995. At the same time, most countries made attempts to strengthen the profile of prevention in health policy (see chapter 8, below).

Convergence

As this summary suggests, there is a remarkable similarity of tone and purpose to health reform in different countries, even if varying institutional arrangements have meant that different instruments have been employed in realising it. In broad terms, Italy, Sweden and the UK have all sought to improve the micro-economic efficiency of their health systems by increasing elements of management and competition, albeit to different degrees and in different ways. France and Germany have sought to increase macro-economic control over costs with more assertive central regulation, while also enhancing the element of selectivity in agreements formed between purchasers and providers (Freeman 1998a, Ranade 1998b). What emerges from this is some convergence between systems, from different directions, on what the OECD has identified as the 'public contract' model of health provision (OECD 1992). In essence, this means that health care is financed from public sources, either through taxation or through compulsory insurance contributions; that health finance is administered by public agencies who are not also health care providers, and that providers, if not independent or even private bodies, are invested with the organisational and managerial autonomy to compete for contracts with purchasers. What is important about the model is that it seems suited to both macro-economic and micro-economic efficiency (OECD 1992).

In many respects, reform appears to have had a common functional or technical rationality. In part this reflects the commonality of problems faced by policy makers in different countries – notably the achievement of both micro- and macro-efficiency in the context of resource constraint. But it also points to wider and deeper social processes of convergence and diffusion. At the most general level, the health care state in Europe had emerged in the course of the nineteenth and twentieth centuries as a correlate of industrial capitalism and liberal democracy. Its concomitants were theirs: urbanisation, party politics, free professions and economic boom (chapter 2, above). A generalised pattern of reform indicated a turning point – one of the many definitions of 'crisis' – in that development, and also that it was common to all. The reform processes of the

1980s were prompted by changes to the increasingly international economic environment in which governments worked. Meanwhile, the international diffusion of technologies meant that medicine and its management shared common characteristics and concerns. The diffusion of new medical technologies (Kirchberger 1991, Stocking 1991), led often by multinational firms, was matched by that of what might be called new managerial technologies, such as Diagnosis-Related Groups (DRGs) (Kimberley and de Pouvourville 1993). If much of this was driven by commercial interests, cheap air travel and telecommunications meant that professional and research networks also functioned on an increasingly international scale.

These multilayered economic and social processes of convergence and diffusion help to explain why different systems began to change at more or less the same time. But they don't fully explain why they should do so in such strikingly similar ways. For that, a stronger concept of policy transfer is required.[5] By the 1980s, common or at least comparable solutions to health policy problems began to be drawn from a general, international currency of reform ideas. These were propagated by quickly developing, sometimes sector-specific organisations and networks, such as the European Healthcare Management Association (EHMA). The OECD has been influential in defining policy problems, disseminating comparative data on the performance and reform of health care systems with increasing frequency since 1977 (OECD 1977). Most notably, the American health economist Alain Enthoven's idea of managed competition became incorporated into a general discourse of health policy and planning (Enthoven 1993). Policy reform in the UK in 1989–91 drew heavily on his treatment of the NHS (Enthoven 1985), and then, in turn, informed policy discussion and debate in the Italian SSN (Bevan, France and Taroni 1992). Sweden's HSU 2000 Committee, similarly, referred its report to an international panel of health policy advisers for consideration (Garpenby 1995, note 8).

Centring the state

Evidence of convergence, diffusion and transfer raise key questions about the autonomy of states (Bennett 1991). Here, in the health sector, they imply that government action is at best reactive, at worst a *fait accompli*. In almost every instance, however, the paradoxical effect of cross-national pressures has been to extend the power of national governments to regulate and reorder highly complex systems of health provision. For cost containment, management, competition and quality control all predicated on public (state) intervention in what was once thought of as a realm of 'private government'. If, formerly, the role of the health care state was simply to finance and administer health services provided by medical professions,[6] these changes imply that, far from being in retreat, the state has made a significant advance. This applies to the substantive content of reform, that is, to the nature of health policy, as well as to health politics, that is, to the political process by which it was realised.

Some of the more general cost containment measures excepted, most of the instruments of health policy reform are local. They operate at the level of the firm – the practice or hospital – and the district, and sometimes the region. Everywhere, however, they are predicated on the centralisation of regulatory authority. The introduction of managed competition, for example, more characteristic of national health services than social insurance systems (above, and chapter 3), has been dependent on the kind of central government authority only the most integrated systems could generate: '[I]t is precisely the firmness of their external constraints which has permitted them to adopt the freedoms of the market within their publicly funded systems' (OECD 1992, p. 142). The very purpose of management was to enable the 'corporate rationalisers' to make rational decisions, for purchasers to be more discriminating in their relations with providers and for providers to be more efficient in production terms (Freeman 1998a).[7] Even in Germany, where users have become entitled to move between different kinds of sickness fund, a centralised system of redistribution of resources between funds has been required for competition among them to become effective. There, it is a cumulative process of reform which has served to strengthen the hand of government (chapter 4, above); this now seems likely to be deployed in the increased regulation of purchaser–provider contracts (Kamke 1998).

The corollary of the enhanced presence of the state is the exclusion of medicine from health policy decision making (chapter 6, below). As Godt established, 'In devising strategies to deal with overriding macro-economic concerns in an era of intense international competition, the French, British and West German states have come to view the medical profession as simply one interest group among many. There are still important aspects of health policy ... in which physicians' technical expertise prevails ... But in those areas which are crucial to broader public purposes, professional power has had to yield' (Godt 1987, p. 478).[8] One of the clearest examples of this is in the UK, where the *Working for Patients* document which formed the basis of reform discussion in the UK between 1989 and 1991 was drafted by a small group of ministers chaired by the Prime Minister. It published no evidence and undertook little consultation. 'In formulating, publishing and implementing its plans for change, the Thatcher administration ignored the medical profession and defied its campaign of opposition' (Klein 1995, p. 302, Mohan 1995). In Sweden, too, aggressive medical opposition testified to the exclusion of professional interests. The government's proposed Family Doctor Scheme provoked a series of strikes by doctors in early 1994 (Brunsdon and May 1995).[9] This was toward the end of a period of reinvigorated party conflict prompted by the change of government in 1991 (Garpenby 1995), and the liberal-conservative proposal was eventually blocked by the Social Democrats in parliament. In Germany, structural reform in 1993 deserved the name only by virtue of having excluded established provider interests. Here too, the health political arena was briefly reoccupied by parties (Bandelow 1994, below).

Until recently, however, policy change in the health sector has been unusual, big change even more so. For all the conflict of the 1980s and since, it is worth remembering that the universalisation of the health care state in the post-war period had been broadly consensual. Access to health care satisfied patients, doctors and employers, that is, both users and providers as well as those who ultimately paid for it. It also established organisational interests such as sickness funds and health authorities, on whom the administration of existing policy and the implementation of reform depended. Particular policies create particular institutional environments; they sustain particular sets of interests which in turn tend to sustain them. Ordinarily, institutional interests may be described as 'locked-in' to the systems of which they form a part.[10] Change, where it takes place, tends to be incremental. Decision making is shaped by institutions and interests, which have themselves been shaped by previous decisions: later decisions are constrained by earlier ones. In this sense, normal patterns of policy making may be described as 'path dependent' (Wilsford 1994, and chapter 2, above).

So what accounts for deviations from established paths of policy making? Why do they occur in some systems rather than others, at some times rather than others? What are the conditions which make reform possible? Change is a product of the interaction between the institutional and procedural routine characteristic of any given health system, and the pressures on that system from its environment. The different systems of health care finance and administration developed in west European countries in the post-war period afforded greater or lesser opportunities for regulatory steering (even if, ordinarily, governments had intervened relatively little). Sources of growing pressures on those systems were of two kinds, political and economic, and they were naturally interrelated. What mattered for the reform of health care was the combination of relative pressure on government, and its relative capacity to do something about it. Change has to do with the relationship between structure and conjuncture: '[S]tructures are the institutions and processes that form the infrastructural framework for policy (decisions) within which dynamic events unfold over time. This may be thought of as an endogenous universe, which then may be subject to exogenous shocks, that is, conjunctures' (Wilsford 1994, pp. 257–258). Among social insurance systems, the reform process has been more far-reaching in Germany than in France; among national health services, more radical in the UK than Italy or Sweden.

At the end of the 1980s, with even the experienced and ambitious labour minister Norbert Blüm outmanoeuvred by the lobbying of health political interests, it was difficult not to see the post-1975 period in Germany as one of reform blockade (Webber 1988 and 1989, Rosewitz and Webber 1990, Altenstetter 1997).[11] Both doctors and the pharmaceutical industry had links to the liberal FDP, the Christian Democrats' partner in government, and used them well, while the hospitals were protected by the *Länder*. Yet 1992 brought change of a more substantial kind. Horst Seehofer, a new health minister who had formerly been deputy to Blüm, had been appointed early in the year. He was able to use his position – the coalition had had a powerful majority since the first post-unification election in 1990 – to negotiate cross-party agreement on structural reform, working as much with the opposition Social Democrats as with the liberals. The background economic pressure imposed by a combination of world recession, high German wage costs and the deepening effects of unification strengthened Seehofer's hand (Wilsford 1994), and meant, too, that the reform arena belonged to political parties, not the sectional interests of Concerted Action (Bandelow 1994).[12] And the 1993 reform was genuinely structural: it affected physician fee levels and methods of payment, hospital funding and pharmaceutical pricing and effectively ended the segmentation of the insurance system into different kinds of fund. On the strength of those changes, further reform followed in 1997.

Reform in France, meanwhile, has tended to focus on public hospitals, that part of the system for which the government has exclusive and unambiguous responsibility. The key change came as early as 1984, with the shift in hospital funding from *per diem* payment to prospective budgeting. Here, too, contextual political and economic factors were crucial to its being realised. A socialist government had been elected in 1981 and tried unsuccessfully to spend its way out of recession, reverting to a policy of economic austerity in 1983; in the health ministry, the tenacious Kervasdoué was appointed Director of Hospitals at the same time (Wilsford 1994). An increased economic need for reform matched an increased political ability to carry to it through. The government's established institutional strength allowed it to reform mechanisms of hospital planning and management again in 1991.

As long as hospital budgets brought some success in containing costs, there was little to be gained by intervening in ambulatory care. But social security deficits continued to build through the late 1980s and into the 1990s: the government's calculation came to be that there was more to be lost, in respect of broader economic policy, in allowing contributions to grow than in restricting spending. The year 1995 brought a new President (Chirac) and a new Prime Minister (Juppé) who were, moreover (in contrast to the period of 'cohabitation' between Mitterrand and Balladur which had gone before), close political allies. The *Plan Juppé* constituted an extensive project of welfare reform. The proposed reduction of public sector pensions it contained was blocked by public protest, but health reform measures were passed in 1996 (Wilsford 1996). They included setting a prospective budget for the social security system as a whole, and by parliament rather than by the funds themselves, and also began to rewrite the rules governing the provision of ambulatory care. Overspending will now make practitioners liable to financial penalties, while patients consulting GPs first rather than going directly to specialists of their choice are entitled to enhanced reimbursement. The implicit assault is on physician freedom of practice and patient freedom of consultation in turn. The underlying government project, meanwhile, appears to be to universalise the statutory insurance system, increasing the proportion of its finance derived from taxation and legitimating greater central control (Palier 1997).

The 1989–91 period in the UK is described as 'Big Bang' reform (Klein 1995). This can't be explained by immediate economic circumstance: Britain was doing at least as well as, if not better than, most of its European competitors, while spending much less on health care in doing so (although, of course, it was the severity of the UK's economic decline in the 1970s and early 1980s which had pre-cipitated the extended neo-liberal project of successive Conservative administra-tions). This government entered its third term in 1987 with a large majority in parliament and a dominant Prime Minister personally committed to a specific set of market-oriented policy goals. Earlier health policy decisions, such as the introduction of management in 1984–86, had created new organisational inter-ests (managers themselves) who in many cases supported reform of the health sector. In the event, reform was prompted by political crisis in 1987–88, engen-dered by the failing performance, expressed in ward closures and lengthening waiting lists, of a cash-starved NHS. Because, in the UK, central government is responsible for the funding and organisation of health care, their problems were laid at its door. But, for the same reason, the government had greater capacity to respond to them than its counterparts in France and Germany, Italy and Sweden. 'The lesson of the British case ... is that strong, centralized state structures in a policy domain can sometimes lead, paradoxically, to greater departures from the established policy path. That is, wholly new trajectories are made more easily possible by strong structures' (Wilsford 1994, p. 265).

In Italy, a long period of legislative stasis since 1978 was punctuated by reor-ganisation in 1992–93. The USLs had been running deficits throughout the 1980s. In 1988 and 1989, health ministry reform initiatives had been blocked by the parties in parliament and under pressure from health sector lobbies (France 1996a). But the party system was to collapse in the early 1990s, leading to the for-mation of two so-called 'technical' governments, the first in mid-1992. While Italian public debt continued to worsen, the new government was charged with managing public finances so as to meet the Maastricht criteria for European monetary integration. Legislation was passed allowing the government wide dis-cretion to design and implement reform in key sectors, including health care (France 1996a).

The Swedish economy experienced a sharp and unexpected downturn at the end of the 1980s. In 1991, the Social Democrat government was replaced by a multiparty coalition led by Bildt and committed to economic deregulation, tax reform and the reduction of public spending. The HSU 2000 committee was con-voked to consider wholesale alternatives to existing arrangements for the finance and organisation of health care, though its proposals were buried among the claims of different parties in the nonsocialist coalition. Its work had petered out even before the election of 1994 (Garpenby 1995). The economic position had steadily and significantly worsened, despite the new government's austerity measures, and the Social Democrats were returned to power. The economic incentive to reform was undoubtedly significant, but the authority of the centre was insufficient to change the rules of the institutional game. Major reform would have implied renegotiating the position of county councils in relation to central government, a constitutional reordering clearly beyond the power of a fragile and short-lived administration (Garpenby 1995). Instead, less systematic change has occurred at sub-central level, taken up by the counties themselves.

The experience of the health sector in the 1980s and 1990s is that political and economic conjunctures in different countries have shaped reform as decisively as the performance of respective systems. That said, structural features of those systems – essentially the regulatory power they afford to government – filter conjunctural pressures in different ways. What matters in each case is the relative effect of structure and conjuncture. In Germany, the limited institutional authority of the centre was overcome by both political and economic factors, creating an opening for government which it continues to exploit. In France, structural limitations have restricted change by and large to hospital care. A new conjunctural moment seemed to arrive in 1995, though whether it established sufficient authority for government to pursue a more extended project of reform remains an open question. In both cases, the real significance of environmental pressures lies in the extent to which they facilitated (or even forced) changes in institutional arrangements: conjuncture changes structure. In the UK, the endogenous power of the centre, already higher than elsewhere, was made greater by external political factors. There, structure worked with, rather than against, conjuncture. In Italy and Sweden, reforming governments were offered brief windows of opportunity: severe economic constraint was common to both, but while the conjunctural weakness of parties in Italy worked in favour of systemic change there, the structural decentralisation of policy competence worked against it in Sweden.

Decentring the system?

The picture of an increasingly state-centred health politics is complemented by what might be described as a decentring of health systems. Health care states were invariably built on the sub-central government of finance and administration, and recent reform has consolidated the regional structure of health governance. Reform has instigated processes of scaling up from the district or locality as well as down from the centre, aggregating local administrations and interests as well as disaggregating national ones, often as an indirect effect of other changes. In many cases, financial and managerial responsibilities have been devolved more clearly than before to sub-central bureaux, and the number of those bureaux has been reduced. But regionalisation is the reverse of disintegration: it is best read as part of the formalisation of public control of health care. Meanwhile, there is little evidence of regulatory authority in the health sector being lost by national governments to supranational bodies such as the European Commission.

As the NHS reform in the UK took effect, some neighbouring Health

Authorities (then known as District Health Authorities as distinct from Regions) began to merge, as some DHAs did with Family Health Service Authorities, the separate bodies which had formerly administered GP contracts. In 1995, Regional Health Authorities were replaced by half the number of Regional Offices of the NHS Executive. Some fundholding general practices made group purchasing arrangements – which are now to be replaced by Primary Care Groups comprising all practitioners in a local area – with hospital providers (trusts). In Italy, the number of local administrative bodies (formerly USLs, now ASLs) was also reduced, while the financial accountability of regional government was more clearly defined. In France, regional systems for planning hospital care and the use of expensive medical technology were introduced in 1991, as they were in Italy in 1984. In France, too, new regional organisations[13] are being established to coordinate social insurance administration at regional level (Palier 1997). The reform of health insurance in Germany opened the way for the amalgamation of district funds. Earlier, exclusive responsibility for hospital building had been allocated to the regional states in 1985, and new arrangements made for authorising registrations of new physicians on the basis of regionally defined need. In Sweden, the counties were made responsible for all aspects of health service planning in 1983. They have become increasingly self-confident vis-à-vis the National Board of Health and Welfare, while some are being merged to form 'super-counties' (Saltman 1998). Questions of access and entitlement continue to be regulated by the centre, though regional autonomy in respect of reform has left the counties operating what are in administrative terms a number of different health care systems.

Across countries, there were economies of scale to be made by doing things on a regional basis which had formerly been done locally, if at all. But more than that, by increasing their relative size, regionalisation has strengthened the hand of the planners and purchasers against that of the providers. In determining the allocation of health care resources, public bodies – health authorities, sickness funds and local and regional governments – have been made increasingly ready and able to punch their weight. Third party payers had always met access and insurance functions – guaranteeing citizens' access to health care and covering its costs – though their agency function had been relatively underdeveloped (Ranade 1998b).[14] Now, as buyers, they were to become more discriminating. In turn, this has tended to increase the local and regional diversity of the health care state, as different administrative agencies have taken up, often with central encouragement, a new freedom to experiment. Coupled with macro-level convergence, this may make for a pattern of increasing regional variety within increasing national similarity among west European health care states.

Convergence has made for regionalisation, but not for internationalisation. Convergence is the result of systems with similar functions (the finance and provision of health care) being subjected to similar cross-national pressures. It does not erode their distinct identities, nor imply that the health care state is about to be supplanted by authorities which operate across national boundaries. Though the reform of health care in Europe has been paralleled by a process of international integration, institutionalised in the widening and deepening of the European Union, it is remarkable how little one has had to do with the other. For the moment, the development of European integration appears perfectly compatible with continued cross-national diversity in the health sector (Altenstetter 1992).

In principle, EU intervention in national policy making is legitimate only where it is required to facilitate or protect the mobility of goods, services, capital and labour between member states. In practice, as far as health issues are concerned, this has meant some standardisation of health and safety regulations in the workplace, and the issuing of reciprocal guarantees of the validity of worker entitlements and professional qualifications across countries. The Commission has no explicit competence in health policy as such, though it is beginning to stake such a claim in respect of public health (chapter 8, below). Title X (Article 129) of the Maastricht Treaty on European Union declared that 'The Community shall contribute towards ensuring a high level of human health protection by encouraging cooperation between the Member States and, if necessary, lending support to their action.' Specific programmes (Europe against AIDS, Europe against Cancer) have been funded, though it is notable that while they address areas of high legitimacy they require limited substantial intervention. Both here and in respect of health care, EU regulation complements, but does not replace, national provisions. It is concerned primarily and specifically with cross-border issues and claims as raised, for example, by the increased mobility of workers, pensioners and tourists (Altenstetter 1992).

This is not to deny that the movement of goods, services, capital and labour between countries takes place in the health sector as in other areas of service-based economies. For the most part, however, this would be classified as private sector activity. Some commercial insurers operate across national boundaries; American corporate providers have set up clinics and other facilities in Britain, and there is an international (if not global) market in specialised goods, such as medical equipment and pharmaceuticals (above). But these markets remain closely regulated by states, and interest representation on the part of industry, as in pharmaceuticals, continues to be organised at national level (Moran and Wood 1996). There is some movement of skilled medical labour as individuals move away from areas of high physician density (and unemployment) such as Germany. Historically, however, greater numbers of doctors have come to Britain from former colonial countries. Medical migration then and now is shaped by national authorities. Some patients travel to other countries for treatment although, here again, this is neither new nor yet substantial enough to be significant (chapter 7, below). In the eighteenth and nineteenth centuries, the wealthy might travel to visit spas and sanatoria; now they might travel to specialist private clinics. Other, more routine movement across borders seems to be determined by geographical proximity, as takes place between the Benelux countries or from health authorities in south-east England to providers in northern France.

The changing governance of the health care state

The idea that the health care state has three 'faces' – social, economic and political – was introduced in chapter 1, above. This chapter has addressed some of the implications of that idea: simply, that health systems have been changing because their environments have been changing. Processes of social, economic and political change are, of course, interrelated, and they are inevitably reflected in the organisation of health care.

The 'end to growth' was only one aspect (if, for welfare states the defining one) of a more general restructuring of capitalist economies (Mohan 1995). Among its key characteristics has been the emergence of a specialised service sector, rooted in technology-based expansion and entailing the formation of a new managerial class, the deskilling and sometimes reskilling of the traditional workforce and the emergence of a group of newly differentiated and demanding consumers. At the same time, the capacity of states to meet productive and redistributive functions has been called into question, as a resurgent liberalism has turned to market mechanisms for allocating goods and services. In industrial and commercial firms as well as government, meanwhile, administrative hierarchies have been broken down into networks of semi-autonomous units. Hierarchies of knowledge have been challenged, making the privileging of scientific rationality no longer certain or self-evident. The corollary of this was that the political consensus about the pre-eminence of the state and the medical profession in health policy and provision had eroded. The working assumption of the post-war era had been that the role of the state was simply to guarantee the financial and administrative framework within which medical care was to be delivered, according to professional judgement, to increasing proportions of European populations – and it no longer held. The changing positions of professions and users in health policy and politics are explored in chapters 6 and 7, below. This chapter concludes with the idea that, just as environmental change puts systems under pressure, so a key function of reform has been to strengthen their adaptive capacity.

Of the principal reform instruments described here, the purpose of macro-level cost-containment measures has been to ensure the continued viability of public health care. In almost every part of the health system, it has necessitated the development of enhanced management capacities. The function of management (as distinct from administration) is to recognise the constraints under which organisations operate, to define and redefine organisational goals and to promote the organisational change required to meet them. Among its guiding principles are the pursuit of quality and efficiency. Competition, meanwhile, perhaps the signal term in the international discourse of reform, may well turn out to have been one of the more transient. In the UK, where it was promoted most vigorously, and in Sweden, competition has turned relatively quickly into collaboration between larger units with more clearly defined functions of planning and providing care. More than anything, it served its purpose as a destabilising strategy, breaking up old rigidities and expectations (Freeman 1998a).

Regionalisation, for its part, may have been among the least recognised elements of reform. In context, it is the continuing expression of a historic tension in health politics between core and periphery, between central and local authority.[15] In an increasingly tense distributional environment, it served partly as a means of blame diffusion, representing 'states' efforts to distance themselves from hard choices' (White 1993, p. 25). There may have been other ways of doing this, but depoliticisation by decentralisation was both more subtle and more legitimate than by marketisation. As described here, the process of 'decentring' is properly the coalescing of systems (whether fragmented or integrated) into multiple centres. It deserves the name only in so far as the (re)construction of the management responsibilities of regions and localities is predicated on the accretion and assertion of central government authority.

Economic and political change threatened to undo many of the assumptions on which the public provision of health care was based. This made reform of some kind likely, if not inevitable. The question remains, however, why state regulation of health care not only persists, but in many ways has been strengthened through reform. And this despite the end to growth and the declining influence of organised labour, both of which had been so important in the universalisation of the health care state in the period following the Second World War. In part, new policies have created a new politics, in which the health care state has become, in a sense, self-sustaining. In economic terms, public health care represents a key market, a prime source of employment and a highly prized benefit. In turn, these are sources of political demand that it be maintained.[16] But what is significant here is that, in order that it be maintained, it must reach some accommodation with other, external sources of economic and political pressure. As these multiply, state intervention becomes ever more essential as the regulator of external pressure and internal demand.

Notes

1 Other recent reviews, taking a wider range of European and other countries, include Ham (1997b), Raffel (1997), WHO (1997), Ranade (1998b), Saltman and Figueras (1998). Mohan (1996) reviews different theoretical approaches to understanding reform in the UK.

2 As proportions of GDP, both total health spending and the proportion of health spending derived from public sources have risen consistently across OECD countries from 1960 (when comparative data series begin) (Schieber and Poullier 1990; appendices 2 and 3). In most countries, health spending has grown less quickly since the economic crisis induced by the OPEC oil price rise in 1973, though this has not meant that economic pressure for reform has gone away. The immediate effect of that was to reduce manufacturing activity and so, in relative terms, to increase the share of national income devoted to health more quickly than might otherwise have been expected (Gray 1993).

3 The Private Finance Initiative (PFI), by which new hospital building in the UK has been opened to private sector investment, is rather different, being an opportunity for capital rather than a burden to it.

4   For detail, see Ferrera (1995).

5   Discussion of policy transfer in general has been reinvigorated in the 1990s. For a review, see Dolowitz and Marsh (1996). For initial treatments of 'lesson drawing' in health policy communities, see Klein (1991, 1997) and Marmor and Plowden (1991).

6   For Bevan, the function of the Ministry of Health in the UK's new National Health Service was 'to provide the medical profession with the best and most modern apparatus of medicine, and to enable them freely to use it, in accordance with their training for the benefit of the people of this country. Every doctor must be free to use that apparatus without interference from secular organisations' (cit Allsop 1984, p. 17).

7   Interestingly, it may be that the proliferation of management at local and regional levels compensates for the low administrative capacity of the central state (chapter 2).

8   Cit. Klein (1993b, pp. 204–205).

9   The Seven Crowns legislation of 1970 had by-passed medical consultation, similarly (Björkman 1985).

10 For further theoretical discussion, see Pierson (1994, pp. 39–50).

11 For summary explanation, see Alber on 'Why the German health system is so hard to reform' (Alber 1991, pp. 263–267).

12 For detail and discussion, see Blanke and Perschke-Hartmann (1994).

13 *Unions Regionales des Caisses d'Assurances Maladie.*

14 Ranade draws on a conceptual schema outlined by Van de Ven, Schut and Rutten (1994).

15 'The history of health policy ... could be written as a history of balancing centrifugal and centripetal forces' (Altenstetter 1992, p. 824).

16 'The main source of durability comes from the high political costs associated with retrenchment initiatives ... The maturation of social programs has produced a new network of organized interests – the consumers and providers of social services – that are well placed to defend the welfare state' (Pierson 1994, pp. 180–181).

6

Doctors and states

Medical power

Health care systems are the means by which, in European countries, states ensure the supply of medical services to populations. To all intents and purposes, health care in Europe means medical care. And it is doctors who practise medicine; medicine is what doctors do.

There is some consensus among social scientists and historians that, by the third quarter of the twentieth century, the medical profession was the most powerful interest in the health sector. Its status was reflected in its political or organisational autonomy, its economic affluence and its social or cultural authority. Doctors themselves determined the nature and volume of the work they did and for which they were very highly paid. Their professional interests were promoted and protected by exclusive, monopolistic organisations. They were reinforced by the social status of medicine in societies in which legitimate and useful knowledge was based in scientific rationality and in which individual physical health had become a core value.

Up to and including most of the nineteenth century, however, few doctors had had any sort of affluence or authority. Large numbers of healers of various kinds competed for the custom of the small numbers able to pay for their services; the practice of medicine was characterised by occupational insecurity rather than institutionalised autonomy. And by the end of the twentieth century, similarly, there was much talk of the deprofessionalisation, proletarianisation and corporatisation of medicine.[1] Medical power, this suggests, is extrinsic rather than intrinsic: it is contingent on the social, economic and political contexts in which medical interests are pursued. If it varies over time, the likelihood is that it varies between countries, too.

This chapter assembles some of the empirical evidence of differences in the pattern of employment of doctors in European countries.[2] It looks at the political organisation of medicine in different countries in the context of differences in the organisation of government, and uses the evidence of recent reform to assess the relative strengths of professions and states. The purpose is to understand the interaction between doctors and government: the chapter paints a

picture of interdependence as much as competition and conflict. It begins by out-
lining what might be understood as the core interests of doctors and states
respectively, paying particular attention to the bases of accommodation between
them.

Doctors, like anyone else, want a degree of security in which to apply their
skills and want to be rewarded for doing so. Their professional security lies in
establishing and protecting the collective freedom to determine the conditions
under which they work. Doctors want to treat patients as they see fit, not as they
are required to by any third party, and they want to negotiate and define the
terms of their own employment. Professional rewards, meanwhile, lie in high
earnings and in the respect of peers and patients alike.

Medicine pays well, but only under certain conditions. Few individual
patients can afford to pay doctors directly for their treatment. It is the state which
makes the demand for health care effective by guaranteeing its collective finance,
either from tax revenues or through mandated insurance premia. On the other
hand, large numbers of doctors tend to drive down individual earnings, as each
is subjected to market competition from new entrants. Again, it is the state which
controls the supply of doctors or affords the profession itself the authority to do
so. This is the paradox of professionalism, what might be described as medicine's
guilty secret: the security and autonomy of medicine are necessarily endorsed by
the state.

But professional autonomy may also be threatened by the state. For example,
doctors' economic interests are best served where the profession acts as a monopoly supplier of services to individual clients. The effect of any form of third party
payment, however, is to aggregate the interests of patient-clients. Where health
care is publicly financed, some of the market advantages of monopoly are
counteracted by what amounts to the monopsony power of the state (Frenk and
Durán-Arenas 1993). State interests lie, in Wilsford's words, in 'provid[ing] relatively adequate coverage to most citizens without breaking the national bank'
(Wilsford 1995, p. 575): these may converge with medical interests, but they may
conflict with them, too. Public agencies may use their purchasing power to shape
professional activity in various ways, placing restrictions on physician income,
for example, or on clinical freedom, or both.

At the same time, however, the state requires that medicine perform important distributive functions in welfare states. The allocation of health care
resources is determined by doctors, both individually and collectively; it is
doctors who decide what treatment, if any, individual patients receive. Yet while
public resources are finite, the demand for health care appears limitless. In so far
as politics, in Lasswell's phrase, is about 'who gets what, when, how', key decisions in the health sector are depoliticised by consigning them to a seemingly
private, local, professional domain. This applies to other sorts of decisions, too.
In most circumstances, for example, absence from work is allowable only against
medical certification. In most countries, abortion is legally carried out only on
medical authority. Key social processes of reproduction and employment – also

including fitness for military service, or to stand trial – are regulated by medical decisions. What this means is that 'Political problems are, in effect, converted into clinical problems' (Klein 1989, p. 86). This works because, while the weaker party in each case sees its interests protected and supported by medical authority, the stronger party ensures that generic problems are isolated and individualised (Swaan 1990). For this process – what Swaan terms the 'medicalisation of discontent' – to appear legitimate, however, medicine itself must seem to be both authoritative and independent (Johnson 1993). Medical autonomy is functional to state interests.

The relationship between doctors and states may be best described as one of mutual dependence, though the risks each party runs mean that it is one which is necessarily conducted at arm's length. Doctors are dependent on states for their legal monopoly of medical practice, for guaranteeing the demand for health care and the resources to meet it; states in turn need doctors to provide care to patients, and to assume responsibility for making rationing decisions of various kinds (Day and Klein 1992). Medicine is threatened by the loss of autonomy, government by the prospect of intractable social and political conflict. That said, the two parties appear to have reached different settlements in different countries.

Doctors in Europe

The number of doctors varies markedly between countries. In 1994, while there were approximately three doctors for every thousand inhabitants in France, Germany and Sweden, there were more than five in Italy and less than two in the UK (table 6.1). Across countries, meanwhile, numbers of doctors have increased significantly since 1970. In France, Germany and Sweden, the physician to population ratio more than doubled. The corresponding increase in Italy appears much greater, while that in the UK was much smaller. This growth can be attributed to the general expansion of health care systems – probably driven more by supply-side factors, such as the increased technical capacity of medicine and the attractiveness of medical employment, rather than demand-side ones, since the

Table 6.1 Practising doctors, 1970–1994[a]

	1970	1980	1990	1994
France	1.3	2.0	2.6	2.8
Germany	1.3	1.8	2.5	3.3
Italy	1.1	2.6	4.7	5.3
Sweden	1.3	2.2	2.9	3.0
UK	1.1[b]	1.3	1.5	1.6

Notes: [a]Numbers per 1000 population; [b]not listed by OECD, but derived from Garpenby (1989, tables 4, 5 and 7).
Source: OECD (1998), except where otherwise stated.

Table 6.2 Practising doctors, generalist and specialist, 1992[a]

	GPs	Ambulatory specialists	Hospital specialists	Ratio of GPs to specialists
France	1.0	0.8	0.8	0.8
Germany	0.5	0.7	1.5	0.2
Sweden	0.4	0.1	2.1	0.2
UK	0.6	0.0	1.0	0.6

Note: [a]Numbers per 1000 population.
Source: Westert (1997, tables 1 and 2).

expansion of access to publicly funded health care was more or less complete by 1970 (chapter 2, above). Just as with absolute numbers, however, it is notable that professional expansion has been more restricted in some systems than in others.

Patterns in the distribution of doctors between general and specialist practice and between ambulatory and hospital care are difficult to discern (table 6.2). France has a relatively high number of GPs. The ratio of GPs to specialists is higher there and in the UK than in Sweden or Germany. Germany and Sweden have high numbers of specialists, proportionately more than twice as many as the UK. Specialists in France are evenly divided between ambulatory and hospital settings. In Germany, there are twice as many specialists in hospitals as in local practice. Sweden has very few specialists in local practice, and the UK effectively none.

The implications they have for clinical freedom, as well as for potential earnings, make the different ways in which doctors are paid in different countries politically significant (table 6.3). In each of the five countries here, doctors working in public hospitals are paid salaries. But this does not mean that doctors everywhere have exchanged – whether freely or under pressure – the autonomy of the independent contractor for the dependent status of the employee. Except in Sweden, most hospital doctors have retained the right to work privately, either in ambulatory care (France), in private sector hospitals (Italy) or by using public facilities for private work (the UK). A normal pattern of career progression in Germany, meanwhile, is from hospital employment to independent local practice. As for doctors working in ambulatory care, those in France are paid fees according to the services they provide. In Italy, Sweden and the UK, however, and now also in Germany, doctors' practice earnings are derived predominantly from capitation and salary payments though they may also earn fees from private work.

Italy has proportionately more doctors than other countries, though their average income is lower than elsewhere. In most countries, as the number of doctors has risen, so physician earnings relative to average earnings have fallen (table 6.4).[3] In Germany, oversupply has played a part in driving down the cost of medical labour. In 1957, the federal government proposed restricting the number of doctors licensed to treat statutory sickness fund patients to a ratio of

Table 6.3 Doctors' employment status and payment mechanisms

	Hospital care	*Ambulatory care*
France	Doctors in public hospitals are salaried civil servants, though half also work in ambulatory care.	Doctors in ambulatory care are self-employed, independent practitioners, paid on a fee-for-service basis. Almost all doctors contract with the national insurance system, but up to a quarter depart from the negotiated fee schedule in favour of extra billing.
Germany	Most hospital doctors are salaried employees.	Doctors working in local practice are independent practitioners. Until 1996, their earnings were derived from a fee-for-service system, while being ultimately constrained by global budgeting; this has now been replaced by payment according to type of doctor and the number of cases treated each quarter.
Italy	Doctors in public hospitals are salaried. Many doctors in private hospitals have part-time contracts, allowing them to work independently.	GPs are independent contractors to ASLs, earning income from capitation and additional service payments; most have comparatively few patients and many also work privately.
Sweden	Almost all doctors, in both hospital and ambulatory care, are salaried, public sector employees.	A small proportion of physicians works full-time in private practice, paid through the national insurance system according to a fee-for-service schedule.
UK	Hospital doctors are salaried, but may hold part-time contracts with the NHS and also work privately. Basic salaries may be supplemented by merit awards.	GPs are self-employed, independent practitioners: their earnings are derived from a combination of capitation payments, fees and practice allowances.

Sources: chapters 3 and 4, above.

one doctor for every 1500 patients. The proposal was challenged by the *Marburger Bund*, the association of hospital doctors, many of whose members normally plan to progress from hospital employment to independent local practice. In 1960, the Constitutional Court ruled against panelling, on the grounds that it represented an unreasonable restraint of trade. By 1980, however, the profession was threatened by the prospect of an oversupply, or 'glut', of trained

Table 6.4 Doctors' earnings, 1970–1990[a]

	1970	1975	1980	1985	1990
France	3.0	2.6	2.0	2.0	2.0
Germany[b]	6.5		6.1	5.2	4.9
Italy	1.5	1.2	1.1		
Sweden			2.1[c]		
UK		2.6	2.5	2.3	2.3

Notes: [a]Average physician earnings expressed as a multiple of average employee earnings; [b]Figures listed for Germany are for 1971, 1980, 1986 and 1989 respectively; [c]Early 1980s figure, from Klein (1990).
Source: OECD (1998).

doctors (Moran 1990). Increased numbers of doctors implied greater competition for patients, and diminishing earnings, among those already practising. Bargaining for protection from government, the associations of sickness fund doctors undertook some voluntary cost containment measures in 1983 and 1984. A post-qualifying position of *Arzt im Praktikum* was subsequently created, paid at one third of the usual hospital doctor's salary.

Significantly, however, physician incomes across countries have not fallen as much as the number of doctors has risen. In France, for example, though the relative number of doctors doubled between 1970 and 1990, the relative difference between their average earnings and average employee earnings remained two-thirds of its previous level. Increased technical scope and heightened economic competition seem to combine to encourage doctors to carry out a greater number of procedures than before, in order to maintain their earnings. '[T]he power of the medical profession is sufficient to safeguard the income of its members even without limiting entry: it simply generates more activity' (Klein 1990, p. 250). This power is not in the first instance collective or 'political': it consists in the very local – even bedside – capacity to allocate resources by individual decision making.

In combination, data about numbers of doctors, patterns of specialisation, payment mechanisms and earnings make for different national profiles of medical professional employment – even if, because the data are fragmented and insecure, these patterns can be taken as no more than suggestive. Of the five countries treated here, Italy has the highest number of doctors, though they are apparently the least well paid. Germany has a relatively high number of doctors and also a high number of specialists, a significant proportion of whom work in ambulatory care. German doctors remain exceptionally well paid, though their relative earnings have declined from the extraordinary high of more than six times average earnings in 1970. The way doctors in independent local practice are paid has recently been changed, in the interest of cost control. Sweden has almost as many doctors and specialists as Germany, though almost all of its specialists work in hospitals. Swedish doctors are almost all salaried employees.

France has slightly fewer doctors, though a much higher ratio (the highest) of GPs to specialists; French doctors work in general practice, as specialists in ambulatory settings and in hospital settings in roughly equal proportions. Independent practitioners in ambulatory care are paid on a fee-for-service basis, a feature which now distinguishes them from colleagues in other countries. The UK has the lowest number of doctors in proportion to its population, but a relatively high ratio of GPs to specialists. In recent decades, the relative number of doctors in the UK, and their earnings appear to have changed less than elsewhere. In different countries, then, professional interests appear to be realised in different ways. To understand how and why that might be so means knowing something about the way those interests are represented.

The organisation of interests

Medical professional bodies carry out two sets of functions, though these are not always clearly distinguished. The first includes those essential to self-regulation, and have to do with registration or licensing and also, if only by implication, with education and training. The second is more directly concerned with political representation and lobbying. Different professional interests are organised in different countries in different ways (table 6.5). Some are more cohesive than others, just as some states are more unitary or integrated than others. The standardisation and exclusivity implicit in professionalism – only licensed members with approved qualifications are entitled to call themselves medical practitioners – give the impression of homogeneity and cohesion. But strong latent tendencies to fragmentation also exist: generalism against specialism, one specialism against another, hospital against local practice. These prompt what may be described as intra-occupational turf wars, the kind of demarcation disputes which are an almost inevitable concomitant of work processes composed of a set of differentiated tasks. Disputes between groups of junior and senior doctors are common: while expansion brings new members into a profession, as long as traditional hierarchical forms of organisation remain in place they are allowed limited opportunities to progress.

The organisation of both states and professions can be thought of as more or less concentrated or diffuse (Marmor 1983)[4]. 'The most advantageous position for physicians is one in which they have managed to achieve corporatist organization under a pluralist system in which the state plays a limited role' (Frenk and Durán-Arenas 1993, p. 39). The paradigmatic example of such a situation is the US, though the closest approximation to it in Europe is probably Germany. There, though the medical profession itself is not centrally organised, the interests ranged against it are even more fragmented (Moran and Wood 1993). While regulatory and representative functions are carried out by diverse bodies, their leadership tends to be drawn from a comparatively small group of doctors in local practice, making for greater cohesion than might be expected. State interests, meanwhile, are weakened not only by federal structures (which the profession

Table 6.5 The political organisation of medicine

	Professional licensing	*Union representation*
France	The *Ordre des Médecins*, established in 1940, is organised at departmental, regional and national levels. It registers physicians, and also acts as a board of peers for the consideration of disciplinary and ethics questions.	Labour organisation among doctors in France is characterised by a relatively low rate of membership (less than 40%) and high fragmentation. This occurs along occupational, geographical and ideological lines. Three principal unions compete in claiming to represent both generalists and specialists in local, private practice: the CSMF (*Confédération des Syndicats Médicaux Français*), the FMF (*Fédération des Médecins de France*), and MG France (*Médecins généralistes de France*). Learned societies, of which there is a wide variety and whose principal purpose is to promote and discuss scientific advances in medicine, also play a lobbying role.
Germany	Professional licensing, and with it matters of ethics, discipline and continuing education, is controlled at regional state (*Land*) level by physicians' chambers (*Ärztekammer*). These are public bodies: doctors are legally obliged to become members, and chambers' decisions are legally binding. In order to treat patients under the statutory sickness insurance scheme (GKV), a doctor must also be a member of the relevant regional Association of Sickness Fund Doctors (*Kassenärztliche Vereinigung*).	Two principal organisations, the *Hartmannbund* and the *Marburger Bund* represent doctors in independent local practice and in hospitals respectively. Where the *Hartmannbund* tends to act as an interest group, lobbying at different stages of the policy making process, the *Marburger Bund* exerts more direct trade union functions, acting on behalf of what are salaried employees.
Italy	Doctors must belong to regional, semipublic organisations, the medical *Ordini*, in order to practise. Created in 1910, the *ordini* have licensing and disciplinary functions, and are run by doctors with the assistance of legally trained staff. A national federation of regional *ordini* (FNOM) is based in Rome. Since the formation of the SSN, and because they are the bodies to which all doctors belong, the ordini have become increasingly important as political agents.	Until very recently, Italian political processes centred on parties and their clientelist relations with groups. Doctors' interests (and especially those of the specialist elite) tend to have been represented through the Christian Democrats (DC), until 1993 the dominant party of government, rather than by medical professional associations.

Table 6.5 (*cont.*)

	Professional licensing	Union representation
Sweden	Medical licensing rests with the National Board of Health and Welfare. A separate Responsibility Board is charged with the investigation of alleged professional incompetence.	The Swedish Medical Association (SMA) exercises an effective monopoly of professional organisation, with a consistent membership rate of 90% since the 1940s. Sectional interests, such as those of consultants and junior doctors tend be subsumed within it. This works to maintain collective cohesion, although sometimes at the price of relative inactivity. The SMA is in turn affiliated to Sweden's peak organisation of professionals.
UK	The 1858 Medical Act established a General Medical Council charged with licensing individual practitioners and approving medical schools. The majority of its members are doctors. It investigates cases of professional misconduct, though a separate disciplinary machinery exists for those arising in the course of NHS practice. Specialist medical qualifications are approved by Royal Colleges, such as those of Physicians, of Surgeons and of General Practitioners.	The British Medical Association is taken to represent all doctors in negotiations over pay and conditions, though its membership rate fluctuates between 50% and 80%. Unlike the BMA, the much smaller Medical Practitioners' Union is affiliated to the general Trades Union Congress (TUC). There are other, separate organisations of consultants and junior doctors.

Sources: Ferrera (1989), Garpenby (1989), Krause (1988), Moran and Wood (1993), Pomey and Poullier (1997), Wilsford (1989, 1996).

shares) but by fragmentation among and between payers (funds) and providers (hospitals). Recent changes in German health politics, however, may be read as a process of the state's 'shoring up' its policy making autonomy (chapters 4 and 5, above).

In the UK, the power of the profession and of the state are both relatively concentrated. 'The pattern that flows from this is one of mutual accommodation institutionalized in a corporatist relationship between the profession and the state, punctuated every few decades by a major confrontation' (Klein 1993b, p. 204). Such confrontations include the passage of health insurance legislation in 1908–11, the foundation of the NHS in 1946–48, and the Working for Patients reform of 1989–91 (Day and Klein 1992). A similar model may be applied to Sweden where, though the delegation of regulatory responsibilities for health care to the county councils affords the state less unitary authority than in the UK, the corporatist pattern of accommodation with, if not coercion by, the state is much stronger than, say, in France, Germany or Italy (Lane and Arvidson 1989).

As in the UK, however, this occasionally dissolves into open confontation, as over outpatient fees in the 1950s, the Seven Crowns Reform of 1968–70 and the more recent Family Doctor Scheme (Garpenby 1989, Rehnberg 1997).

What has been described as the splintered 'organizational particularism' of the medical profession in France weakens its ability to press claims against what is a relatively strong state (Wilsford 1987, 1991), though perhaps not quite as much as might be expected. The relative strengths of state and profession differ markedly between ambulatory and hospital sectors (chapters 4 and 5, above). What is interesting about the French example is the way it suggests that state strength may be counter-productive in so far as it makes for frequent recourse to direct action among doctors, typically including demonstration and the collective withdrawal from administrative tasks.

In Italy, the organisation both of the state and of the medical profession remains relatively diffuse. A weak executive, uncertain relations between centre and region and the continuing importance of private providers in the SSN face a profession with very limited independent political organisation. Until recently, party politics mattered more in health care decision-making than either public or professional bodies. Significantly, however, the slow increase of the state presence in health care has served to strengthen the formal organisation of doctors (Krause 1988). A professional organisation of GPs was formed in 1982, not long after the passing of SSN legislation in 1978 (just as, in Germany, the formation of the *Hartmannbund* in 1900 was a response to the introduction of sickness insurance schemes). By the same token, it appears that the hold of parties on the Italian political process is now in relative decline.

The reform of medicine

Because they were attempts to restructure the environment in which doctors work, almost all aspects of health care reform affected medical practice (chapter 5). The introduction and extension of copayments for drugs, hospital stays and some ambulatory consultations, for example, though they affect the users of health services directly, indirectly modify physician activity by strengthening the economic interest of the patient against that of the professional. At the same time, though, some changes affected doctors more directly than others. They include certain restrictions on medical practice, changes in the ways doctors are paid and in the balance between primary and secondary care, and the introduction of managerial functions and responsibilities.

Medical practice is affected by limitations on where doctors work and what they do. In 1979, UK consultants' contracts were revised, encouraging many to undertake more private practice; in France, 'sector 2' arrangements for ambulatory care doctors were introduced in 1981 and then extended in 1986, but then frozen in 1990. Recruitment to the SSN was blocked in Italy in 1983, and staffing cuts imposed in Sweden in 1988. New specialist registrations were restricted in Germany in 1986, and doctor–patient ratios established in 1993. A system of medical audit, meanwhile, had been introduced in Germany in 1977; in 1989, arrangements for monitoring physicians' prescribing practice were strengthened and the medical auditing of sickness fund payments reformed. The 1990 reform of the NHS required doctors to implement medical audit schemes, though their purpose is ostensibly educational rather than regulatory and compliance is voluntary (Hatcher 1997). In France, similarly, the fee schedule agreed in 1993 included the introduction of quality guidelines (*Références Médicales Opposables*) for medical practice.

Changing the ways in which doctors are paid alters the pattern of economic incentives which partly inform their practice. This has been done in different countries for different reasons, and in different ways. In Germany, earnings have been capped as the fee-for-service system has evolved into one of collective prospective budgeting (1977) and, subsequently, a combination of capitation and service complex payments (1993). Sweden's Dagmar reform, similarly, changed the retrospective fee-for-service funding of ambulatory care to a prospective, capitation-based system in 1985. In contrast, fee payments to GPs in the UK were extended in 1989 to reward preventive screening.[5]

One of the principal effects of reform in the UK has been to change the status of general practice in relation to hospital medicine (Klein 1995). Fundholding GPs, for example, have found themselves for the first time in a position to make demands of hospital consultants – not in respect of the nature of their patients' treatment, but more of its promptness and location. Contracts with specialist providers may specify treatment within a certain time, or in a local clinic. Amalgamations between District Health Authorities and Family Health Service Authorities into purchasing consortia have brought primary care, for the first time in England, into the administrative core of the NHS. As in the UK, provision has been made in Germany for local practitioners to conduct minor surgery outside hospital. German hospitals were entitled to provide outpatient care for the first time in 1993, as the attempt was made to increase the proportion of primary care doctors among those in local practice by improving their fee levels. In 1996, the French government sought to promote a gatekeeping function for GPs by offering a higher rate of insurance reimbursement to patients accepting their referral decisions.[6]

The emergence of a management function in health care may be formulated explicitly, or it may occur as a concomitant of other kinds of system change. General managers began to be appointed to hospital and health authority positions in the UK in 1984–86, following the Griffiths report.[7] Clinical directorates were formed under the Resource Management Initiative in 1986. French public sector hospitals were accorded managerial autonomy in 1991 (Bach 1993), and Italian USLs appointed general managers in 1992–93. At the same time, both budgeting and contracting – keynotes of reform across countries – imply significant managerial capacity. The imposition of budgets requires that someone take responsibility for managing them, as does planned investment in medical technology. In order to draft contracts between payers and providers, services must be defined and costed, and volumes negotiated. In many instances, this has merely added to the work of existing administrative agencies such as health authorities, county councils and sickness funds. To many doctors, however, managerial constraints and responsibilities seemed new. In the UK, many GPs came to manage practice budgets; in Germany, reform in 1989 obliged doctors to consider the cost-effectiveness of referrals to different hospitals and in 1993 provided for individual indicative drugs budgets.

Taken together, these measures constitute a significant rewriting of the terms of medical practice. But their effect appears uncertain and ambivalent. Conceived in the pursuit of governmental rather than professional interests, they seem to serve as an indication of increasing state strength, but it is not always clear that this has taken place at doctors' expense. Where global budgets have been introduced, for example, doctors play an important part in the process by which they are negotiated, as in Germany and France. Similarly, medical audit appears less an imposition by government than a defensive strategy on the part of the profession. While peer review of medical practice may limit the autonomy of an individual practitioner (though probably not as much as non-medical assessment might), it protects and may even promote the collective autonomy of the profession as a whole (Mechanic 1991,[8] Klein 1995). Meanwhile, a heightened management function may be part of the 'organisational rationality' (Freddi 1989) of contemporary health systems. The increasing complexity of health care administration means that 'the physician alone simply can no longer cope with the new task domains' (Freddi 1989, p. 8). The relationship between physicians and managers is not necessarily a zero-sum game: both parties have an interest in sustaining the organisations to which they belong (Klein 1995). The impact of management on the work of nursing and ancillary staff is much greater than it is on medicine.

Medicine and government

In comparative perspective, there are two approaches to understanding the relationship between doctors and the state. One focuses on difference, and ways of explaining it, while the other deals in patterns of broad similarity. They represent different levels of analysis, though they are not necessarily incompatible. The first approach is essentially pluralist and institutionalist (chapter 1, above). The assumption is that professions and states are discrete entities, and that they have sometimes complementary, sometimes competing interests. In different countries, they are shaped by different histories and draw on different kinds of economic, social and political resources. Different patterns of medical earnings and employment, for example, reflect differences in the strength and organisation of interests and in the institutions which mediate them. This perspective takes settlements between states and doctors to constitute highly complex sets of variables. Methodologically, it tends to encourage partial explanations of limited groups of phenomena rather than more general readings of trends and patterns.

For example, where medical specialisation is concerned, it may be that the respective interests of doctors and governments diverge. Professional interest lies in specialisation and in the higher rewards, in terms of both status and earnings, that it brings. State interests lie in access and affordability, keynotes of primary rather than specialist care. It follows from this that, where state intervention in health care is stronger, state interests are likely to be better realised. Greater levels of executive, central and public integration of the health sector (chapter 3) ought to enable states to be more directive about patterns of medical employment. If this is true, national health services will provide higher levels of general and ambulatory care than social insurance systems do (Westert 1997).

By and large, the hypothesis is borne out by the evidence presented here (tables 6.1 and 6.2 above). The UK, the most integrated of the five systems, has not only the lowest number of doctors but by a long way the lowest number of specialists and at the same time a relatively high number of GPs. The German system, the least integrated, has a relatively high number of doctors and the highest proportion of specialists. Similarly, that France has the lowest number of hospital specialists of all five countries here may reflect the distinctive, centralised public control of its hospital sector. Though the number of doctors in Italy is high, the growth in numbers of public hospital doctors between 1970 and 1990 was low (OECD 1993, Abel-Smith *et al.* 1995, note 42). Its high number of hospital specialists makes Sweden the exception to the rule, reflecting the long-standing bias of the county councils toward hospital provision (Westert 1997).

Across countries, however, there is as much evidence of change in the relationship between doctors and governments as there is of stable and structured difference. For the most part, too, it is change in which general patterns – of the regulation and reregulation of medicine by the state – appear stronger than local differences.

It is public spending constraint, or the 'fiscal imperative' which has come to give states leverage over medical professions (chapter 5, above). Its effect has been to exert downward pressure on fees, salaries and clinical autonomy (Wilsford 1994, 1995). On its own, the increasing public finance of health care (chapter 2) seems to have little fundamental effect on professionalism; if anything, it increases its scope and security. What matters is that government becomes responsible for raising and allocating an increasing proportion of health care finance and then is faced by macro-economic constraint. It is this which causes the medical paradigm to give way, at least in part, to an economic paradigm (Klein 1993b). A discourse in which collective arrangements – such as social insurance – serve to support the treatment of individual patients by individual doctors comes to be replaced by one of the public management of the allocation of health services to populations.

Successful reform seems predicated on the exclusion of medicine from the policy making process (chapter 5). Reform in Germany and Sweden as well as the UK, for example – very different kinds of health system – indicated that the medical profession had lost its privileged place in decision making. What distinguishes these reforms and the conflicts that accompanied them is that they were about constitutional rather than more routine distributional issues (Day and Klein 1992). They were first order questions about the way in which health care should be organised, and the decision making process by which it should be governed; only indirectly were they about more of this and less of that, about who gets what. Those are the ordinary, secondary, distributional questions over which doctors and governments consistently find themselves at loggerheads. But when push comes to shove, it seems that states win out. And the stronger the state, the greater the shove is likely to be. '[S]ubstantial change occurs in all systems in the face of economic challenges to financing the system. The traditional prerogatives of a powerful and strategic interest – providers – are thereby diminished in every country. State autonomy is strengthened, beginning to triumph over even well-endowed, well-mobilized interests. However, change occurs more comprehensively and more rapidly in some countries than in others' (Wilsford 1995, p. 605). In Europe, medical interests and state interests are sometimes congruent, sometimes divergent; where they diverge too much, state action seems almost inevitable. This over-riding of professional autonomy is readily explicable in terms of the simple understanding of professionalism with which this chapter began: it is sanctioned by the state in the first place. The state giveth, and the state taketh away.

The underlying question here is why it should do so. Part of the answer lies in the contextual features of health care politics discussed in chapters 2 and 5, above. In the final quarter of the twentieth century, the economic and political conditions of the professional dominance that had been established over the preceding hundred years or so had altered (Moran 1995b). The insulation of medicine from economic and political competition – which is what professionalism signified – had become impossible to sustain. Much of the rest of the answer lies in the character and dynamic of professionalism itself.

Professional dominance

What was signally defined by Eliot Freidson as professional dominance (Freidson 1970) is assured rather than undermined by state intervention in health care. The public funding of health care does not represent the establishment of government power over doctors; rather, the health care state seems to guarantee demand for medical services, without seriously limiting clinical freedom or even physician income. Across countries, medical power is institutionalised in self-government and in quasi-corporatist negotiation between professional leaders and civil servants. Though these can be interrupted by serious policy making conflict, and though comparative differences exist in both collective organisation and individual career structures, by and large universalisation has consolidated the position of medical professions in Europe. Doctors do well.

But professional dominance is essentially unstable (Light 1995). One of the reasons why professionals enjoy high social standing is that they are seen to operate above both states and markets, serving the public interest – both individual and collective – of their clients. Over time, however, dominance can look like self-indulgence. The ever increasing elaboration and specialisation of the medical project makes it seem over-extended. It makes for increased cost, which affects everybody, while specialised therapeutic interventions directly affect only a few. It also tends to distance doctors from the ordinary and immediate concerns of their patients. At worst, professionals can be seen to be self-serving, standing above states and markets in order to manipulate them both, in accordance with personal and professional interests.

The first two or three decades after the Second World War represented a 'golden age' of medical professionalism. Medicine was suddenly available to all, and it was provided in newly built, distinctively modern facilities. Practising a form of magic which combined the technical brilliance of the scientist with the authority of the priest, doctors' social status seemed unimpeachable. During the 1970s, however, the societal consensus over welfare in general, and health care in particular, began to dissolve. The health care state was beset by crises both of resources and of legitimacy (chapter 2). Once the end of the long post-war boom became evident, health care spending was newly questioned. Arguments for retrenchment were compounded by growing scepticism over the inherent virtues of professional power, or what has been described as the 'cultural crisis of modern medicine' (Ehrenreich 1978). The multiple and sustained challenges to medicine have been brought by other professional groups including lawyers and nurses, by the media in various forms, by social movements among women, black people and gay men as well as among patients (Gabe, Kelleher and Williams 1994). These complex pressures have made it almost inevitable that the poles of the relationship between state and profession should be reversed, that the pendulum should start to swing back.

This notion is formalised by Light (1991, 1995) in the concept of countervailing power. Put simply, it supposes that an excess of power on one side of a relationship will generate a reciprocal increase on the other in order to counteract it. 'In those states where the government has played a central role in nurturing professions within the state structure but has allowed the professions to establish their own institutions and power base, the professions and the state go through phases of harmony and discord in which countervailing actions take place' (Light 1995, pp. 26–7). The idea is essentially dialectical, derived from Hegel through Marx,[9] and Light is drawn to it by his work on the history of German health care: the medical profession began to organise at the end of the nineteenth century (the *Hartmannbund* was formed in 1900) in order to challenge the dominant position of the sickness funds as employers of medical labour; the profession was granted legal status in 1935 as the funds, as representative organisations of workers, were being systematically deprived of influence; counter-measures, led by the state, began in the 1970s. These long cycles of interaction (Light 1991, 1995) echo the long periods of accommodation between state and profession interrupted by conflict in the UK and Sweden (Day and Klein 1992, Klein 1993b, above). The difference is that the concept of countervailing power says something about the logic of the sequence as a whole. Now what is interesting about medical professional autonomy is less its 'paradoxical' basis (above) than its 'ironic consequences' (Light 1995). The health care reform projects of the 1980s and 1990s may be read as countervailing actions undertaken by European states against their medical professions.

Medicine as government

Interpretations of the relationship between doctors and the state struggle with what appears to be a characteristic ambiguity. The construction of medical professional autonomy is 'paradoxical', in that it is sponsored and supported by the state. Its effects are 'ironic', in that it invites countervailing actions on the part of governments and others. The effects of those actions (health care reform) on doctors, meanwhile, are 'ambivalent'. Can these ambiguities be resolved?

An anglo-american tradition in the study of the professions has tended to conceive states and doctors as distinct entities, and the interaction between them as an instance of pluralist, group-based politics. A very different, continental tradition sees professions not as interests to be accommodated but as aspects or instruments of the state itself. In Europe, medical professions have been created by and through the activities of states. In Italian city-states and in Swedish rural districts, for example, medical professionalism begins rather than ends with practising doctors working as public employees (Krause 1988, Garpenby 1989). In this tradition, the emphasis is on interdependence, even identity between the profession and the state: what is otherwise taken to be a dichotomous relationship is in fact a symbiotic one.

Underlying conflicts between states and interests, which are essentially about the government of medicine, is a different (Foucauldian) problematic, that of government *through* medicine. For the state as such

> emerges out of a complex interplay of political activities, including the struggle for occupational jurisdictions. The state forms, in the context of the exercise of power, systems of technique and instrumentality: of notation, documentation, evaluation, monitoring and calculation, all of which function to construct the social world as arenas of action. It is in the context of such processes that expertise in the form of professionalism has become part of the state. Expert technologies, the practical activities of professional occupations, and the social authority attaching to professionalism are all implicated in the process of rendering the complexities of modern social and economic life knowable, practicable and amenable to governing. (Johnson 1995, p. 151)

This is not to say that the construction and manipulation of ideas about states and interests is in any way redundant, but it is to claim that these problems can usefully be situated within some broader theoretical propositions. The construction and regulation of professionalism is a means of governing medicine, and it is the government *of* medicine which makes government *through* medicine possible. Ideas about states acting *versus* interests only make sense in terms of the possibility of their acting *via* interests, too.

Medical practice in Europe is characterised by liberal professionalism. Its liberal aspect is articulated explicitly in French *médecine libérale*, though it inheres in health care organisation elsewhere, too. The idea captures the individualism of the relationship between patient and practitioner, the clinical freedom of the doctor and the freedom of choice of most patients in choosing whom to consult. It expresses the contractual rather than employment status of much medical work, and the nature of ambulatory care as an essentially private, entrepreneurial activity. Medical independence from government is guaranteed by the state, and the independence and autonomy accorded to the profession as a collectivity is assumed by individuals in practising without reference to or interference by other practitioners, as long as general rules of medical and ethical conduct are kept. The liberal character of medicine predominates, despite the apparent illiberalism of state-sponsored occupational closure, and the collectivism of third-party public finance.

The notion of autonomy or self-regulation which is intrinsic to professionalism means that medicine is governed at a distance (Osborne 1993). The distance between them is functional to both doctors and states. For doctors, autonomy is essential to the pursuit of professional and economic interests. For states, remember, one of the key functions of professionalism is to convert what are political problems of resources allocation into clinical decisions. As with the regionalisation of health care (chapter 5, above), '[C]onceding medical autonomy may represent a sensible political strategy for diffusing blame rather than conclusive evidence of professional power' (Klein 1993b, p. 204). Limiting the government *of* medicine enhances the prospect of government *through* medicine.

In the context of reform, however, the problem for government is that its challenges to professional autonomy risk the repoliticisation of medical decision-making. '[A]ny government that pursues policies with the effect of politicizing established areas of expertise and destabilizing existing professional jurisdictions also risks undermining the entrenched conditions that sustain legitimate official action' (Johnson 1993, p. 151). Opening professional autonomy to the public gaze – as held by the hospital manager, the lawyer or the patient organisation, for example – exposes medicine and government to complex, potentially uncontainable conflict.

What this implies, in turn, is that occupational closure in health care reflects not only the power of the professional but also the relative impotence of the patient or client. State intervention in health care is perfectly compatible with private (medical) interest, and does not necessarily advance public participation. This is the subject of the next chapter.

Notes

1 For introductions, see Light and Levine (1988) and Elston (1991).
2 At this level of generalisation, the available indicators are mostly crude. The analytic

statements they generate must remain tentative and their significance relative rather than absolute.

3 Comparative data on physician earnings are particularly incomplete and insecure. Evidence of patterns of change is more reliable than indications of absolute levels of income (OECD 1993).

4 Cit. Klein (1993b).

5 These were subsequently abandoned. For detail and discussion, see Lewis (1998).

6 The fate of this measure is unclear. It seems to be carried by a higher level of administration, having little immediate impact on patient or physician (Wilsford, personal communication).

7 For analytic accounts of the introduction of management to the NHS, see Strong and Robinson (1990), Harrison *et al.* (1992) and Harrison and Pollitt (1994).

8 Cit. Klein (1993b).

9 Light cites its application in economics by Galbraith: '[P]ower on one side of a market creates both the need for, and the prospect of reward to the exercise of countervailing power from the other side' (Galbraith 1956, cit. Light 1995, p. 26), also acknowledging earlier work in the sociology of the professions by Johnson (1972) and Larson (1977).

7

The users of health care

Introduction

Over time, patients have slowly lost some of the power they once had to determine the conditions under which they use health services. In England, in the sixteenth and seventeenth centuries, those individuals who could might have
bargained with any one of an array of practitioners over a particular treatment
or cure (Pelling 1985, Stacey 1988). In the eighteenth century, the establishment
of hospital medicine was led by lay initiatives; in the nineteenth century, in different countries, cooperative and mutual aid societies formed among industrial
workers would negotiate and contract for the services of a doctor (Deppe 1987,
Widgery 1988). By the early twentieth century, however, the organisational
strength of physicians had come to supersede that of their patients (chapter 2,
above). Until recently, and perhaps still, doctors have been seen to dominate
health politics (chapter 6). The doctor–patient relationship is constructed as a
relationship between individuals, and is dominated by the doctor. As a group,
patients (and those acting on their behalf) have been understood to be a
'repressed interest' (Alford 1975 and chapter 1, above).

A more recent cultural shift has taken place from the idea of the passive
patient to one of the active health care client (Herzlich and Pierret 1987). In part,
this reflects a new assertiveness among some of the users of the health care,
which has to do with critiques both of professional power and of science and
technology: 'The structure of lay thought and perceptions of modern medicine
is complex, subtle and sophisticated, and individuals are not simply passive consumers who are duped by medical ideology ... in late modernity, a far more "critical distance" is beginning to open up between modern medicine and the lay
populace' (Williams and Calnan 1996, pp. 1613, 1617). In part, too, it has been
prompted by other interests, such as commercial providers of medical insurance
and health care facilities, as well as by government. The patient interest has been
an essential part of the rhetoric of health reform in Europe, whether patients are
seen as consumers of health and medical goods and services or as individuals
with restated responsibilities for health maintenance (Crawford 1977, Freeman
1995; chapters 5, above, and 8, below).

This chapter sets out to explore the political behaviour of the users of health care in different European countries. It begins by assessing the nature and extent of health citizenship as well as general measures of public opinion. It uses Hirschman's concepts of exit, voice and loyalty to explore movement within and between sectors as well as patterns of representation, asking how far these have changed in the process of health care reform. One of the first problems it confronts, however, is that of terminology. The idea of the patient is strongly associated with passivity. It is a shared professional and common sense construction, but not an analytic one. More empirically, it captures only those people who have entered the health care delivery system. The alternative concept of the consumer seems essentially flawed, too, not least because of what economists refer to as the agency relationship. In health care, the interests of the consumer (known as the principal) are almost always mediated (defined and sometimes met) by an agent (usually a doctor) acting on the so-called consumer's behalf. In any case, if the idea of the patient is too passive and too trusting, that of the consumer is too rational and too active to reflect the real relationship of the user to health care. The concept of the client is heavily legalistic; unlike social work, health care has little basis in law. All three usages are highly individualistic: they tend to inhibit talking about the users of health care as a collectivity. For these reasons, the concept of the user seems preferable.[1]

Health citizenship: access and equity

By 1970, most people in most countries in Europe were entitled to publicly financed health care (Moran 1992; chapter 2, above, and table 7.1).[2] Almost everywhere (in every country except the Netherlands), more than 90 per cent of populations were covered; in more than half of all European countries, coverage had reached 100 per cent. The proportion of health care costs which continued to be borne by users was low, especially where the most expensive services (those provided in hospitals) were concerned (table 7.2). Coverage remains less complete for ambulatory care and less again for medical goods such as pharmaceuticals, which is to say that it is access to the centre of the health care system, the

Table 7.1 Health care coverage, 1960–1995[a]

	1960	1965	1970	1975	1980	1985	1990	1995
France	76.3	85.0	95.7	96.0	99.3	99.0	99.5	99.5
Germany	85.0	85.8	88.0	90.3	91.0	92.2	92.2	92.2
Italy	87.0	91.0	93.0	95.0	100.0	100.0	100.0	100.0
Sweden	100.0	100.0	100.0	100.0	100.0	100.0	100.0	100.0
United Kingdom	100.0	100.0	100.0	100.0	100.0	100.0	100.0	100.0

Note: [a]The share of the population which is eligible to medical goods and services that are included in total public health expenditure (OECD 1998).
Source: OECD (1998).

Table 7.2 Cost-sharing, 1960–1995[a]

	1960	1965	1970	1975	1980	1985	1990	1995
Inpatient care								
France	85.0	85.0	91.0	90.1	91.4	89.9	91.0	92.0
Germany	99.0	99.0	99.0	99.0	99.0	98.0	98.0	98.0
Italy	96.0	95.0	93.0	93.0	86.5	84.1	85.2	85.0
Sweden	100.0	100.0	100.0	100.0	98.6	96.6	99.7	98.0
United Kingdom	98.0	99.0	99.0	99.0	99.3	99.2	99.3	99.0
Ambulatory care								
France	60.0	60.0	68.0	67.6	67.6	64.8	60.0	57.0
Germany	93.0	93.0	93.0	93.0	93.0	92.0	92.0	90.0
Italy	71.0	78.0	70.0	70.0	82.6	77.4	73.8	73.0
Sweden	47.0	47.0	78.0	78.0	88.1	83.8	84.0	74.4
United Kingdom	88.0	89.0	90.0	91.0	89.0	88.0	88.0	88.0
Pharmaceutical goods								
France	60.0	60.0	63.0	62.4	61.9	63.5	58.7	54.0
Germany	60.0	60.0	60.0	60.0	60.0	57.0	50.0	48.0
Italy	68.0	84.0	90.0	84.0	70.8	68.1	66.4	65.0
Sweden	45.0	45.0	53.0	73.0	71.8	70.1	71.7	71.4
United Kingdom	88.0	88.0	90.0	93.0	92.7	92.3	91.0	90.0

Note: [a]The part of total medical care outlays (or outlays on hospital, ambulatory services, pharmaceuticals) which is covered under public programmes and which is actually paid from public sources of financing, i.e. after the deduction of co-insurance, deductibles and other forms of cost-sharing by private households.
Source: OECD (1998).

hospital, which is guaranteed by the state. Closer to the periphery, systems begin to diverge according to the extent to which the market becomes important as the regulator of access (Moran 1992). There is evidence that the public share of billing dropped slightly in the 1980s – again, more so for ambulatory care and pharmaceuticals – though coverage did not (chapter 5).

Equity is a common goal of European health systems (OECD 1992), though it is pursued in different countries by different means and with different degrees of success. A distinction might be drawn between financial equity and equity in access or delivery (Wagstaff, van Doorslaer *et al.* 1992, van Doorslaer, Wagstaff *et al.* 1992). Progessivity in revenue raising for health is predicated on the mix of mechanisms used; in most countries, these will include direct taxation, social insurance, private insurance and out-of-pocket payments. In predominantly tax-financed systems, health finance tends to be proportional or mildly progressive. In social insurance systems, it is regressive: while social insurance premia themselves are either proportional or progressive, they are often, as in Germany, only payable on incomes up to a given ceiling (Wagstaff, van Doorslaer *et al.* 1992).

Table 7.3 Satisfaction with health care systems, 1996

	France	Germany	Italy	Sweden	UK
Very satisfied	10.0	12.8	0.8	13.1	7.6
Fairly satisfied	55.1	53.2	15.5	54.2	40.5
Neither satisfied nor dissatisfied	18.7	21.4	23.1	16.7	10.0
Fairly dissatisfied	12.8	9.8	33.5	11.4	25.7
Very dissatisfied	1.8	1.1	25.9	2.8	15.2
Other	1.6	1.7	1.3	1.9	1.0
Per capita health spending 1995, US$ PPP	1971	2128	1503	1590	1234

Note: The original question read: 'In general, would you say you are very satisfied, fairly satisfied, neither satisfied nor dissatisfied, fairly dissatisfied or very dissatisfied with the way health care runs in (our country)?'
Sources: Mossialos (1997), OECD (1998).

However, if equity is taken to mean that individuals in equal need should receive the same treatment, irrespective of income, a different pattern emerges. Inequity continues to exist in countries where public cover is universal and comprehensive, that is in what might be referred to as the national health systems of Italy and the UK (as well as others such as Denmark and Spain). Conversely, segmented and much less comprehensive systems (such as the Netherlands and Switzerland) are not necessarily those with lower levels of equity (van Doorslaer, Wagstaff *et al.* 1992).

Satisfaction

Access to health care in Europe is effectively universal: the right to health care is certainly universal in principle and is almost wholly realised in practice, even if not always in wholly equitable ways. Meanwhile, the available survey data suggests that user satisfaction with health care systems varies between countries and over time. In 1996, among the five countries studied here, satisfaction with health systems appeared highest in France, Germany and Sweden, where those either 'very' or 'fairly' satisfied with the way health care is run represented something like 65 per cent of the population in each case (table 7.3). It was lowest in Italy, where almost 60 per cent were dissatisfied. The UK lay somewhere in between: half the population there was more or less satisfied, but a third dissatisfied. It may be that there is some general, positive correlation between user satisfaction and per capita health spending (Blendon *et al.* 1990, Mossialos 1997; table 7.3): satisfaction was higher in those countries which spent more on health care per head of population, probably because higher spending serves as an indicator of the relative modernity of facilities and the wider availability of medical technologies, of greater freedom of choice of physician and less waiting for elective and specialist

Table 7.4 Support for the reform of health care, 1996

	France	Germany	Italy	Sweden	UK
On the whole, health care in (our country) runs quite well	25.6	36.9	3.4	28.5	14.6
There are some good things ... and some minor changes would make it work better	40.9	38.5	15.1	44.1	27.4
There are some good things ... but only fundamental changes would make it work better	24.6	16.7	43.8	21.8	42.0
Health care in (our country) runs so badly that we need to rebuild it completely	5.0	2.2	33.1	3.4	14.0
Other	3.9	5.7	4.5	2.2	2.0

Note: The original question read: 'Now, I will read you four statements about the way health care runs in (our country). Which one comes closest to your own point of view?'
Source: Mossialos (1997).

Table 7.5 Support for the reform of health care, 1990

	France	West Germany	Italy	Sweden	UK
On the whole, the health care system works pretty well, and only minor changes are necessary to make it work better	41	41	12	32	27
There are some good things in our health care system, but fundamental changes are needed to make it work better	42	35	46	58	52
Our health care system has so much wrong with it that we need to completely rebuild it	10	13	40	6	17

Source: Blendon *et al.* (1990).

treatment (Blendon *et al.* 1990). That said, significant differences emerge for comparable levels of spending: in 1995, Italy spent much more per capita than the UK and almost as much as Sweden, though it satisfied few of its users.

Interestingly, support for health care reform across countries was higher in 1996 than measured levels of satisfaction might suggest (Mossialos 1997; table 7.4), though it was lower than that reported in a slightly different but comparable survey for 1990 (Blendon *et al.* 1990; table 7.5). At that time, there was significant support for fundamental reform in each of the five countries considered here. It was more radical in Italy than elsewhere, but still strong in Sweden and the UK. Even in France and Germany, there was as much support for fundamental changes as for minor ones. By 1996, majority support for a degree of change in each country remained, though the balance of opinion now seemed to be for minor changes in France, Germany and Sweden, for fundamental change in the UK, and still for more radical, thoroughgoing change in Italy.

It is important to recognise that there is a distinction to be made between perceptions of the efficiency of health systems and of the quality of health care. Users tend to be more satisfied with their own health care than with their country's health care system, though there is naturally some correlation between the two. Hsiao reports levels of satisfaction with care as such consistently higher than 80 per cent in Germany, Sweden and the UK (Hsiao 1992). This is echoed by other Eurobarometer data from 1992: in the social insurance systems, more than 90 per cent of users thought the quality of care they received was good, though a third saw services as inefficient. In the UK, 81 per cent thought their quality of care was good, but 43 per cent thought services were inefficient. Less than half the users of health services in Italy – in common with those in Spain, Portugal and Greece – saw those services as good while a majority, around four-fifths, saw them as inefficient (Ferrera 1993). Unsurprisingly, perhaps, patients seem to appreciate doctors and nurses much more than they do politicians, policy makers and administrators.

What all of this means is that large numbers of the users of health care, though they enjoy access to health services, are critical – sometimes highly critical – of the ways health care systems seem, to them, to work (or not work). How is this dissatisfaction processed, and what are its political effects? To understand dissatisfaction requires a more dynamic modelling of health citizenship. One way of providing that is to draw on Hirschman's concepts of exit, voice and loyalty (Hirschman 1970). His model is appropriate here for two reasons. First, it is attractive for its combination of economic and political theory: both analytically and prescriptively, recent comparative work in health policy is notable for its integration of political and economic considerations, and exit and voice are meant as 'impersonations' of economic and political behaviour in turn. Second, Hirschman's contextual problematic is the organisation in decline: across Europe, health services are certainly in question (OECD 1992, Gabe, Kelleher and Williams 1994), if not in decline. Indeed, the deepening mix of organisational forms in the funding and delivery of health care, and the increased politicisation of health issues which is the corollary of reform, seem to make their analysis in terms of exit, voice and loyalty increasingly salient. In the next section, exit and voice are examined in turn. The meaning of loyalty is reserved for a concluding discussion.

Exit

There are three levels of exit from public health care open to the dissatisfied user. The first is between providers within public health systems, the second is between public providers as such and others. The third, much rarer, is from one national system to another.

In the national health services considered here (chapter 3), patients register with doctors in ambulatory care: with GPs in Italy and the UK, and with local health centres in Sweden. Movement between doctors is partly constrained in Germany by the obligation for users to stay with one doctor for the whole of an accounting period (three months), but is much less restricted in France. Similarly, patient choice of clinician is limited by referral systems in the UK and Italy, as it is increasingly in Sweden. Access to hospital in Germany is similarly by referral from a doctor in ambulatory care. A comparative assessment of how much this matters, of how much and how often choice is exercised, is difficult to establish. In France and Germany, where specialists work in local practice, patients consult different doctors for different conditions, but this can't be construed as exit. Anecdotal evidence suggests that patients actively change their doctor rather rarely, except in France, where mobility, and consultation rates, are relatively high. For the most part, user movement within the public sector appears heavily controlled, usually by public or professional agents.

There is a distinction to be made between health care delivery and its administration, which in essence amounts to the difference between the provision of finance and the provision of care. In national health services, the jurisdictions of health authorities, agencies and councils are territorial. In Germany, similarly, sickness insurance has been ordinarily provided by local funds, unless an individual's occupation or employment gives them rights of access to substitute funds, or others organised in the workplace or among different trades.[3] Recently, there appears to be an increased propensity for members to move between funds at the point at which their insurance status changes as a result of gaining, losing or changing employment (Müller and Schneider 1997). Meanwhile, following reform in 1993, free choice of insurer became effective for most fund members at the beginning of 1997. There is initial evidence that this will accelerate a long-term drift in the west from local to substitute insurers, though such movement has recently been more pronounced in the east, where labour market volatility is higher (Müller and Schneider 1997, Freeman 1998a). Across the country, the pattern of movement is closely associated with contribution rates: users are moving to funds where premia are lower.

Movement out of the public sector, meanwhile, is indicated by levels of private spending. The sector as a whole, of course, is dominated by public spending, which now accounts for four-fifths of total health expenditure in France and Germany, Sweden and the UK (slightly more in Sweden and the UK and slightly less in Germany), and for 70 per cent of health spending in Italy (appendix 1). Private spending is composed primarily of out-of-pocket payments but includes premia paid to private insurers. Private insurance has a variety of functions: it may buy cover against public sector copayments, as in France; it may buy cover for services which supplement state provision (and may therefore be classed as a luxury good), as in Italy and the UK; it may be a sole source of cover, as it is for some people in Germany (Wagstaff, van Doorslaer *et al.* 1992). There, only high earners are allowed to rely on private health insurance, which is usually supplied by non-profit making agencies. About half of those entitled to opt out in fact stay with statutory funds (OECD 1992 and chapter 4, above). For families, premia tend to be lower in the GKV; it is single people who choose to be insured privately, and then primarily because it makes financial sense for them to do so (Schneider 1991). Six per cent of members of statutory schemes also have supplementary private cover, for example to provide better accommodation in a hospital or to enable them to be seen by a senior physician (Schulenburg 1994, Greiner and Schulenburg 1997).

In Italy, 10 per cent of the population has private health insurance (Ferrera 1995). Since 1995, private insurance payments have been deductible from compulsory contributions; there is no such arrangement in Sweden, where private health insurance remains comparatively very low. In the UK, 12 per cent of the population is insured with private third-party payers. The market there is dominated by non-profit rather than profit making organisations: BUPA, PPP and WPA are provident associations, which do not distribute profits but retain surpluses for reinvestment. Individuals insured privately tend to be concentrated in outer metropolitan areas and among professional and managerial socio-economic groups. As in Sweden, many of them have their premia paid either wholly or partly by their employers as part of an employment package. In the UK, private care is used principally for elective surgery, that is for acute but non-emergency hospital care. As such, it seems to provide evidence of a level of unsatisfied demand among some users of health services – 'people of working age, suffering from relatively minor conditions, who want to be treated by their own consultant in a room of their own at a time of their own choice' (Klein 1989, p. 155).

The public–private distinction is a feature of national health services much more than social insurance systems (chapter 3, above). Even there, the relationship between public and private sectors tends to be complementary rather than competitive, both at the level of the system and of the individual user. Where public systems address need, private systems cater for demand; while public systems cannot always meet demand, private systems can never fully meet need. In the UK, individuals who use private medicine are highly likely to use state medicine, too – precisely because their insurance coverage tends to be limited to elective rather than emergency surgery, to short-term rather than long-term care, to hospital rather than primary or rehabilitative services. The effective significance of the distinction between public and private sectors is questionable (Busfield 1990).

In a social insurance system such as Germany, meanwhile, movement between public and private amounts to movement between payers rather than between providers and facilities. In France, to consult a sector 2 doctor perhaps because he or she has a specialist reputation is simply to be subject to extra billing. In each case, to 'go private' is not to enter a different world. Differences between public and private, if any, are of degree (quicker, cheaper, more luxurious) rather than of kind. Intersectoral exit in health care is partial, and limited to a relatively small percentage of the users of any given public health care system.

Transnational exit, from one country to another, does also take place but it is rare. What has been described as 'medical tourism' tends to be between specialist private facilities (Moran and Wood 1996 and chapter 5, above). In the EU, cross-border care can be publicly financed for migrant workers (using designated form E106) and in the case of temporary stays, usually by tourists (E111). Care provided in another country can also be pre-authorised by a home country (E112). Across member states, this kind of health care funding represented no more than an estimated 0.13 per cent total health expenditure in 1993, most of which (60 per cent) was E112 care (Hermesse, Lewalle and Palm 1997). Until 1989, E112 authorisations were relatively easy to obtain in Italy, which effectively amounted to a public recognition of the inadequacy of SSN facilities (France 1997, Hermans and France 1998). Though the number of successful applications has dropped by up to 50 per cent since vetting by referral committee was introduced, Italy remains by far the largest net exporter of patients in the EU: in 1993 only 540 UK residents travelled abroad for treatment, while 14 000 Italians did so, mostly to France (Crivelli and Rhodes 1995, cit. France 1996a). This pattern also reflects a high rate of interregional mobility among Italian patients: in 1992, 6 per cent of hospital admissions crossed regional boundaries, mostly from south to north in search of a higher quality of care (France 1997).

Voice

Opportunities for the expression of voice may be divided into representation and redress in turn. Representation refers to the ways in which users may participate in decision-making at the level of policy, redress to procedures for hearing grievances or complaints about decisions already taken, usually by professionals in respect of individual patients.

Different countries allow the users of health care different opportunities for representation. These exist in the political system more broadly conceived as well as in systems of health administration. Because health systems everywhere are public systems governed by public policy, their development is subject, however indirectly, to electoral approval. This may be greater in centralised, public systems (like the UK) than in decentralised, parapublic ones (Germany). In the UK, a more or less unitary health service is controlled by central government. The Department of Health is one of the major spending ministries: health policy in the UK is articulated at national level. That may sometimes make pressure on government quite acute (chapter 5, above), though it can also mean that health policy issues must compete with others for national attention while the centre remains unresponsive to local needs. Unprecedented concern about the NHS was not sufficent to determine the outcome of general elections in 1987 or 1992. In Sweden, by contrast, though central government (as in Germany) retains responsibility for the legislative framework of health provision, health services remain the administrative – and importantly financial – responsibility of the county councils. Health spending forms the larger part of county council budgets. County council elections in Sweden, for example, have the propensity to be much more 'about' health services than local elections in the UK or regional state (*Land*) elections in Germany. There is some evidence that county councillors in Sweden have a greater 'felt legitimacy' than do appointees to Health Authorities in the UK although, because they are large bodies with stable political majorities, their electoral sensitivity is relatively weak (Ham 1988).

Some health systems have their own political structures, separate from the political systems in which they are embedded. Some national health services, such as those in Italy and the UK, are organised into local or regional health authorities, distinctive bodies charged with the administration of health services covering the population of a given geographical area. Social insurance systems tend to be regulated not through separate bodies, but through processes of negotiation between payers and providers. User participation is sometimes gained by the election of representatives to sickness fund boards, as in Germany and France.

Between 1978 and 1992, health services in Italy were run by elective committees drawn from local authorities, making for a high degree of penetration of local health politics by political parties. Individual membership of committees was a matter of the distribution of party political favours, unrelated to managerial or technical expertise. This made for a sometimes chaotic, even fraudulent local health administration (Ferrera 1989, 1995). Following reform in 1992, the districts are now run not by politicised committees but by general managers appointed by the regions on the basis of professional competence. In the UK, Health Authorities are governed by a mixture of executive and non-executive directors or members. Membership of authorities is appointive rather than elective; non-executive individuals are chosen for the personal contribution they might make to decision making rather than for the sake of representation. While there is some assumption that they act on behalf of those served by respective authorities, they tend to be seen as remote from those communities, their political influence diminished by their lack of a coherent programme or power base (Allsop 1984, Ham 1992).

Local democratic accountability in the NHS has always been weak (Ranade 1994), despite the creation in 1974 of a distinctive, additional system of local representation. Community Health Councils (CHCs) are statutory bodies, with rights to some strategic information from local NHS authorities, including access to certain premises. They have the right to be consulted on developments or changes in health services, and also serve as a source of information and advice to the public. Their members are mainly local government and voluntary sector nominees. CHCs were instituted 'from above' in order to articulate a potentially useful user interest in what the NHS saw as an underdeveloped chronic sector: they were a way of devising a constituency for under-served patient groups. Yet they hold few formal powers; their influence, if any, lies in persuasion, information giving and advice. The power of 'consultation', which takes place at Health Authorities' discretion, is limited (Ham 1992), and may be decreasing. Few newly independent provider trusts allowed CHC representatives to their board meetings, for example (Ashburner and Cairncross 1992).[4]

In the German social insurance system, sickness funds are governed by elective boards composed of representatives of employers and employees. In 1951, in the process of post-war reformation of social insurance, the labour membership of boards was reduced from two-thirds to one-half. Formally, this was to reflect the establishment of the social partnership. Its effect was to complete the depoliticisation of sickness fund administration, neutralising the funds as foci of union activity (chapter 2). The funds are described as self-managing, because their boards are comprised of elected members working in an honorary capacity. However, members represent fund contributors (workers) and not, at least in the first instance, dependants and health care users. The highest users of health services are those with the lowest labour market participation, and are therefore the least represented in decision-making (Alber 1995). In any case, funds are managed on a day-to-day basis by professional administrators. While administrators are bound to comply with board decisions, the board, for its part, is effectively dependent on the information and advice they supply (Göckenjan 1980). The participation of contributors in board elections is extremely low, and communication between sickness fund technocrats and local populations is poor (Ferber 1985). In sum, there is no effective coupling of consumer interests to payers and providers in German sickness insurance (Alber 1995).[5]

If user participation in health politics through political systems is indirect, that through the health systems reviewed here seems little more than symbolic. Most systems make for some form of structured user representation, though it tends to be ineffective and mostly unused. Meanwhile, a different kind of 'voice' results from the ways in which the direct relationships between the users and providers of health care are regulated. As the tension between a universal right to health care and the limited availability of resources with which to meet it becomes more acute, this regulation tends to become more explicit. In the UK, for example, a Patient's Charter was introduced by the Department of Health in 1991 as part of a broader attempt to define and specify the rights of public service users. Its principal use has been as a lever in the reduction of waiting times (Ham 1997a). In other countries, the law comes to serve as a mediating institution between citizens and health care administrations. Article 32 of the Italian constitution guarantees the right to health, which has been interpreted by the courts as a right to health care. Even here, though, judicial protection of access and of freedom of choice of provider has come to be qualified by a formal acceptance of the implications of resource constraint (Hermans and France 1998). Explicit restriction has been deemed legally acceptable; the right to health care is not subjective, but is taken to allow both national and regional governments discretionary power over which services should be provided publicly and how. And in countries where health care rights 'have a weaker legal basis and/or where the judiciary is reluctant to intervene in the sphere of health care resource allocation and/or where patients ... are less aware of their rights ... the scales will tend to be heavily weighted in favour of payers' (Hermans and France 1998, p. 281). As Dingwall argues more generally, legal conceptions of such responsibilities tend to be much narrower and more closely defined than those of common understanding. Medicine is no longer set to realise 'national health'. 'It is, rather, to be directed towards the servicing of human bodies under a series of specific agreements between purchaser, provider and consumer ... The intervention of law becomes a way to limit the apparently infinite demand for a health care that represents a collective panacea' (Dingwall 1994, p. 60).

At the same time, rights to health care are rights to consultation rather than treatment. Effective provision tends to be determined by medical professional judgement rather than by law. In this context, the basis for patient complaint against doctors is always fundamentally insecure. Furthermore, the procedures through which grievances are heard tend to be dominated by doctors themselves. The self-regulation of medical professions in such matters is almost axiomatic. In Germany, for example, responsibility for complaint investigation lies with the doctors' chambers, membership of which is restricted to doctors, though complaints may also be pursued in the courts (Moran and Wood 1993). Lay membership of the General Medical Council, the UK body charged with licensing individual doctors, is small and not really significant (Stacey 1992, Moran and Wood 1993). In the UK, negligence claims increased rapidly in the early 1980s, by a factor of five in frequency and three in severity, though the rate of increase has slowed since then (Dingwall 1994). Claims may reflect a real increase in the damage done to patients by doctors, perhaps because the medico-technological opportunity to do so is greater, or they may reflect an increased awareness by patients of their rights and a willingness to use them. Increased litigation has increased self-consciousness among clinicians, and to some recourse to the security of peer review. It has also been marked by the emergence of specialist lawyers. On both counts, it seems as though the effect of medical error has been less to improve the articulation of patient power than to provide a new niche for the professional arbiters of medical power.

Reform

What part has the user interest played in recent health care reform? Users have been protected from radical cuts in entitlement by largely indirect but compelling political pressures (chapter 5). 'More than a decade after the end of the long boom, the frontiers of citizenship in health care remain largely unbreached. There have been a few incursions, represented by the widening of copayment arrangements; but there are other areas where the entitlement system has actually expanded. The resources needed to fund entitlements have continued to grow. The coalition of interests supporting generous entitlements of a universalist character remains overwhelmingly strong' (Moran 1991, p. 54). Some of these interests are structural, indicating institutional and professional investment in expansion. But public opinion is probably not the least of them: certainly, comparative historical research on health reform in the UK and the US indicates that the influence of different interest groups on public policy was contingent on public opinion (Jacobs 1993). More recent experience in Europe in the 1980s and 1990s suggests that public opinion and media coverage are mutually reinforcing, and can constrain the freedom of activity of governments. In liberal democracies, health policy is ordinarily subject to the tensions of pluralist politics (Moran 1995a).

Opportunities for the more direct engagement of users in health policy decision making – the use of voice – have been limited. Where they do exist, they seem as much an effect of change as an essential part of its process. In the UK, for example, consumer surveys, health panels and user groups have become part of the political landscape of the new NHS, though recent research is critical of their capacity to represent user interests genuinely or effectively (Harrison and Mort 1998, Pickard 1998). More often, it is doctors and managers (and politicians) who appeal to users in the course of their own conflicts: the user interest is to some extent constructed by them. User involvement and public consultation may be understood as 'technologies of legitimation' for managerial decision making (Harrison and Mort 1998). Across countries, the payers and providers of health care remain better organised and better represented than its users (though even they may claim that reforming governments have ignored them).

Some governments have sought to encourage user movement within public systems, whether between payers (as between sickness funds in Germany) or providers (GPs in the UK). Coupled with the declining political relevance of representative bodies such as Community Health Councils and sickness fund boards, this seems to indicate an exchange of voice for exit, though it is significant that this is something which has been presented to users rather than demanded by them. Nowhere did user dissatisfaction with health care states imply a demand for the quasi-marketisation of health care, though that is the way in which, in part, governments have sought to meet it (Moran 1998). Health policy continues to be determined by providers, payers and regulators – by doctors, health insurers and government. Even if the government of health care is now more public than private (chapters 2 and 5, above), it can scarcely be said to be democratic. At the same time, the boundaries of the health care state are being drawn in. The provision of public health care is increasingly rule-bound, and it is bound by rules which users play little part in making. In this context, both exit and voice may be expressions of patient anxiety as much as of patient power (Mackenzie 1979).

Understanding the users of health care in Europe

Exit and voice attract attention because they are bright, noisy and deviant, but they are probably not the normal experience of the users of health care in

Europe. In each of the countries reviewed here, some patients will choose to make arrangements for their health care in the market, some will participate in local decision-making bodies, some will complain and some will have recourse to law. But most will do none of these things. In comparative terms, we know little about the majority of users who neither exit nor exercise voice and who, though they are mostly grateful to their doctors and nurses, are not always satisfied with the way their health care is organised, paid for and delivered. As far as we can tell, they are inactive, non-participatory.[6] This may be testament to an enduring fatalism among the users of health care (Thompson 1997): for many, going to the doctor has a metaphysical aspect as much as a rational, interest-based one. And it may also be not least because active participation requires energy and imagination as well as material resources, and these are not things which sick people have. Some groups of users, typically those in chronic need such as older people and the mentally ill, have a low capacity for either voice or exit. In this way, the Hirschman framework provides a means of explaining their disadvantaged position in all health systems. Populations of health care users are not homogenous (just as health services are not monolithic) and the ability to use exit and voice is always likely to be inequitably distributed (Klein 1980b).

Exit and voice point to variation within systems as much as between them. It is not that some systems promote exit and some voice; both options exist everywhere, though institutional differences mean that they are expressed in slightly different ways. Exit and voice seem to tell us a lot about relatively little: the small proportions of users who can be said to be actively engaged in decision making about the terms and conditions of their access to health care. This may be because Hirschman's concept is essentially two-dimensional: *Exit, Voice and Loyalty* is really about exit and voice (economics and politics) and the relationship between them. The nature of loyalty remains problematic. It is introduced late into the argument, without carrying the same analytic weight as exit or voice. Crucially, it is not a third pattern of behaviour, but a way of explaining selection between the first two. It is of interest here because it is a phenomenon associated particularly with public goods – Hirschman originally used the example of public education (Hirschman 1970, ch. 7). There is a sense in which loyalty appears as a residual construct, needed to account for behaviour which the exit-voice framework would not immediately predict (Klein 1980b). As Hirschman himself explains, 'loyalty holds exit at bay and activates voice', although 'While loyalty postpones exit, its very existence is predicated on the possibility of exit ... the effectiveness of the voice mechanism is strengthened by the possibility of exit' (Hirschman 1970, pp. 78, 82, 83). Loyalty is indicated by voice and predicated on the possibility of exit but, as we have seen, the use of either is limited to a minority of users in any given health care system. If not loyalty, what lies between (or behind or beyond) exit and voice? Is it really 'satisfaction'?

Discovering more about the users of health care in Europe may mean identifying analytic frames other than the one used here. Klein suggests that the economic and political thinking of exit and voice may require a sociological complement (Klein 1980b). Cross-national work in medical sociology, however, remains relatively underdeveloped. The Parsonian sick role concept might well form the basis of useful comparative inquiry (Turner 1987), as might Everett Hughes's construction of the user as health worker (Hughes 1958, cit. Allsop 1984). Do responses to illness vary significantly between European countries? Are responsibilities for the production and maintenance of health allocated and assumed in different ways? These are key questions in understanding user behaviour in health care across countries and, for the moment, it doesn't seem possible to answer them fully.

An English study of people discharged from hospital after stroke (Baldock and Ungerson 1996) suggests an alternative way of rethinking 'loyalty' and 'satisfaction'. In explaining differences in the use of continuing care, it draws on the sociology of consumption rather than of health and illness, and on ideas about what Tocqueville described as 'habits of the heart': beliefs, attitudes and opinions, moral and intellectual dispositions as well as ordinary patterns of participation in religious, political and economic life (Bellah *et al.* 1988).[7] It attempts to characterise the varieties of 'script' according to which people make decisions (or non-decisions) about their care, using individual–collective and active–passive axes to construct a typology of different relationships to the consumption of welfare. The *consumerist* approach denotes an active use of market, family and household resources, in the context of minimal expectations of the state and some uncertainty about the loss of autonomy which the use of voluntary or public services might bring; *privatist* attitudes are similarly individualistic and independent, but much more passive in the way they are realised, often resulting in an inability to capture goods not advertised or made available in familiar ways. A *welfarist* position reflects a committed belief in public services and the right to use them, usually supported by a high level of awareness of the range of services on offer and the ability to exploit it actively. *Clientism* describes the passive receipt of public sector services. What is valuable about this framework is its specification of a variety of relationships between users and given constellations of services. It amplifies and enriches the range of behaviours which begin to be treated by exit and voice in such a way as to include all users of health care.

On this basis, differences between systems might be conceived in terms of the differences among different groups of users within them, and the extent to which these are promoted or inhibited by institutional (both organisational and cultural) factors. This is to restate the essential character of health care systems as complex arrangements of solidarities – between employers and employees, for example, and between them and those outside the labour market, as well as between different geographical regions – and to suggest that user behaviour is shaped by the ways in which these are maintained and expressed. In the case of the NHS, for example, '[I]t could be argued that its most important symbolic output is equity – ie, perceived fairness in dealing with people, regardless of their financial circumstance – which inhibits both voice and exit' (Klein 1980b, p. 424).

By the same token, the continuing legitimacy of specific institutional arrangements in health and welfare is dependent on their capacity to reproduce the cultural norms on which they depend. Hinrichs has argued that Germany's health insurance system rests on a specific 'moral infrastructure'. Reform there, in promoting cost-benefit calculation and user mobility, has risked undermining the 'culture of solidarity' by which the system as a whole is sustained (Hinrichs 1995). In different kinds of system, such as the national health services of Italy, Sweden and the UK, the growth of private health insurance tends to reduce the commitment of influential sections of the population to universalist arrangements (Holliday 1992, Ferrera 1995, Garpenby 1995). This is by way of saying no more – and no less – than that the organisation, finance and delivery of health care in Europe are embedded in particular normative frameworks: they shape and are shaped by the cultures which penetrate and surround them.

Notes

1   That said, it has its own, different weaknesses: to some, it appears impersonal and even alienating. For the moment, however, this distancing seems methodologically useful.

2   Figures for Germany, which are lower than for other countries treated here, include only those covered by statutory schemes.

3   In 1995, of all those insured in statutory schemes, 38 per cent were members of local funds and 41 per cent belonged to white collar substitute funds (Müller and Schneider 1997).

4   Cit. Ranade (1994).

5   Compare Björkman on Britain, Sweden and the United States: '[P]olicy options selected by professional elites are legitimated by arrangements for citizen participation. Yet when citizens sit on planning boards, operational committees and health councils, lay participants are rarely active' (Björkman 1985, p. 415).

6   In general, 'non-decisions ... appear more common than decisions' (Klein and Millar 1995, p. 310).

7   Cit. Baldock and Ungerson (1996).

8

Health, the public and public health

Introduction

This closing chapter is about prevention in health policy. For the most part, this book has been concerned with health care in different European countries and the political significance of the ways it is organised and paid for. As the idea of the health care state implies, the bulk of government activity in the twentieth century, as of medical professional activity, has been about responding to illness rather than preventing it. Prevention – a marginal activity of medicine and a peripheral aspect of public policy – provides a place to stand outside the health system, from which it is cast in a different light. It presents an opportunity to review many of the ideas and problems raised in the course of earlier discussion: the differences and similarities between systems, the logic of reform, the nature of governmental, professional and user interests and the relationships between them. In a sense, the book ends where it began, with the ordering and reordering of public responsibility for health.

The chapter begins by noting what marked something of a rediscovery of prevention on the part of governments and policy makers in the 1970s, describing the strategies by which they sought to promote it and the contexts in which they did so. The discussion then focuses on government responses to AIDS in the 1980s, showing how they illustrate more generic issues. It points to a liberal order in public health, consistent with the political culture of advanced industrial democracies and their prevailing patterns of public policy, but consonant also with dominant interests in the health sector. Prevention illuminates key relationships between medicine and government and between core and periphery, as well as the positioning of the state in health politics at the end of the twentieth century. The chapter closes by returning to the idea of the system as such, summarising the various pressures – economic, political and ideological – to which health systems in western Europe are subject. Prevention is explained as one of the ways of regulating the tensions they produce.

The rediscovery of prevention

Since the 1970s, different national governments have produced signal declarations on the health status of their populations and the role of prevention in health policy. In Germany, the new Social Democrat-led administration published a *Health Report* in 1970, stating a core commitment to health protection; in 1985, prevention was an important feature of the first major health policy statement made by the conservative-liberal government on regaining power. The UK government has published a series of green papers, beginning with *Prevention and Health: everybody's business* in 1976, including *Promoting Better Health* (1987), *The Health of the Nation* (1991) and *Our Healthier Nation* (1998). The Swedish National Board of Health and Welfare issued a *Public Health Report* in 1987, following *Health in Sweden* (1982) and *The Swedish Health Services in the 1990s* (1985). *Selected Public Health Issues*, submitted to parliament in 1991, drew on the Public Health Commission's *National Strategy for Health*.[1] In 1982, the French government issued a *Health Charter*, intending to promote 'a new social impetus in public health' (Steudler 1986), while its Public Health Commission more recently published a report on *Health in France* (Pomey and Poullier 1997). Implicit in most, if not all of these statements was a recognition of the threats to health posed by cancer and heart disease, among other chronic conditions. In response to them, governments adopted a shared set of policy instruments, albeit with different emphases. These included a degree of institutional reform, the advocacy of intersectoral working, improved provision of screening, some new legislation and, a *sine qua non* of these statements, the assertion of individual, personal responsibility for health supported by health education programmes.

As with the reform of health care (chapter 5), governments sought to create or assume a greater central capacity for the monitoring and regulation of health issues, combined with a multisectoral approach to implementation. In Germany, a research department for environmental health was set up in 1967 at the Federal Health Office in Berlin, and a Federal Centre for Health Education in Cologne. There followed protracted wrangling between federal and regional state governments over constitutional responsibilities for public health in the period 1968–70, the centre seeking to add a more general remit to its exclusive responsibilities for infectious disease. In Italy, similarly, the transfer of environmental health from health authorities to central government was subject to a referendum in 1993. In 1974 in the UK, the long-established local government post of Medical Officer of Health (MoH) was abolished, to be replaced by the Medical Officer of Environmental Health (MOEH) and a new health services specialism (Community Medicine). Blurred boundaries of responsibility were eventually resolved by the *Report of the Committee of Inquiry into the Future Development of the Public Health Function* in 1988, which identified a clear managerial accountability for public health matters, fixing it in health authorities (and so making it more readily subject to central direction) rather than local government.

At the same time, prevention and health were clearly identified, in the UK government's words, as 'everybody's business'. Health issues were the concern not only of health services and central and local governments, but also of employers, unions, schools and community groups. Much of this was sustained by World Health Organization (WHO) initiatives, as the agency looked to develop a role in the European region. Drawing for its part on the Canadian *Lalonde Report* of 1974 (Ministry of National Health and Welfare (Canada) 1974), WHO proclaimed a commitment to 'Health for All' in 1977, made more concrete in its advocacy of primary health care at Alma-Ata in 1978 (WHO 1978). A *Charter for Health Promotion* was drawn up at Ottawa in 1986 (WHO 1986), and a *Healthy Cities* symposium met in Lisbon the same year (Ashton, Grey and Barnard 1986). In Europe, WHO strategy was perhaps most strongly endorsed among Nordic countries (Salmela 1991), as expressed in the Swedish Ministry of Welfare, Health and Current Affairs's *Health 2000* document (1986). In 1987, the Swedish government set up a Public Health Commission to develop its intersectoral health policy.

Statutory provision for screening was included in amendments to health insurance regulations in Germany in 1970, covering health checks for children younger than 4; cancer screening for adults over 45; cervical screening for women over 20 and breast screening for those over 30. The Health Care Reform Act of 1989 required sickness funds to finance dental checks for children of school age, as well as annual screening for cancer for the over 35s and heart, kidney and diabetes screening every 2 years. In France, a National Fund for Preventive Screening was set up in 1988 to finance similar health checks, while insurance funds were requested to notify individual members as tests became due (Schneider *et al.* 1992). In the UK, new GP contracts were issued in 1990, derived from proposals contained in the green paper *Promoting Better Health* (1987). Doctors were now paid a fee for screening new patients, sessional fees for health promotion clinics and received further payments for meeting targets for screening older people, vaccinating and immunising children, and for cervical cytology. In Italy, from 1992, 6 per cent of the central government's health allocation was to be used to fund preventive programmes (OECD 1994).

There is mixed evidence, meanwhile, of legislation being used for preventive health purposes. In 1970, Sweden was one of only two European countries to ban alcohol advertising (Saffer 1991). In 1990, legislation prohibiting almost all advertising of alcohol and tobacco products was passed in France (Sulkunen 1997); the UK, by contrast, has sought to limit tobacco advertising by voluntary agreement with industry (Calnan 1991). British governments have applied relatively high rates of taxation to cigarettes in particular, at least in part for health promotion purposes (Leichter 1991). At the end of 1997, EU health ministers agreed a phased ban on tobacco advertising and sponsorship, to be implemented in stages over 3–8 years. At the same time, however, the harmonisation of tax regimes required by the formation of a Single European Market is driving down alcohol and tobacco duties in Britain and Sweden (Baggott 1990, Sulkunen 1997). UK restrictions on licensing hours were relaxed in 1988 while the distribution and sale of alcohol in Scandinavian countries, for a long time a state monopoly, has been liberalised in the 1990s. Early in 1998, a draft bill to ban smoking in public offices and on public transport was rejected by the German Bundestag.

Public health questions present a fundamental political dilemma, which is such that government action in this field almost inevitably seems partial and fragmented, if not contradictory and inconsistent. In recent decades, the specific risks associated with patterns of behaviour ('lifestyles') have become better understood, not least by government scientists. They also quickly tend to become the object of general public concern. At the same time, however, consumption has become an expression of individual autonomy and identity.[2] The idea that governments should actively seek to restrict it is much less legitimate than it was. The dominant tone of economic and public policy in the 1980s and 1990s has been one of deregulation. As far as prevention is concerned, governments are increasingly compelled to act while being increasingly uncertain of the bases, both ideological and material, of their doing so. In the 1980s, this uncertainty was made critical by the emergence of AIDS.

AIDS

AIDS politics is complicated. In part, this has to do with the breadth and multiplicity of actors it has involved, some of them established players, some new to health politics, many of them only intermittent participants. To central, regional and local government, doctors, health authorities and insurance funds, employers and employees have been added community organisations, churches, schools and social workers, print and broadcast media, international organisations and life assurance companies. Simply, it has concerned (and to some extent perhaps constructed) the entire health polity (chapter 1). Even within the health sector more narrowly conceived, it brought marginal agencies and specialisms to the fore: epidemiological institutes, blood suppliers, genito-urinary (GU) doctors and health educators. In part, too, however, its complexity is derived from the depth and intensity of the issue. Within a few years of the public finance of health care having 'grown to limits' (chapter 2), HIV and AIDS tested the limits of biomedical research, of public authority in the realm of the private, and of tolerance and community between groups.

First diagnoses of AIDS were made in 1981 in France and the UK, and in 1982 in Germany, Italy and Sweden (Fox, Day and Klein 1989, Moss 1990, Pollak 1990a and 1990b). Table 8.1 gives case rates for each country for the period 1982–90, and for 1997. All five countries conformed to the 'type 1' pattern of AIDS epidemiology, common to western industrialised countries, in which the group predominantly affected was that of homosexual and bisexual men, along

Table 8.1 Reported cases of AIDS, 1982–1990 and 1997[a]

	France	Germany	Italy	Sweden	UK
1982	31	5			3
1984	209	95	1	16	106
1986	1207	694	46	91	562
1988	5570	2550	2081	256	1957
1990	13146	5138	7300	508	4066
1997	47407	17048	40950	1557	15081

Note: [a]Cumulative totals.
Source: derived from UNAIDS/WHO Epidemiological Fact Sheet, June 1998.

with a variably sized (and increasing) cohort of intravenous drug users.[3] At the end of 1988, roughly the middle of the key period of policy making described below, gay men accounted for 75 per cent of known cases in Germany, 80 per cent in Sweden, and 83 per cent in the UK. In France, the equivalent figure was 57 per cent and that for drug users 17 per cent, while a relatively high proportion (7 per cent) of cases were attributable to HIV transmission by blood transfusion. In Italy, two thirds of cases were injecting drug users.

The prevention of HIV and AIDS has been based around three strategies. *Infection control* has been applied for the most part in clinical settings, concerned with the safe disposal of clinical and other waste and the protection of health care workers. It has been characterised by the production of guidelines which have been refined in the light of emerging scientific knowledge. The use of *HIV testing* has been much more contentious: screening provides epidemiological information and may be used as a basis for both counselling and secondary chemotherapeutic prevention, but it can also be used to discriminate between infected and non-infected individuals. *Health education* in relation to HIV and AIDS has been oriented to individual behavioural change and to the alleviation of discrimination against groups. For the most part, these strategies are complementary, and governments have employed all three. At each stage, though, the process of policy formulation has been fraught with political tension – over the proper use of testing, for example, or the appropriate form and content of health education.

In most west European countries, a conflict was discernible between two ideal-typical approaches to HIV and AIDS prevention, one authoritarian and one more liberal. The authoritarian 'contain-and-control' approach, usually referring to pre-existing public health legislation, advocated mandatory testing, detention or quarantine as necessary, and repressive measures against 'risk groups' (Bayer and Kirp 1992). The liberal 'cooperation-and-inclusion' strategy rested principally on voluntary testing, counselling and widespread health education. As Moss and Misztal put it, 'Essentially the choice has lain between persuasion through education and obligation through law' (Moss and Misztal 1990, p. 13).[4]

Policy responses to AIDS in the 1980s are summarised in table 8.2. Across countries, they followed a more or less typical trajectory.[5] In the early period, from 1982 until 1985–86, cases began to be monitored by interested doctors, operating through offices and institutes of epidemiology and public health. The first preventive responses took place among groups of those affected, who were invariably gay men. Local, community-based information campaigns were organised, sometimes in collaboration with public health agencies. Infection control guidelines were promulgated, both locally and centrally, and early moves were made to protect the blood supply by requesting individuals at risk not to donate blood. When a test for HIV became available in 1985, blood and blood products were systematically screened. Media interest in AIDS increased, and became increasingly alarmist.

The period 1986–87 brought a flurry of policy making. In most cases, government intervention was prompted by a number of factors, including an anticipated spread of HIV and AIDS to heterosexual populations, their actual spread to marginalised populations other than that of gay men, a need for national guidance for policy making at the local level, and the increasing financial burden of care for people with AIDS. Governments did what governments do, defining new institutional responsibilities and modifying others, reviewing and revising legislation and providing money – principally for health education, medical research and specialist care. Most formed expert-led, multi-interest and cross-party advisory bodies in an attempt to repair what had been a deeply fractured consensus over the form and extent of public health intervention.

By the end of 1988 a process of normalisation had been set in train. Though conflicts continued, notably over the place of harm reduction in drugs policy, AIDS would slowly be absorbed into existing (if invigorated) programmes for the prevention of sexually transmitted diseases, the funding of medical research and the provision of chronic care. No longer a generalised and intensely debated political issue it became 'a professional problem in the management of what was increasingly seen as a chronic condition' (Fox, Day and Klein 1989, p. 93).[6]

The response to AIDS in France was dominated by science, medicine and public administration (Pollak 1990a, Steffen 1992). A French research team, led by Luc Montagnier at the Pasteur Institute in France, was the first to isolate the virus (then named LAV) which causes AIDS in 1983. Early moves by doctors and officials were concerned to 'de-dramatise' the issue, resisting calls for regulatory measures and emphasising individual responsibility in avoiding the disease. As elsewhere, individuals at particular risk of HIV were asked not to donate blood in 1983, and all blood and blood products were screened once a test for HIV became available in 1985. Though some dialogue took place, collaborative working with gay groups was limited (Pollak 1990a). A more widespread education campaign came later, in 1987, with AIDS being declared a national *cause*; this was reinvigorated in 1989, following a highly critical evaluative report on HIV and AIDS strategy conducted for the Minister of Health. A central agency for AIDS prevention and an advisory AIDS Council were formed at the same time.

Table 8.2 Government responses to AIDS, 1982–1990

	France	Germany	Italy	Sweden	United Kingdom
1982	March: small epidemiological study financed by Ministry of Health	AIDS case register established at the Federal Health Office (BGA); reporting remains anonymous and non-compulsory		First cases of AIDS diagnosed	First recorded deaths from AIDS; voluntary, confidential reporting of further cases of AIDS and, from the end of 1984, positive HIV test results to the Communicable Disease Surveillance Centre
1983	Individuals at particular risk asked not to donate blood Association for Research on AIDS (ARSIDA) formed among medical experts	Government press release designates AIDS a national problem AIDS included in government research programme	*Ad hoc* AIDS study group formed at National Health Institute		Medical Research Council working party on AIDS August: government issues request to individuals at high risk not to give blood
1984	Epidemiological data collection centralised at Ministry of Health 1984–85	Informal advisory body on AIDS established at Ministry of Health November: government considers new legislation to control sexually transmitted diseases			Government Advisory Committee on Dangerous Pathogens produced interim guidelines on handling of HIV infected laboratory specimens

1985				
Policy recommendations issued by health ministry ethics committee that no testing be performed without consent, and that results be communicated to all seropositives July: government circular to hospitals stipulated that individuals with HIV or AIDS entitled to inpatient or outpatient care; no special units were to be created; guidelines issued on appropriate treatment and on communicating with HIV-infected patients August: screening of donated blood and blood products made compulsory	October: all blood and blood products tested for HIV Parliamentary health committee first briefed on AIDS December: government information leaflet distributed to all households	June: (anonymous) notification of cases of AIDS made compulsory in Lazio July: government recommends regions that blood donated by individuals at risk of HIV infection not be used, and that all donated blood be screened Government recommends screening of prison population November: government recommends mandatory screening of IV drug users attending treatment centres	AIDS Delegation formed to coordinate policy response to AIDS, headed by the Minister of Health and Social Affairs and composed of representatives of the National Board of Health and Welfare, the national bacteriological laboratory, medical experts, the county councils and local authorities, and political parties September: AIDS classified as a venereal disease under Infectious Diseases Act, requiring obligatory consultation by infected individuals and contact tracing of their partners and providing for penal sanction in the event of non-cooperation	January: Expert Advisory Group on AIDS formed to advise the Chief Medical Officer All imported factor VIII (a blood clotting agent used in the treatment of haemophilia) heat treated to destroy HIV October: all blood donations screened for HIV Public Health (Infectious Disease) regulations, made under the Public Health (Control of Diseases) Act (1984) extended to cover AIDS, though AIDS not made a notifiable disease AIDS Unit established at DoH

Table 8.2 (*cont.*)

	France	Germany	Italy	Sueden	United Kingdom
1986	Notification of cases of AIDS made compulsory, though anonymous	First (brief) parliamentary debate on AIDS	January: (anonymous) notification of cases of AIDS made compulsory in Lombardy	Major AIDS education campaign	May: District Health Authority general managers asked by the government to set up AIDS action groups
	June: Second International Conference on AIDS, Paris	November: AIDS conference in Berlin			October: Cabinet Committee on AIDS formed
	Liberalisation of sale of condoms and widespread health education campaign announced by Minister of Health Barzach, including broadcast media slots and household leafletting				November: first major parliamentary debate on AIDS
					National AIDS Helpline established
	Front National campaigns for compulsory testing and quarantining				
1987	May: creation of anonymous test centres in each administrative *département* announced, the first opening in March 1988	March: coalition agreement commits incoming government to a liberal AIDS policy, centred on health education, voluntary	January: NHI group formally established as AIDS Centre (COA) National Committee for Campaign Against AIDS (CNLA) formed to	Gay saunas closed	January: AIDS information leaflet distributed to all households February: 'AIDS week' – a coordinated schedule of

Pilot epidemiological study blocked by Ministry of Health; proposed by authorities in south-east, it would have included named registration of seropositive individuals

July: central government made exclusively responsible for AIDS policy making

AIDS declared *cause nationale*

In Paris, a schoolteacher with AIDS is refused tenure, later granted on appeal at the end of 1988

testing and support for those directly affected; this includes funding specialist AIDS posts in local public health departments and the formation of a National AIDS Council as a permanent advisory body to government, as well as a Parliamentary Commission of Inquiry on AIDS

The federal government position is endorsed by health ministers of the *Länder*; in May, Bavaria dissents, publishing legal-repressive measures including compulsory testing on suspicion of HIV infection and the criminalisation of HIV transmission

October: laboratories obliged to report positive HIV test results to BGA in Berlin; AIDS Coordinating Unit set up at Ministry of Health

provide advice and coordination, composed of medical researchers and administrators

Named notification of all cases of AIDS to national authorities made compulsory

May: national AIDS conference in Rome

health education programmes in broadcast media

May: House of Commons Select Committee on the Social Services report *Problems Associated with AIDS*

AIDS (Control) Act passed, obliging health authorities (RHAs, DHAs and Scottish Health Boards) to provide reports of AIDS case numbers and accounts of local facilities for prevention, testing, treatment, counselling and care

Table 8.2 (*cont.*)

	France	Germany	Italy	Sweden	United Kingdom
1988	January: Ministry of Education to run AIDS education programmes in schools	January: AIDS Centre established at the Federal Health Office	January: screening of donated blood made mandatory	Legal provision for compulsory HIV testing in sexual assault cases	January: World Summit of Ministers of Health on Programmes of AIDS Prevention, London
	June: new health minister Schwartzenberg forced to resign by reaction to his proposals for testing before marriage and during pregnancy, and for methadone programme	November: Federal Supreme Court upholds judgment of a district court in Nuremberg that a man who had not informed his sexual partners of his (positive) HIV status had been guilty of an attempt to inflict grievous bodily harm	July: national media campaign on AIDS	June: Fourth International Conference on AIDS, Stockholm	July: DoH planning guidelines ask health authorities to develop community-based prevention initiatives
	November: following an evaluative report on AIDS policy, new minister Evin presents a plan against AIDS, with substantial funding for prevention following in 1989		August: national research plan on AIDS launched December: letter from Minister of Health delivered to all households		

1989	National agency for AIDS prevention created at Ministry of Health		Cabinet committee on AIDS dissolved
	Expert National AIDS Council formed to advise Minister of Health		DoH guidance to health authority general managers requires that each DHA has a named officer responsible for HIV/AIDS prevention
1990		National AIDS strategy voted through parliament, centring on voluntary testing, condom promotion and clinical services	

Sources: BMJFFG (1990), Fox, Day and Klein (1989), Frankenberg (1992), Henriksson and Ytterberg (1992), Moss (1990), Pollak (1990a, 1990b), Steffen (1992, 1998), Street (1988), Street and Weale (1992).

AIDS politics in France experienced severe and sustained 'aftershocks' from 1991, when litigation on the part of individuals infected with HIV through transfusion of contaminated blood escalated into a national scandal. Criminal investigations were undertaken against a number of officials, including former health ministers and a former prime minister (Fabius), and the Director and Scientific Director of the national blood transfusion service were imprisoned for fraud. Both the transfusion service and regulations for the safety of medicines have been completely reformed, effectively reinforcing the responsibilities of the Ministry of Health (Steffen 1998, 1999).[7]

German AIDS politics became highly polarised, providing perhaps the clearest example of the dichotomy between maximalist (repressive) and minimalist (liberal) approaches to prevention (Frankenberg 1992). During 1986–87, a conflict emerged between the Federal Ministry of Health and the state of Bavaria over the applicability to AIDS of longstanding epidemic legislation. Having flirted with the idea of new legislation as early as 1984, the federal government formally adopted a liberal line, which was quickly endorsed by most of the *Länder*. Bavaria, by contrast, identified prostitutes and injecting drug users as particular risk groups, while closely regulating gay bars and saunas. Mass screening was carried out on civil servants, prisoners and foreigners applying for a residence permit, and HIV transmission was made subject to criminal prosecution. Meanwhile, the *AIDS-Hilfen*, voluntary organisations of gay men set up in the major cities in 1983–84, had become an established interlocutor and partner of public health administration. The *Deutsche AIDS-Hilfe*, the national association of local groups, gained substantial federal funding during 1985–87, its representatives holding an established presence at expert hearings and on advisory bodies. The prominence of the voluntary sector in AIDS politics, as well as the conflict between Bavaria and the centre, are characteristic of the legalism, federalism and subsidiarism of German social and public policy more generally (Freeman and Clasen 1994).

Like Germany, AIDS policy making in Italy was subject to central–regional antagonisms. Conflict here was less about the content of policy than about the authority by which it was promulgated. Institutional weakness of various kinds meant that policy leadership on AIDS was slow to be established (Moss 1990). Religious (catholic) organisations in Italy are stronger and more influential than elsewhere, though the impact they had on AIDS policy is difficult to determine. By the same token, other voluntary organisations, including groups of those affected, are weaker. While education, the media and health and medical research were organised centrally, health service administration was decentralised. Their responsibilities for public health meant that responses to AIDS tended to be formulated first by the regions, in an uncoordinated way, with central direction being given in the form of recommendations. A national AIDS centre was set up early in 1987, as well as a national policy advisory committee, and health education campaigns and a research strategy followed in 1988. The national strategy approved in 1990 focused on voluntary testing and clinical services, though regional governments protested at the centralisation of policy it implied (Steffen 1998).

In comparative context, Swedish AIDS policy appears an exceptional case (Henriksson and Ytterberg 1992). Sweden was almost alone in applying sexually transmitted disease legislation to HIV and AIDS, in 1985. The authoritarian measures prescribed by the Infectious Diseases Act included a legal obligation on HIV-infected individuals to consult a public health doctor, and to provide information to enable their sexual partners or contacts to be traced, who might then themselves be subject to mandatory testing. Infected individuals were required to inform their sexual partners of their HIV status, as well as doctors or dentists who might be treating them. The Act also made provision for the compulsory isolation of individuals deemed to constitute a risk to others. In practice, however, the full panoply of possible measures has been brought to bear in no more than a handful of cases. As in Bavaria, quasi-judicial measures have been complemented by the active encouragement of voluntary testing among the general population, supported by extensive health education campaigning, and echoed in the refusal to countenance needle exchange and other harm reduction programmes for drug users. Although radical, Sweden's repressive strategy was the product of a broad political consensus, promoted by a national advisory body, the AIDS Delegation. Its discussions did much to resolve what amounted to disarray among government, officials, politicians, doctors and interest group leaders during 1985, and later when government inactivity was criticised in 1987 (Fox, Day and Klein 1989). That Swedish strategy should have taken the form it did is attributable to the paternalist ideology of the 'Moral Left' that has shaped other elements of its welfare state (Henriksson and Ytterberg 1992).

In the UK, although comparable infectious disease legislation was extended to cover AIDS in 1985, it was scarcely invoked. AIDS was not made a notifiable disease. Other legislation in 1987 merely obliged health authorities to report on their programmes of prevention, treatment and care. What was distinctive about AIDS policy making in the UK was its relatively centralised, elitist and exclusive nature (Street and Weale 1992). Though groups such as the Terrence Higgins Trust and others had some influence on the Department of Health in the early period (Strong and Berridge 1990), the intense politicisation of 1986 was defined by the government's assumption of control. The clearest evidence of this was the special cabinet committee on AIDS which began meeting in October 1986, and the budget allocation which funded the mass health education campaigns which began at the end of the year. The access of medicine to policy making was privileged over other interests (Street and Weale 1992, Fox, Day and Klein 1989), while the government used the organisational structure of the NHS to fund and regulate local responses. Parliamentary committee hearings and an All-Party Parliamentary Group on AIDS helped to foster consensus around a liberal strategy.

AIDS, prevention and health politics

AIDS represented an explosive kind of health politics. Because it quickly and deeply involved an unusually wide array of actors, AIDS policy making was an effective indicator of the embeddedness of health systems in their social, cultural, economic and political contexts.[8] AIDS affected whole sets of political actors and interests, and these in turn affected the way the disease was addressed. They included government, the law and public administration, but also pharmaceutical and insurance industries and blood and sperm banks; they included doctors and scientists and groups directly affected by HIV and AIDS, as well as broader societal interests, often articulated through the media. In different countries, the contours of AIDS politics were set by specific arrangements of and between state, market, associations and community, or what can be identified as the bases of social order itself (Moss and Misztal 1990). The problem which AIDS presented for government was essentially a problem of managing relations between these elements.

In retrospect perhaps unremarkably, though the outcome rarely seemed certain at the time, the solution to the problem was a liberal one. AIDS policy rested principally on health education and voluntary testing, and improved resources for treatment and care. Significantly, too, this held across countries. If AIDS serves as an indicator of the embeddedness of health politics in particular contexts, these were typical of advanced industrial – and liberal – democracies. Assumptions about individual behavioural change consequent upon voluntary testing and counselling (and, equally, of the effectiveness of excluding those compulsorily screened) were, at the time of their conception, little more than assumptions. But voluntary testing accorded with prevailing liberal ideas about the private and ultimately rational nature of individual behaviour, including sexual behaviour, and not only with them but with an associated professional value system in which the freely contracted and confidential nature of the relationship between doctor and patient remains paramount (Day and Klein 1989).

It fitted with pre-existing patterns in preventive health policy making, too. Responses to AIDS were consistent with responses to heart disease or asthma: as a policy problem, AIDS differed from these only in degree, not in kind. Across the field of preventive health policy making, substantive change has focused on extending the scope of preventive screening and on improved capacities for epidemiological monitoring and health education, while legislation has been used in very limited ways. Across countries, policy has expressed the liberal individualism of pluralist democracies in which, in Leichter's phrase, citizens invariably remain 'free to be foolish' (Leichter 1991). In Germany and the UK most notably, a succession of health policy statements has emphasised the responsibility of individuals for their own health (Freeman 1995). If Swedish policy statements tend to have been less individualist, more egalitarian, placing greater emphasis on government and workplace intervention (Gustaffson and Nettleton 1992), their benevolent paternalism has much the same ideological and cultural roots as the more discriminatory authoritarianism which characterised the response to AIDS.[9]

In a very general way, then, prevention is a fair indicator of the nature of the health polity. But it also serves as a something of a litmus test of health political interests more specifically (cf. Ferber 1985). It reveals and expresses key characteristics of the relationship between medicine and government, between government, parties and groups and between central, sub-central and supranational levels of policy making. In doing so, it echoes patterns and problems raised in earlier chapters.

AIDS was first identified and tracked by doctors working in public epidemiological and research facilities. The first organised responses were those by community groups. In many countries, the crisis period of the mid- to late 1980s saw these displaced by state intervention, which also tended to entail a shift of authority and responsibility in favour of the medical profession. What is interesting is that the epidemiological uncertainty surrounding AIDS served to heighten rather than diminish medical authority. The 'power of professionalism' was to provide an invaluable source of political consensus and legitimate public policy. 'Given uncertainty, it has suited everyone to leave AIDS, like most areas of policy, to the professionals' (Fox, Day and Klein 1989, p. 111). On AIDS as on other prevention issues, medicine and government operated in tandem (chapter 6, above).

This is part of what has been a long process of the medicalisation of prevention: if there is cross-national evidence of the screening activity of doctors in local practice (both specialists and generalists) being extended, there is as much to suggest that public health specialists and services have lost out. Prevention is a key instrument of inter-and intra-professional turf wars. In Germany as in France, the extension of screening served to bolster the occupational identity as well as the more immediate economic interests of doctors in local private practice (Göckenjan 1980, Letourmy 1986). At the end of the previous century, similarly, the concept of preventive medicine had been deployed in the UK 'as a way of reconceptualising and reconstituting the old environmentally oriented public health in terms of curative medicine and personal health care services' (Sturdy and Cooter 1998, p. 13). In turn, the Royal College of General Practitioners' 1981 document, *Health and Prevention in Primary Care*, represented simply a stage in the continuing search for an effective occupational rationale for general practice (Davies 1984).

Professional dominance in health care is replicated, perhaps even established and protected in prevention. Yet one of the key features of AIDS politics is the degree to which user interests were mobilised. The *AIDS-Hilfen* in Germany and the Terrence Higgins Trust in the UK were both formed in the absence of any existing resource on which those immediately and directly affected by AIDS could draw, becoming important government interlocutors as public policy responses were first formulated (Freeman 1992a).[10] Voluntary organisations in France and Italy, however, played a more limited role. In Sweden, representatives of those affected were not members of the AIDS Delegation, leaving them minimal access to the policy process. As they became more involved, providing more and more money for specialist services, governments began to turn away from organisations based in the communities of those affected to seek new voluntary sector partners:

the National AIDS Trust (rather than THT) in the UK and Noah's Ark (not RFSL) in Sweden. Even in Germany, the DAH's grant funding was of limited duration (Pollak 1990b). Though differences between countries are significant, reflecting different national policy styles, organisations based in the communities of those directly affected by HIV and AIDS have been critics of as much as participants in continuing AIDS policy making.

At the same time, the politics of prevention matches the low level of party politicisation evident on other health issues. Though prevention is sometimes thought of as a Left goal, it was revived by liberal-conservative governments. With the possible exception of Sweden, the Left version of prevention has been a victim of the reaction against social planning and public intervention in Europe which has taken place in the 1980s and 1990s. Responses to AIDS, similarly, were delayed rather than altered by parliamentary elections (in France in 1986 and 1988, in Germany in January 1987 and in the UK in June). The issue was conflict-ridden – and governments near the end of their parliamentary terms sought to avoid conflict – but not on party political lines. Only small parties saw any mileage in exploiting the populist appeal of radical measures, setting themselves against the prevailing national consensus: the CSU in Bavaria, and Le Pen in campaigning as Front National candidate for the French presidency in 1988.

Prevention says as much about the contested relationship between centre and region in health politics. In Germany and Italy, AIDS set the centre against one or more regions, exposing weaknesses in the structure of federal administrations (Misztal and Moss 1990). In Britain, typically, NHS organisation meant that the central–local relationship was more easily managed. In all three countries, governments have attempted to use prevention in an instrumental way for the accretion of central authority in the health sector, while the identification of regional or sub-central responsibilities has served as an effective means of depoliticisation (cf. chapter 5, above). In Germany, the federal government failed to gain generic responsibility for prevention in 1968–69 and nor did it acquire more than passing responsibility for HIV and AIDS. Later, in Britain, public health management was successfully incorporated into the territorial structure of the NHS. Meanwhile, just like national governments, the European Commission has used prevention to claim increased powers and resources in environmental and consumer affairs, as well as in social policy (Bomberg and Peterson 1993).

In many ways, AIDS expresses the international, if not global interrelatedness of problems of health and disease (Christakis 1989, O'Neill 1990).[11] Across countries, health officials and AIDS Service Organisations (ASOs), as well as doctors and clinical researchers, are linked by international networks. That said, international organisations have been less important players in AIDS politics in the advanced industrial countries of western Europe, North America, Australia and New Zealand than elsewhere. Again, this exemplifies a pattern discernible in health policy more generally. WHO's Global Programme on AIDS, announced in 1986, was designed to assist member states to draw on first world resources. A World Summit of health ministers met under WHO auspices in London in

January 1988 to discuss AIDS prevention strategies. Supranational policy initiatives on the part of the European Union came later, and were largely symbolic (Altenstetter 1994). A 'Europe against AIDS' programme was adopted in June 1991 for the period 1991–93, aiming to strengthen national preventive programmes by promoting the exchange of information and experience among experts and policy makers; some support for medical research had been provided from 1983. In the end, however, in European countries, 'national considerations and AIDS control programs remain dominant, and hopes for a gradual erosion of national control over AIDS prevention programs are ill-founded' (Altenstetter 1994, p. 435).

Prevention, modernity and the state

What is the significance of policy making for prevention, including responses to AIDS, for understanding the way in which health issues are governed at the end of the twentieth century?

Since the 1970s, health and disease have become a symbolic container of public and social concerns, much as they were in the second half of the nineteenth century (cf. Baggott 1991).[12] In both periods, ideological concern for health is related to the management of broad social change (Göpel 1986). At the beginning of the modern era 'health' became a social and political ordering mechanism, a principle of social discipline. In the period of industrialisation it became a touchstone of national economic and military capacity. That 'health' should again become a subject of public discussion in the 1970s and 1980s is an indication of the extent to which social roles have seemed to lose their self-evident quality and have been subject to renegotiation and reorientation (Göpel 1986).[13] This is to say that the regulation and reregulation of health as such was a key aspect of the transition to modernity, and is again of the transition out of or beyond it. The regulation of access to medical care (chapters 2, 5 and 7, above) is only a part of this more general problematic. Deindustrialisation begs as many questions about the relationship between individuals and their environments, and the way these are expressed as health problems, as did industrialisation. Issues of employment, diet and morality are as salient now as they were then, even if the context in which they are articulated has shifted from the realm of production to consumption, from the workplace to the household. At the same time, health issues are coincident with the reinvigoration of prevention, for similar reasons, in other areas of social welfare, such as child protection.

Public action on AIDS was conceived and carried out at a time in which the form and extent of public (state) action as such was being critically revised. Public health capacity had atrophied, and health care policy was fixed on cost containment, if not retrenchment. Across countries, laws on divorce, contraception and abortion, sexuality and drug use had been liberalised (Moss and Misztal 1990).[14] Strategies for dealing with AIDS were necessarily very different to the way sexually transmitted diseases had been addressed at the end of the nineteenth century. Across western Europe, governments chose not to apply the legislation which public health tradition had left at their disposal. For public health services have become functionally inert. When they were established in the nineteenth century, they were concerned primarily with the provision of amenities such as drainage and some medical services, while their academic inspiration was derived from medicine and civil engineering (Fraser 1984). Public health was an institutionalised form of prevention, both reproducing and dependent on the premisses on which it was based. In time, it suffered a form of institutional sclerosis, in which a gulf opened between the order of health problems perceived as preventable and the organisational and technical capacity available to deal with them. In the course of the twentieth century, the expert gaze was to move from the external to the internal, from the boundary between individuals and their environments (sanitation) to the boundaries between people (the management of infection and contagion), and ultimately to the boundaries of the body itself (the effects of behaviours on individual bodies) (Armstrong 1993).[15] Public policy, in turn, was to witness a broad shift from regulation to persuasion (Allsop 1984). In effect, public health practice became increasingly divorced from the ideological discourse of late twentieth century health care and the relationships between government and society it characterised (cf. Schülein 1983). Public health has been displaced as much by the erosion of the concept of the public as of changing understandings of health and disease.

Of course, the state has not withered away any more than it has in the process of the reform of health care (chapter 5). Statistical information-gathering, the foundation of the public health movements of the nineteenth century, has been reinvigorated.[16] France, for example, has established regional health 'observatories' for epidemiological surveillance and forecasting, including the management of individual health records (Towers 1992). A telematic network of communicable disease surveillance was set up in 1984 (Hubert and Roure 1993), while a *carnet de santé*, revised in 1995, monitors preventable conditions in childhood, including weight problems, dental decay and domestic accidents (Pomey and Poullier 1997). Preventive discourse is expressed in a new vocabulary of '*securité sanitaire*' (Steffen 1998). Meanwhile, in the UK, the Communicable Disease Surveillance Centre's work on HIV and AIDS secured the future of the Public Health Laboratory Service at a time when its continued existence was under threat (Berridge and Strong 1992). The establishment by most governments of administrative centres for coordinating responses to AIDS indicates both the relative atrophy of public health capacity and its needful reconstitution. Now, the state appears as less the backbone of public health than the carapace within which it is contained.

In some countries and contexts, prevention expresses a new managerialism in the health sector, marking an increased government presence. In the UK, in 1992, the *Health of the Nation* white paper set priorities and targets for the reduction of preventable morbidity and mortality. In France, Germany, and Italy at more or less the same time, specific allocations of public funding were made for screening. These moves represent small but significant attempts by government to redirect or manipulate the activity of doctors, health authorities and sickness funds. The common sense legitimacy of the goal ('prevention is better than cure') – especially if linked to new money – may have made new obligations of this kind difficult to resist. But even if prevention is a legitimate requirement of health care actors and organisations, it is also a way of making new requirements appear legitimate (Freeman 1995).

Prevention, health and social systems

In the 1980s and 1990s, action on prevention parallelled intense, sustained processes of health care reform (chapter 5). Reform was driven by multiple pressures: perhaps the first and most prominent among them was the relative financial burden the public finance of health care had come to represent. Equally significant, however, were underlying uncertainties about both medicine and government (chapter 2). For all the criticism, too, both medicine and government were faced with increasing demand for more health care of better quality. Health systems, that is to say, were presented with increasing demand at precisely the point of decreasing capacity to meet it. Reform consequently addressed the problem of providing more for less, relying on a set of policy instruments including budget-setting, the replacement of routine resource allocations by competitive processes, enhanced management and dehospitalisation. One of the side-effects of reform, however, was to deepen public and professional uncertainties, and to challenge the legitimacy of existing health systems. In this context, prevention was essential to, not simply a distraction from, the distributional politics of health care.

Preventive policy making was a 'panacea' with regard to the 'dual crisis of cost and efficacy' (Taylor 1984). For it satisfied two of the most important criteria of social policy making in the post-crisis welfare state. It offered opportunities both for a retreat from big government and for the extension of control over the health sector. The point is not simply that prevention is characteristic of a changing (late modern) order of health politics, but that it fulfils a specific function in continuing processes of transition and adaptation. This can be explicated by returning to one of the key concepts with which this book began, that of the health system.

Politics (including health politics) can be conceived as a system of interactions (Easton 1965a, 1965b). The idea of the political system designates those interactions through which authoritative allocations of values or valued things are made. Political systems must be able to allocate values effectively, but must also be able to induce most of their members to accept those allocations as authoritative, or binding. These are the 'essential variables' of political life (Easton 1965b, p. 24). At the same time, political systems (including health systems) are open, subject to influences and pressures to which in turn they adapt: 'a system has the capacity for creative and constructive regulation of disturbances' (Easton 1965b, p. 21).

Systems exist in environments, which are themselves composed of other systems, such as families, states, cultures and economies. These constitute sources of pressure, but also resources by which consequent disturbance might be managed.

Prevention is a marginal aspect of medicine, and an equally marginal feature of health policy. But these margins are also borders: between medicine's treatment of disease and the promotion and protection of health; between professional judgement and public policy; between the individual and the public. Preventive policy making is a way of maintaining the boundaries between health care and its political, economic and cultural environment.[17] It is one of the ways in which a health system is adjusted to its environment: it forms part of the policy traffic between the health care system and the other systems – social, political and economic – which it serves and on which it draws.

'Boundary maintenance' can be achieved in two ways: by blocking or rejecting demands and pressures, or by mediating, adapting and amending them, rendering them into manageable form. Prevention serves to moderate the pressure on both medicine and government, while at the same time promoting the legitimacy of each. The role of prevention in health policy is not to secure the health of populations, but to secure the conditions of the continued functioning of health services.

Policy statements on prevention are made at points of significant structural change in health care systems, at times in which pressure of all kinds on governments and health care systems is most acute. Preventive measures ease this pressure in various ways. In part, they seek to regulate the demand for health care by asserting individual responsibility for health and its maintenance. In this they are something like user charges (another area of recently increased regulation and reregulation): their symbolic aspect is more significant than their functional one. At the same time, in the reform packages of the 1980s and 1990s screening represents one of the few areas (if not the only one) of expanded entitlement, a political 'sweetener'. Similarly, and in different national contexts, responses to AIDS represented a form of political education as much as health education. Governments were as concerned to send out general messages about the nature of the epidemic, to reduce panic and social division, as much as to amend specific sexual behaviours (Day and Klein 1989).

The expansion of individualist and medical forms of prevention (health education and screening), meanwhile, is designed to promote government's authority as much as its active responsibility. Primary strategies which address the social, cultural and environmental causes of ill-health come only at great cost, both financial and political. Governments which incur such costs are unlikely to derive any benefit from the policies they implement, which will have at best long-term results which in turn will be difficult to attribute to specific interventions. Immediate pressures are much better displaced into the individual and medical realms (Vobruba 1983): the medicalisation of prevention is the concomitant, if not one of the principal vehicles, of its depoliticisation.[18] Its transfer from (usually local) government to health care is in essence a shift from a political to a professional sphere of activity: 'The great service which professionals render to government is that they both express social concern and exalt expert solutions to social problems at the expense of political solutions ... Professionals stand for the solution of problems within the existing social system, they are the technicians and tacticians of piecemeal social engineering rather than the strategic planners of social change' (Wilding 1982, p. 16).

The arena of preventive policy-making may be characterised as a political frontier space between the state, medicine and other health political actors. It is a space in which power struggles in the health sector are played out. What are recognisable as typical health political conflicts are reproduced in respect of prevention: between medicine and government, between centre and region, between market and state and between the state and the individual citizen (above, and preceding chapters). They have to do both with the definition and redefinition of the boundaries of the health sector as such, and with the limits of competence of those working within it. As the location of the health care system in the health world becomes increasingly uncertain, its borders are more actively and intensively patrolled. The point is not so much that prevention should be thought of in terms of its technical effectiveness or efficiency, or even primarily as a way of extending or contracting the boundaries of the health care state, but that its central function is to maintain the capacity of the state to act in respect of health policy.

Notes

1 For more detail on the UK, see Allsop and Freeman (1993); on Germany, Freeman (1994); on Sweden, Diderichsen and Lindberg (1989) and Gustaffson and Nettleton (1992).
2 'On the one hand, consumers need protection against risks; on the other they build their identities as sovereign and independent decision makers for their own pleasure and satisfaction' (Sulkunen 1997, p. 257).
3 The classification was proposed by WHO in 1986. Type 2, common to the Caribbean and sub-Saharan Africa, was characterised by the transmission of HIV through heterosexual intercourse; type 3 referred to countries in which few cases have been recorded. For later refinements, see Blaxter (1991).
4 For more detailed discussion, see Frankenberg (1992) and Scott and Freeman (1995).
5 Mildred Blaxter provides an important caveat: 'Many countries' reaction has been cyclical, with periods of action and reaction, waves of concern followed by periods when the problem is down-played' (Blaxter 1991, p. 31).
6 For more discussion, see also Fee and Krieger (1993).
7 Similarly, in Germany in 1993, a commercial supplier was found to have failed to screen blood products adequately for HIV; patients infected as a result sued health ministers (Gow and Tomforde 1993).
8 As Jonathan Mann, former Director of WHO's Global Programme on AIDS put it 'the response to AIDS illuminates each nation's political culture ... as HIV dissects the immune system, so HIV/AIDS lays bare the social, cultural, and political character of entire societies' (Mann 1992, p. x).

9   For extended discussion of the controlling aspects of Swedish welfare, see Gould (1988).

10 There are interesting echoes here of the complex relationship between charity, medicine and the state in the early modern period (Barry and Jones 1991 and chapter 2, above).

11 'When confronting the AIDS pandemic, a national AIDS epidemic, or an AIDS patient, one must keep in mind that each exists because of the others, each acquires some of its properties from its relation to the others, and aspects of all three evolve because of their interaction. The AIDS pandemic is not simply the sum of the epidemics faced in all the nations of the world nor simply the sum of the AIDS problems faced by all the inhabitants of the globe. The whole is greater than the sum of the parts' (Christakis 1989, p. 126). For a study of international cooperation in response to AIDS, see Gordenker *et al.* (1995).

12 The predecessor to Sweden's *Public Health Report* of 1987 was published, significantly, in 1911 (Diderichsen and Lindberg 1989).

13 There is an interesting parallel with the environment, which, Howard Newby suggests, constitutes 'a readily available idiom in which anxieties can be articulated' (Newby 1991, p. 2). Environmentalism, meanwhile – prevention in a different context – may be 'little more than a vocabulary which cloaks certain sectional interests and presents them as the common good' (Newby 1991, p. 6).

14 Jeffrey Weeks goes further, arguing that 'the response to the AIDS crisis has been very much shaped by the development of a much wider crisis, which is external to the health crisis ... that is a complex crisis in sex relations, in race relations and in class relations which most of the Western world has been undergoing over the past twenty or thirty years' (Weeks 1989, p. 127).

15 For a critical account of the focus on individual behaviour in preventing HIV and AIDS, see Scott and Freeman (1995).

16 'Nineteenth-century public health was primarily an administrative discipline: it was closely linked with the growth of national and local government, and was concerned with managing the growth of populations rather than individuals ... New theories of epidemic disease developed primarily as technologies of surveillance and classification' (Sturdy and Cooter 1998, p. 17).

17 Recall here Moran's conception of the 'three faces' of the health care state: the welfare state, the capitalist industrial state and the pluralist democratic state (Moran 1995a, and chapter 1, above). The task of government is maintain some kind of equilibrium among these three sets of structural demands.

18 For more extended commentary and discussion, see Freeman (1992b).

Appendix

Table A.1 Health care finance and delivery indicators, 1995

	Total health spending, % GDP	Public spending on health, % GDP	Public spending on health, % total health spending	Practising doctors per 1000 inhabitants[a]	Health care coverage, % population	Cost-sharing (inpatient care), %	Cost-sharing (ambulatory care), %	Life expectancy at birth, women, years	Life expectancy at birth, men, years
France	9.9	8.0	80.6	2.8	99.5	92.0	57.0	81.9	73.9
Germany	10.4	8.1	78.2	3.3	92.2	98.0	90.0	79.8	73.3
Italy	7.7	5.4	69.3	5.3	100.0	85.0	73.0	80.8	74.4
Sweden	8.5	7.1	83.4	3.0	100.0	98.0	74.4	81.3	75.9
United Kingdom	6.9	5.8	84.4	1.6	100.0	99.0	88.0	79.7	74.3

Note: [a] 1994 figures.
Source: OECD (1998).

Table A.2 Total expenditure on health, % GDP, 1960–1995

	1960	1965	1970	1975	1980	1985	1990	1995
France	4.2	5.2	5.8	7.0	7.6	8.5	8.9	9.9
Germany	4.8	4.6	6.3	8.8	8.8	9.3	8.7	10.4
Italy	3.6	4.3	5.2	6.2	7.0	7.1	8.1	7.7
Sweden	4.7	5.5	7.1	7.9	9.4	9.0	8.8	8.5
United Kingdom	3.9	4.1	4.5	5.5	5.6	5.9	6.0	6.9

Source: OECD (1998).

Table A.3 Public expenditure on health, % GDP, 1960–1995[a]

	1960	1965	1970	1975	1980	1985	1990	1995
France	2.4	3.6	4.3	5.4	6.0	6.5	6.6	8.0
Germany	3.2	3.2	4.6	7.0	7.0	7.2	6.7	8.1
Italy	3.0	3.8	4.5	5.2	5.6	5.5	6.3	5.4
Sweden	3.4	4.4	6.1	7.1	8.7	8.1	7.9	7.1
United Kingdom	3.3	3.5	3.9	5.0	5.0	5.0	5.1	5.8

Note: [a]Publicly funded care in institutions, whether publicly or privately owned, and where public refers to central and local authorities, health boards and social insurance institutions. Public capital formation on health includes publicly financed investment in health facilities plus capital transfers to the private sector for hospital construction and equipment and subsidies from government to health care service providers.
Source: OECD (1998).

References

Abel-Smith, B. and Mossialos, E. (1994), 'Cost containment and health care reform: a study of the European Union', *Health Policy*, 28, 89–132.

Abel-Smith, B., Figueras, J., Holland, W., McKee, M. and Mossialos, E. (1995), *Choices in Health Policy. An agenda for the European Union*, Aldershot, Dartmouth.

Aggleton, P. (1990), *Health*, London, Routledge.

Alber, J. (1991), 'The West German health care system in comparative perspective', in Kolinsky, E. (ed.) *The Federal Republic of Germany: the end of an era*, Oxford, Berg.

Alber, J. (1995), 'A framework for the comparative study of social services', *Journal of European Social Policy*, 5:2, 131–149.

Albritton, F. P. (1993), *Health Care Insurance Reform in the United States. A market approach with application from the Federal Republic of Germany*, Lanham, Maryland, University Press of America.

Alford, R. R. (1975), *Health Care Politics. Ideological and interest group barriers to reform*, Chicago, University of Chicago Press.

Allsop, J. (1984), *Health Policy and the National Health Service*, Harlow, Longman.

Allsop, J. and Freeman, R. (1993), 'Prevention in health policy in the United Kingdom and the NHS', in Mills, M. (ed.) *Prevention, Health and British Politics*, Aldershot, Avebury.

Altenstetter, C. (1989), 'Hospital planners and medical professionals in the Federal Republic of Germany', in Freddi, G. and Björkman, J. W. (eds) *Controlling medical professionals: the comparative politics of health governance*, London, Sage/ECPR.

Altenstetter, C. (1992), 'Health policy regimes and the Single European Market', *Journal of Health Politics, Policy and Law*, 17:4, 813–846.

Altenstetter, C. (1994), 'European Union responses to AIDS/HIV and policy networks in the pre-Maastricht era', *Journal of European Public Policy*, 1:3, 413–440.

Altenstetter, C. (1997), 'Health policy-making in Germany: stability and dynamics', in Altenstetter, C. and Björkman, J. W. (eds) *Health Policy Reform, National Variations and Globalization*, Basingstoke, Macmillan.

Anderson, O. (1972), *Health Care: can there be equity? The United States, Sweden and England*, New York, John Wiley.

Appleby, J. (1998), 'Economic perspectives on markets and health care', in Ranade, W. (ed.) *Markets and Health Care. A comparative analysis*, Harlow, Longman.

Armstrong, D. (1993), 'Public health spaces and the fabrication of identity', *Sociology*, 27:3, 393–410.

Ashburner, L. and Cairncross, L. (1992), 'Just trust us', *Health Service Journal*, 14 May, 20–22.

Ashton, J., Grey, P. and Barnard, K. (1986), 'Healthy Cities: WHO's New Public Health initiative, *Health Promotion*, 1:3, 319–324.

Atteveld, L. van, Broeders, V. and Lapré, R. (1987), 'International comparative research in health care. A study of the literature', *Health Policy*, 8, 105–136.

Bach, S. (1993), 'Health care reforms in the French hospital system', *International Journal of Health Planning and Management*, 8:3, 189–200.

Bach, S. (1994), 'Managing a pluralist health system: the case of health care reform in France', *International Journal of Health Services*, 24:4, 593–606.

Baggott, R. (1990), *Alcohol, Politics and Social Policy*, Aldershot, Gower.

Baggott, R. (1991), 'Looking forward to the past? The politics of public health', *Journal of Social Policy*, 20:2, 191–213.

Baggott, R. (1994), *Health and Health Care in Britain*, Basingstoke, Macmillan.

Baldock, J. and Ungerson, C. (1996), 'Money, care and consumption: families in the new mixed economy of social care', in Jones, H. and Millar, J. (eds) *The Politics of the Family*, Avebury, Aldershot.

Bandelow, N. (1994), 'Ist Politik wieder autonom? Das Beispiel Gesundheitsreform', *Gegenwartskunde*, 4, 445–456.

Barry, J. and Jones, C. (1991), *Medicine and Charity before the Welfare State*, London, Routledge.

Bayer, R. and Kirp, D. (1992), 'An epidemic in political and policy perspective', in Kirp, D. and Bayer, R. (eds) *AIDS in the Industrialised Democracies: passions, politics and policies*, New Brunswick, Rutgers University Press.

Bell, D. (1987), 'The world and the United States in 2013', *Daedalus*, 116:3, 1–31.

Bellah, R. N., Madsen, R., Sullivan, W. M., Swidler, A. and Tipton, S. M. (1988), *Habits of the Heart: middle America observed*, London, Hutchison Education.

Bennett, C. J. (1991), 'Review article: what is policy convergence and what causes it?', *British Journal of Political Science*, 21:2, 215–233.

Berridge, V. and Strong, P. (1992), 'AIDS policies in the United Kingdom: a preliminary analysis', in Fee, E. and Fox, D. (eds) *AIDS: the making of a chronic disease*, Berkeley, University of California Press.

Bevan, G., France, G. and Taroni, F. (1992), 'Dolce Vita. Inside Italy's NHS', *Health Service Journal*, 27 February, 20–23.

Björkman, J. W. (1985), 'Who governs the health sector?' *Comparative Politics*, 17:4, 399–420.

Björkman, J. W. (1989), 'Politicizing medicine and medicalizing politics: physician power in the United States', in Freddi, G. and Björkman, J. W. (eds) *Controlling Medical Professionals: the comparative politics of health governance*, London, Sage/ECPR.

Blanke, B. and Perschke-Hartmann, C. (1994), 'The 1992 health reform: victory over pressure group politics', *German Politics*, 3:2, 233–248.

Blaxter, M. (1983), 'Health services as a defence against the consequences of poverty in industrialised societies', *Social Science and Medicine*, 17:16, 1139–1148.

Blaxter, M. (1991), *AIDS: Worldwide Policies and Problems*, London, Office of Health Economics.

Blendon, R. J., Leitman, R., Morrison, I. and Donelan, K. (1990), 'Satisfaction with health care systems in ten nations', *Health Affairs*, 9:2, 186–192.

BMJFFG (Bundesministerium für Jugend, Familie, Frauen und Gesundheit) (1990), *Aidsbekämpfung in der Bundesrepublik Deutschland*, Bonn, BMJFFG.

Bodenheimer, T. and Grumbach, K. (1992), 'Financing universal health insurance: taxes, premiums and the lessons of social insurance', *Journal of Health Politics, Policy and Law,* 17:3, 439–462.

Bomberg, E. and Peterson, J. (1993), 'Prevention from above? The role of the European Community', in Mills, M. (ed.) *Prevention, Health and British Politics*, Aldershot, Avebury.

Bruno, M. and Sachs, J. D. (1985), *Economics of World Stagflation*, Oxford, Blackwell.

Brunsdon, E. and May, M. (1995), 'Swedish health care in transition?', in Brunsdon, E. and May, M. (eds) *Swedish Welfare: policy and provision*, London, Social Policy Association.

Busfield, J. (1990), 'Sectoral divisions in consumption: the case of medical care', *Sociology,* 24:1, 77–96.

Busse, R. and Schwartz, F. W. (1995), 'Germany: hard choices ahead', *European Health Reform,* 2, 6–7.

Calnan, M. (1991), *Preventing Coronary Heart Disease. Prospects, policies and politics*, London, Routledge.

Cawson, A. (1982), *Corporatism and Welfare,* London, Heinemann Educational Books.

Chambaud, L. (1993), 'À la carte', *Health Service Journal*, 18 March, 24–27.

Christakis, N. A. (1989), 'Responding to a pandemic: international interests in AIDS control', *Daedalus,* 118, 113–134.

Clasen, J. (1997), 'Social insurance in Germany – dismantling or reconstruction?', in Clasen, J. (ed.) *Social Insurance in Europe*, Bristol, Policy Press.

Cochrane, A. L. (1971), *Effectiveness and Efficiency. Random reflections on health services*, London, Nuffield Provincial Hospitals Trust.

Crawford, R. (1977), 'You are dangerous to your health: the ideology and politics of victim blaming', *International Journal of Health Services,* 7:4, 663–680.

Crivelli, L. A. and Rhodes, G. (1995), 'The authorisation process for E112 cross-border care from the perspective of information theory', paper prepared for European Union Concerted Action Project *Health Care Financing and the Single European Market.*

Culyer, A. J. (1990), 'Cost containment in Europe', in OECD *Health Care Systems in Transition. The search for efficiency*, Paris, OECD.

Culyer, A. J. and Meads, A. (1992), 'The United Kingdom: effective, efficient, equitable?', *Journal of Health Politics, Policy and Law,* 17:4, 667–688.

Dahl, R. A. (1961), *Who Governs? Democracy and power in an American city.* New Haven, Yale University Press.

Davies, C. (1984), 'General practitioners and the pull of prevention', *Sociology of Health and Illness,* 6:3, 267–289.

Day, P. and Klein, R. (1989), 'Interpreting the unexpected: the case of AIDS policy making in Britain', *Journal of Public Policy,* 9:3, 337–353.

Day, P. and Klein, R. (1992), 'Constitutional and distributional conflict in British general practice, 1911–1991', *Political Studies,* 40:3, 462–478.

Deppe, H.-U. (1987), *Krankheit ist ohne Politik nicht heilbar*, Frankfurt, Suhrkamp.

Diderichsen, F. and Lindberg, G. (1989), 'Better health – but not for all: the Swedish Public Health Report, 1987', *International Journal of Health Services,* 19:2, 221–255.

Dingwall, R. (1994), 'Litigation and the threat to medicine', in Gabe, J., Kelleher, D. and Williams, G. (eds) *Challenging Medicine*, London, Routledge.

Döhler, M. (1991), 'Policy networks, opportunity structures and neo-Conservative reform strategies in health policy', in Marin, B. and Mayntz, R. (eds) *Policy Networks: empirical evidence and theoretical considerations*, Frankfurt, Campus.

Döhler, M. (1995), 'The state as architect of political order: policy dynamics in German health care', *Governance*, 8:3, 380–404.

Dolowitz, D. and Marsh, D. (1996), 'Who learns what from whom: a review of the policy transfer literature', *Political Studies*, 44:2, 343–357.

Easton, D. (1965a), *A Framework for Political Analysis*, New Jersey, Prentice-Hall.

Easton, D. (1965b), *A Systems Analysis of Political Life*, New York, John Wiley.

Ehrenreich, B. and Ehrenreich, J. (1971), *The American Health Empire: power, profits and politics*, New York, Random House.

Ehrenreich, J. (ed.) (1978), *The Cultural Crisis of Modern Medicine*, New York, Monthly Review Press.

Elston, M. A. (1991), 'The politics of professional power: medicine in a changing health service', in Gabe, J., Calnan, M. and Bury, M. (eds) *The Sociology of the Health Service*, London, Routledge.

Enthoven, A. C. (1985), *Reflections on the Management of the National Health Service*, London, Nuffield Provincial Hospitals Trust.

Enthoven, A. C. (1993), 'The history and principles of managed competition', *Health Affairs*, supplement, 24–48.

Fee, E. and Krieger, N. (1993), 'Thinking and rethinking AIDS: implications for health policy', *International Journal of Health Services*, 23:2, 323–346.

Ferber, C. von (1985), 'Kassen und Prävention: Handlungsbereitschaft, Handlungsmöglichkeiten und Chancen', in Rosenbrock, R. and Hauß, F. (eds) *Krankenkassen und Prävention*, Berlin, Edition Sigma/WZB.

Ferrera, M. (1989), 'The politics of health reform: origins and performance of the Italian health service in comparative perspective', in Freddi, G. and Björkman, J. W. (eds) *Controlling medical professionals: the comparative politics of health governance*, London, Sage/ECPR.

Ferrera, M. (1993), *EC Citizens and Social Protection: main results from a Eurobarometer survey*, Brussels, Commission of the European Communities.

Ferrera, M. (1995), 'The rise and fall of democratic universalism. Health care reform in Italy, 1978–1994', *Journal of Health Politics, Policy and Law*, 20:2, 275–302.

Ferrera, M. (1996a), 'The "southern model" of welfare in social Europe', *Journal of European Social Policy*, 6:1, 17–37.

Ferrera, M. (1996b), 'The partitocracy of health', *Res Publica*, 38:2, 447–460.

Field, M. G. (1973), 'The concept of the "health system" at the macrosociological level', *Social Science and Medicine*, 7:10, 763–785.

Flora, P. (1986), *Growth to Limits: the Western European welfare states since World War II*, Berlin, de Gruyter.

Flora, P. and Alber, J. (1981), 'Modernization, democratization, and the development of welfare states in western Europe', in Flora, P. and Heidenheimer, A. J. (eds) *The Development of Welfare States in Europe and America*, New Brunswick, Transaction Books.

Flora, P. and Heidenheimer, A. J. (1981), 'The historical core and changing boundaries of the welfare state', in Flora, P. and Heidenheimer, A. J. (eds) *The Development of Welfare States in Europe and America*, New Brunswick, Transaction Books.

Fox, D. M. (1988), 'AIDS and the American health polity: the history and prospects of a crisis of authority', in Fee, E. and Fox, D. M. (eds) *AIDS: the burdens of history*, Berkeley, University of California Press.

Fox, D. M., Day, P. and Klein, R. (1989), 'The power of professionalism: AIDS in Britain, Sweden and the United States', *Daedalus*, 118, 93–112.

France, G. (1991), 'Cost containment in a public–private health care system: Italy', *Public Budgeting and Finance*, 11:4, 63–74.

France, G. (1996a), 'Constrained governance and the evolution of the Italian National Health Service since 1980', paper presented to workshop *Beyond the Health Care State. New dimensions in health politics in Europe*, 24th ECPR Joint Sessions of Workshops, Oslo, 29 March to 3 April.

France, G. (1996b), 'Governance of two national health services: Italy and UK compared', in Pola, G. *et al.* (eds) *New Developments in Local Government Finance*, London, Edward Elgar.

France, G. (1997), 'Cross-border flows of Italian patients within the European Union. An international trade approach', *European Journal of Public Health*, 7:3, 18–25.

Frankenberg, G. (1992), 'Germany: the uneasy triumph of pragmatism', in Kirp, D. and Bayer, R. (eds) *AIDS in the Industrialised Democracies: passions, politics and policies*, New Brunswick, Rutgers University Press.

Fraser, D. (1984), *The Evolution of the British Welfare State*, second edition, Basingstoke, Macmillan.

Freddi, G. (1989), 'Problems of organizational rationality in health systems: political controls and policy options', in Freddi, G. and Björkman, J. W. (eds) *Controlling Medical Professionals. The comparative politics of health governance*, London, Sage/ECPR.

Freeman, R. (1992a), 'Governing the voluntary sector response to AIDS: a comparative study of the UK and Germany', *Voluntas*, 3:1, 29–47.

Freeman, R. (1992b), 'The idea of prevention: a critical review', in Scott, S. J., Williams, G. H., Platt, S. D. and Thomas, H. A. (eds) *Private Risks and Public Dangers*, Aldershot, Avebury.

Freeman, R. (1994), 'Prevention in health policy in the Federal Republic of Germany', *Policy and Politics*, 22:1, 3–16.

Freeman, R. (1995), 'Prevention and government: health policy making in the United Kingdom and Germany', *Journal of Health Politics, Policy and Law*, 20:3, 745–765.

Freeman, R. (1998a), 'Competition in context: the politics of health care reform in Europe, *International Journal for Quality in Health Care*, 10:5, 395–401.

Freeman, R. (1998b), 'The German model: the state and the market in health care', in Ranade, W. (ed.) *Markets and Health Care. A comparative analysis*, Harlow, Longman.

Freeman, R. (1999), 'Institutions, states and cultures: health policy and politics in Europe', in Clasen, J. (ed.) *Comparative Social Policy. Concepts, theories and methods*, Oxford, Blackwell.

Freeman, R. and Clasen, J. (1994), 'The German Social State: an introduction', in Clasen, J. and Freeman, R. (eds) *Social Policy in Germany*, Hemel Hempstead, Harvester Wheatsheaf.

Freidson, E. (1970), *Professional Dominance. The social structure of medical care*, New York, Atherton.

Frenk, J. and Durán-Arenas, L. (1993), 'The medical profession and the state', in Hafferty, F. and McKinlay, J. B. (eds) *The Changing Medical Profession: an international perspective*, New York, Oxford University Press.

Friedman, M. (1962), *Capitalism and Freedom*, Chicago, University of Chicago Press.

Fry, J. (1991), 'Comparative analysis of approaches to the provision and financing of health care', in Holland, W. W., Detels, R. and Knox, G. (eds) *Oxford Textbook of Public Health*, second edition, Oxford, Oxford University Press.

Gabe, J., Kelleher, D. and Williams, G. (eds) (1994), *Challenging Medicine*, London, Routledge.

Galbraith, J. K. (1956), *American Capitalism: the concept of countervailing power*, Boston, Houghton Mifflin.

Garpenby, P. (1989), *The State and the Medical Profession. A cross-national comparison of the health policy arena in the United Kingdom and Sweden 1945–1985*, Linköping Studies in Arts and Science 39, Linköping, University of Linköping.

Garpenby, P. (1995), 'Health care reform in Sweden in the 1990s: local pluralism versus national coordination', *Journal of Health Politics, Policy and Law*, 20:3, 695–717.

George, V. and Wilding, P. (1976), *Ideology and Social Welfare*, London, Routledge and Kegan Paul.

George, V. and Wilding, P. (1984), *The Impact of Social Policy*, London, Routledge and Kegan Paul.

Glennerster, H. and Matsaganis, M. (1994), 'The English and Swedish health care reforms', *International Journal of Health Services*, 24:2, 231–251.

Göckenjan, G. (1980), 'Politik und Verwaltung präventiver Gesundheitssicherung', *Soziale Welt*, 31, 156–175.

Godt, P. (1987), 'Confrontation, consent and corporatism: state strategies and the medical profession in France, Great Britain and West Germany', *Journal of Health Politics, Policy and Law*, 12:3, 459–480.

Godt, P. (1996), 'The politics of health care reform in France', paper presented to workshop *Beyond the Health Care State. New dimensions in health politics in Europe*, ECPR Joint Sessions of Workshops, Oslo, 29 March–3 April.

Göpel, E. (1986), 'Wohin treibt die 'Gesundheitsbewegung'? Überlegungen zur politisch kulturellen Bedeutung des Gesundheitsmotivs', *Das Argument*, Argument Sonderband AS 131, 115–125.

Gordenker, L., Coate, R. A., Jönsson, C. and Söderholm, P. (1995), *International Cooperation in Response to AIDS*, London, Pinter.

Gould, A. (1988), *Conflict and Control in Welfare Policy. The Swedish experience*, Harlow, Longman.

Gow, D. and Tomforde, A. (1993), 'Bad blood on their hands', *Guardian*, 6–7 November, 25.

Gray, A. (1993), 'International patterns of health care, 1960 to the 1990s', in Webster, C. (ed.) *Caring for Health: history and diversity*, Buckingham, Open University Press.

Greiner, W. and Schulenburg, J.-M. Graf v d (1997), 'The health system of Germany', in Raffell, M. W. (ed.) *Health Care and Reform in Industrialized Countries*, University Park, PA, Pennsylvania State University Press.

Gustaffson, U. and Nettleton, S. (1992), 'The health of two nations', *International Journal of Sociology and Social Policy*, 12:3, 1–25.

Habermas, J. (1975), *Legitimation Crisis*, Boston, Beacon Press.

Hage, J., Hanneman, R. and Gargan, E. T. (1989), *State Responsiveness and State Activism. An examination of the social forces that explain the rise in social expenditures in Britain, France, Germany and Italy 1870–1968*, London, Unwin Hyman.

Håkansson, S. and Nordling, S. (1997), 'The health system of Sweden', in Raffell, M. W. (ed.) *Health Care and Reform in Industrialized Countries*, University Park, PA, Pennsylvania State University Press.

Ham, C. (1988), 'Governing the health sector: power and policy-making in the English and Swedish health services', *Milbank Quarterly*, 66:2, 389–414.

Ham, C. (1992), *Health Policy in Britain. The politics and organisation of the National Health Service*, third edition, Basingstoke, Macmillan.

Ham, C. (1997a), 'The United Kingdom', in Ham, C. (ed.) *Health Care Reform. Learning from international experience*, Buckingham, Open University Press.

Ham, C. (1997b), 'Lessons and conclusions', in Ham, C. (ed.) *Health Care Reform. Learning from international experience*, Buckingham, Open University Press.

Ham, C., Robinson, R. and Benzeval, M. (1990), *Health Check: health care reforms in an international context*, London, King's Fund.

Harrison, S., Hunter, D. J., Marnoch, G. and Pollitt, C. (1992), *Just Managing. Power and culture in the National Health Service*, Basingstoke, Macmillan.

Harrison, S., Hunter, D. J. and Pollitt, C. (1990), *The Dynamics of British Health Policy*, London, Unwin Hyman.

Harrison, S. and Mort, M. (1998), 'Which champions? Which people? Public and user involvement in health care as a technology of legitimation', *Social Policy and Administration*, 32:1, 60–70.

Harrison, S. and Pollitt, C. (1994), *Controlling Health Professionals. The future of work and organization in the NHS*, Buckingham, Open University Press.

Hatcher, P. R. (1997), 'The health system of the United Kingdom', in Raffell, M. W. (ed.) *Health Care and Reform in Industrialized Countries*, University Park, PA, Pennsylvania State University Press.

Hayek, F. A. (1944), *The Road to Serfdom*, London, Routledge and Kegan Paul.

Hayek, F. A. (1960), *The Constitution of Liberty*, London, Routledge and Kegan Paul.

Heidenheimer, A. (1979), 'Public capabilities and health care effectiveness: implications from a comparative perspective', *Journal of Health Politics, Policy and Law*, 4:3, 491–506.

Heidenheimer, A. J. (1980), 'Conflict and compromises between professional and bureaucratic health interests 1947–72', in Heidenheimer, A. J. and Elvander, N. with Hultén, C. (eds) *The Shaping of the Swedish Health System*, London, Croom Helm.

Heidenheimer, A. J., Heclo, H. and Teich Adams, C. (1976), *Comparative Public Policy. The politics of social choice in Europe and America*, Basingstoke, Macmillan.

Henke, K.-D. (1986), 'A "concerted" approach to health care financing in the Federal Republic of Germany', *Health Policy*, 6, 341–351.

Henriksson, B. and Ytterberg, H. (1992), 'Sweden: the power of the Moral(istic) Left', in Kirp, D. and Bayer, R. (eds) *AIDS in the Industrialised Democracies: passions, politics and policies*, New Brunswick, Rutgers University Press.

Hermans, H. E. G. M. and France, G. (1998), 'Choices in health care in Italy and the Netherlands: II. Legal dimensions', in Leidl, R. (ed.) *Health Care and its Financing in the Single European Market*, Amsterdam, IOS Press.

Hermesse, J., Lewalle, H. and Palm, W. (1997), 'Patient mobility within the European Union', *European Journal of Public Health*, 7:3, 4–10.

Herzlich, C. and Pierret, J. (1987), *Illness and Self in Society*, Baltimore, Johns Hopkins University Press.

Hinrichs, K. (1995), 'The impact of German health insurance reforms on redistribution and the culture of solidarity', *Journal of Health Politics, Policy and Law*, 20:3, 653–687.

Hirschman, A. O. (1970), *Exit, Voice, and Loyalty: responses to decline in firms, organizations, and states*, Cambridge, MA, Harvard University Press.

Hitiris, T. and Posnett, J. (1992), 'The determinants and effects of health expenditure in developed countries', *Journal of Health Economics*, 11, 173–181.

Holliday, I. (1992), *The NHS Transformed*, Manchester, Baseline Books.

Honigsbaum, F. (1979), *The Division in British Medicine*, London, Kogan Page.

Hsiao, W. C. (1992), 'Introduction: what nations can learn from one another', *Journal of Health Politics, Policy and Law*, 17:4, 613–636.

Hsiao, W. C. (1995), 'Abnormal economics in the health sector', *Health Policy*, 32, 125–139.

Hubert, B. and Roure, C. (1993), 'Communicable disease surveillance in France', in Normand, C. E. M. and Vaughan, P. (eds) *Europe without Frontiers. The implications for health*, Chichester, Wiley.

Hughes, E. C. (1958), *Men and their Work*, Glencoe, IL, Free Press.

Hurst, J. (1991), 'Reform of health care in Germany', *Health Care Financing Review*, 12:3, 73–86.

Hurst, J. and Poullier, J.-P. (1992), 'Paths to health reform', *OECD Observer*, 179, 4–7.

Illich, I. (1976), *Limits to Medicine. Medical nemesis: the expropriation of health*, London, Marion Boyars.

Immergut, E. (1990), 'Institutions, veto points and policy results: a comparative analysis of health care', *Journal of Public Policy*, 10:4, 341–416.

Immergut, E. (1992), *Health Politics. Interests and institutions in western Europe*, Cambridge, Cambridge University Press.

Ito, H. (1980), 'Health insurance and medical services in Sweden and Denmark 1850–1950', in Heidenheimer, A. J. and Elvander, N. with Hultén, C. (eds) *The Shaping of the Swedish Health System*, London, Croom Helm.

Jacobs, L. R. (1993), *The Health of Nations: public opinion and the making of American and British health policy*, Ithaca, Cornell University Press.

Johnson, T. (1972), *Professions and Power*, London, Macmillan.

Johnson, T. (1993), 'Expertise and the state', in Gane, M. and Johnson, T. (eds) *Foucault's New Domains*, London, Routledge.

Johnson, T. (1995), 'Governmentality and the institutionalization of expertise', in Johnson, T., Larkin, G. and Saks, M. (eds) *Health Professions and the State in Europe*, London, Routledge.

Jones, B. (1996), 'Sweden', in Wall, A. (ed.) *Health Care Systems in Liberal Democracies*, London, Routledge.

Jones, C. (1985), *Patterns of Social Policy*, London, Tavistock.

Jordan, G. (1990), 'The pluralism of pluralism: an anti-theory?', *Political Studies*, 38:2, 286–301.

Kamke, K. (1998), 'The German health care system and health care reform', *Health Policy*, 43, 171–194.

Kervasdoué, J. de and Rodwin, V. G. (1984), 'Health policy and the expanding role of the state: 1945–1980', in Kervasdoué, J. de, Kimberley, J. R. and Rodwin, V. G. (eds) *The End of an Illusion. The future of health policy in western industrialised nations*, Berkeley, University of California Press.

Kervasdoué, J. de, Kimberley, J. R. and Rodwin, V. G. (1984), 'Introduction. The end of an illusion', in Kervasdoué, J. de, Kimberley, J. R. and Rodwin, V. G. (eds) *The End of an Illusion. The future of health policy in western industrialised nations*, Berkeley, University of California Press.

Kervasdoué, J. de, Meyer, C., Weill, C. and Couffinhal, A. (1997), 'French health care system: inconsistent regulation', in Altenstetter, C. and Björkman, J. W. (eds) *Health Policy Reform, National Variations and Globalization*, Basingstoke, Macmillan.

Kimberley, J. R. and de Pouvourville, G. (1993), *The Migration of Managerial Innovation. Diagnosis-related groups and health care administration in western Europe*, San Francisco, Jossey-Bass.

King, A. (1975), 'Overload: problems of governing in the 1970s', *Political Studies*, 23:2/3, 284–296.

Kingdom, J. (1996), 'The United Kingdom', in Wall, A. (ed.) *Health Care Systems in Liberal Democracies*, London, Routledge.

Kirchberger, S. (1991), *The Diffusion of Two Technologies for Renal Stone Treatment across Europe*, London, King's Fund Centre.

Kirp, D. and Bayer, R. (1992), 'The second decade of AIDS: the end of exceptionalism?', in Kirp, D. and Bayer, R. (eds) *AIDS in the Industrialised Democracies: passions, politics and policies*, New Brunswick, Rutgers University Press.

Klein, R. (1974), 'Policy problems and policy perceptions in the National Health Service', *Policy and Politics*, 2, 235–236.

Klein, R. (1980a), 'The welfare state: a self-inflicted crisis?', *Political Quarterly*, 51, 24–34.

Klein, R. (1980b), 'Models of Man and models of policy: reflections on *Exit, Voice and Loyalty* ten years later', *Milbank Memorial Fund Quarterly: Health and Society*, 58:3, 416–429.

Klein, R. (1989), *The Politics of the National Health Service*, second edition, Harlow, Longman.

Klein, R. (1990), 'Medical manpower planning: dynamics without direction', *Health Policy*, 15, 247–251.

Klein, R. (1991), 'Risks and benefits of comparative studies: notes from another shore', *Milbank Quarterly*, 69:2, 275–291.

Klein, R. (1993a), 'Health care reform: the global search for Utopia', *British Medical Journal*, 307:6907, 752.

Klein, R. (1993b), 'National variations on international trends', in Hafferty, F. and McKinlay, J. B. (eds) *The Changing Medical Profession: an international perspective*, New York, Oxford University Press.

Klein, R. (1995), 'Big Bang health care reform – does it work?: the case of Britain's 1991 National Health Service reforms', *Milbank Quarterly*, 73:3, 299–337.

Klein, R. (1997), 'Learning from others: shall the last be the first?', *Journal of Health Politics, Policy and Law*, 22:5, 1267–1278.

Klein, R. and Millar, J. (1995), 'Do-It-Yourself social policy: searching for a new paradigm', *Social Policy and Administration*, 29:4, 303–316.

Korpi, W. (1989), 'Power, politics and state autonomy in the development of social citizenship: social rights during sickness in eighteen OECD countries since 1930', *American Sociological Review*, 54, 309–328.

Korpi, W. (1995), 'The development of social citizenship in France since 1930: comparative perspectives, in MIRE, *Comparing Social Welfare Systems in Europe*, vol. 1, Oxford conference France – United Kingdom, Paris, MIRE.

Krause, E. (1988), 'Doctors, partitocrazia and the Italian state', *Milbank Quarterly*, 66:2, 148–166.

Kuhnle, S. (1981), 'The growth of social insurance programs in Scandinavia: outside influences and internal forces', in Flora, P. and Heidenheimer, A. J. (eds) *The Development of Welfare States in Europe and America*, New Brunswick, Transaction Books.

Lane, J.-E. and Arvidson, S. (1989), 'Health professionals in the Swedish system', in Freddi, G. and Björkman, J. W. (eds) *Controlling Medical Professionals: the comparative politics of health governance*, London, Sage/ECPR.

Larson, M. S. (1977), *The Rise of Professionalism: a sociological analysis*, Berkeley, University of California Press.

Le Grand, J., Propper, C. and Robinson, R. (1992), *The Economics of Social Problems*, third edition, Basingstoke, Macmillan.

Leibfried, S. (1993), 'Towards a European welfare state?', in Jones, C. (ed.) *New Perspectives on the Welfare State in Europe*, London, Routledge.

Leichter, H. M. (1979), *A Comparative Approach to Policy Analysis. Health care policy in four nations*, Cambridge, Cambridge University Press.

Leichter, H. M. (1991), *Free to be Foolish*, Princeton, NJ, Princeton University Press.

Letourmy, A. (1986), 'Qui veut, en France, d'un mode de vie plus sain?', *Social Science and Medicine*, 22:2, 125–133.

Letourmy, A. (1995), 'The economic forms of the regulation of health spending in France: negotiated waste', in MIRE, *Comparing Social Welfare Systems in Europe*, vol. 1, Oxford conference France–United Kingdom, Paris, MIRE.

Levitt, R., Wall, A. and Appleby, J. (1995), *The Reorganized National Health Service*, fifth edition, London, Chapman and Hall.

Lewis, J. (1998), 'The medical profession and the state: GPs and the GP contract in the 1960s and the 1990s', *Social Policy and Administration*, 32:2, 132–150.

Light, D. W. (1986), 'Conclusion. Values and health in the two Germanies', in Light, D. W. and Schuller, A. (eds) *Political Values and Health Care. The German experience*, Cambridge, MA, MIT Press.

Light, D. W. (1991), 'Professionalism as a countervailing power', *Journal of Health Politics, Policy and Law*, 16:3, 499–506.

Light, D. W. (1995), 'Countervailing powers: a framework for professions in transition', in Johnson, T., Larkin, G. and Saks, M. (eds) *Health Professions and the State in Europe*, London, Routledge.

Light, D. W. and Levine, S. (1988), 'The changing character of the medical profession: a theoretical overview', *Milbank Quarterly*, 66:2, 10–32.

Mackenbach, J. P. (1991), 'Health care expenditure and mortality from amenable conditions in the European Community', *Health Policy*, 19, 245–255.

Mackenzie, W. J. M. (1979), *Power and Responsibility in Health Care*, Oxford, Oxford University Press/NPHT.

Mann, J. (1992), 'Foreword', in Kirp, D. and Bayer, R. (eds) *AIDS in the Industrialised Democracies: passions, politics and policies*, New Brunswick, Rutgers University Press.

Marmor, T. R. (1983), *Political Analysis and American Medical Care*, New York, Cambridge University Press.

Marmor, T. R. and Plowden, W. (1991), 'Rhetoric and reality in the international jet stream: the export to Britain from America of questionable ideas', *Journal of Health Politics, Policy and Law*, 16:4, 807–812.

Maxwell, R. (1980), *International Comparisons of Health Needs and Services,* project paper RC9, London, King's Fund Centre.

McKeown, T. (1965), *Medicine in Modern Society. Medical planning based on evaluation of medical achievement*, London, Allen and Unwin.

McKeown, T. (1979), *The Role of Medicine. Dream, mirage or nemesis?,* Oxford, Blackwell.

McLennan, G. (1995), *Pluralism*, Buckingham, Open University Press.

Mechanic, D. (1991), 'Sources of countervailing power in medicine', *Journal of Health Politics, Policy and Law,* 16:3, 485–498.

Miguel, J. M. de (1977), 'Policies and politics of the health reforms in southern European countries: a sociological critique', *Social Science and Medicine,* 11:6/7, 379–393.

Ministry of National Health and Welfare (Canada) (1974), *A New Perspective on the Health of Canadians (the Lalonde Report)*, Ottawa, Government of Canada.

Misztal, B. A. and Moss, D. (1990), 'Conclusion', in Misztal, B. A. and Moss, D. (eds) *Action on AIDS: national policies in comparative perspective*, New York, Greenwood.

Mohan, J. (1995), *A National Health Service? The restructuring of health care in Britain since 1979*, Basingstoke, Macmillan.

Mohan, J. (1996), 'Accounts of the NHS reforms: macro-, meso- and micro-level perspectives', *Sociology of Health and Illness*, 18:5, 675–698.

Mohan, J. (1998), 'Uneven development, territorial politics and the British health care reforms', *Political Studies,* 46:2, 309–327.

Moran, M. (1988), 'Review article: crises of the welfare state', *British Journal of Political Science,* 18, 397–414.

Moran, M. (1990), *Distributional Struggles in the German Health Care System: cost containment and the doctor glut*, University of Manchester, EPRU Working Paper 2/90.

Moran, M. (1991), 'The frontiers of social citizenship: the case of health care entitlements', in Vogel, U. and Moran, M. (eds) *The Frontiers of Citizenship*, Basingstoke, Macmillan.

Moran, M. (1992), 'The health-care state in Europe: convergence or divergence', *Environment and Planning C: Government and Policy,* 10, 77–90.

Moran, M. (1994), 'Health care policy', in Clasen, J. and Freeman, R. (eds) *Social Policy in Germany*, Hemel Hempstead, Harvester Wheatsheaf.

Moran, M. (1995a), 'Three faces of the health care state', *Journal of Health Politics, Policy and Law,* 20:3, 767–781.

Moran, M. (1995b), 'Explaining change in the National Health Service: corporatism, closure and democratic capitalism', *Public Policy and Administration*, 10:2, 21–34.

Moran, M. (1998), 'Explaining the rise of the market in health care', in Ranade, W. (ed.) *Markets and Health Care. A comparative analysis*, Harlow, Longman.

Moran, M. and Wood, B. (1993), *States, Regulation and the Medical Profession*, Milton Keynes, Open University Press.

Moran, M. and Wood, B. (1996), 'The globalization of health care policy?', in Gummett, P. (ed.) *Globalization and Public Policy*, Cheltenham, Edward Elgar.

Moss, D. (1990), 'AIDS in Italy: emergency in slow motion', in Misztal, B. A. and Moss, D. (eds) *Action on AIDS: national policies in comparative perspective*, New York, Greenwood.

Moss, D. and Misztal, B. A. (1990), 'Introduction', in Misztal, B. A. and Moss, D. (eds) *Action on AIDS: national policies in comparative perspective*, New York, Greenwood.

Mossialos, E. (1997), 'Citizens' views on health care systems in the 15 member states of the European Union', *Health Economics,* 6, 109–116.

Müller, J. and Schneider, W. (1997), 'Mitgliederbewegungen und Beitragssätze in Zeiten des Kassenwettbewerbs', *Arbeit und Sozialpolitik,* 3–4, 11–24.

Murswieck, A. (1985), 'Health policy making', in Beyme, K. von and Schmidt, M. G. (eds) *Policy and Politics in the Federal Republic of Germany,* Aldershot, Gower.

Navarro, V. (1989), 'Why some countries have national health insurance, others have national health services, and the United States has neither', *International Journal of Health Services,* 19:3, 383–404.

Newby, H. (1991), 'One world, two cultures: sociology and the environment', a lecture given to mark the fiftieth anniversary of the founding of the British Sociological Association, February 1991, *Network,* 50, May, supplement, 1–8.

Newhouse, J. P. (1977), 'Medical-care expenditure: a cross-national survey', *Journal of Human Resources,* 12:1, 115–125.

O'Connor, J. (1973), *The Fiscal Crisis of the State,* New York, St Martin's Press.

O'Neill, J. (1990), 'AIDS as a globalizing panic', in Featherstone, M. (ed.) *Global Culture. Nationalism, globalization and modernity,* London, Sage.

OECD (1977), *Public Expenditure on Health,* Paris, OECD.

OECD (1992), *Reform of Health Care: a comparative analysis of seven OECD countries,* Paris, OECD.

OECD (1993), *OECD Health Systems,* Paris, OECD.

OECD (1994), *The Reform of Health Systems. A review of seventeen OECD countries,* Paris, OECD.

OECD (1998), *OECD Health Data 98. A comparative analysis of 29 countries,* Paris, OECD.

Offe, C. (1990), 'Akzeptanz und Legitimität strategischer Optionen in der Sozialpolitik', in Sachße, C. and Engelhardt, H. F. (eds) *Sicherheit und Freiheit: zur Ethik des Wohlfartsstaates,* Frankfurt, Suhrkamp.

Osborne, T. (1993), 'On liberalism, neo-liberalism and the "liberal profession" of medicine', *Economy and Society,* 22:3, 345–356.

Palier, B. (1997), 'A "liberal" dynamic in the transformation of the French social welfare system', in Clasen, J. (ed.) *Social Insurance in Europe,* Bristol, Policy Press.

Palme, J. (1990), 'Models of old age pensions', in Ware, A. and Goodin, R. E. (eds) *Needs and Welfare,* London, Sage/ECPR.

Parry, R. (1995), 'Redefining the welfare state', in Page, E. and Hayward, J. (eds) *Governing the New Europe,* Cambridge, Polity.

Paton, C. (1993), 'Devolution and centralism in the National Health Service', *Social Policy and Administration,* 27:2, 83–108.

Paton, C. (1997), 'The politics and economics of health care reform: Britain in comparative context', in Altenstetter, C. and Björkman, J. W. (eds) *Health Policy Reform. National variations and globalization,* Basingstoke, Macmillan.

Pelling, M. (1985), 'Medicine and sanitation', in Andrews, J. F. (ed.) *William Shakespeare. His World, His Work, His Influence, vol. 1 His World,* New York, Scribner's.

Pelling, M. and Harrison, M. (1993), 'Pre-industrial health care, 1500 to 1750', in Webster, C. (ed.) *Caring for Health: History and diversity,* Buckingham, Open University Press.

Pfaff, M. (1990), 'Differences in health care spending across countries: statistical evidence' *Journal of Health Politics, Policy and Law,* 15:1, 1–67.

Pickard, S. (1998), 'Citizenship and consumerism in health care: a critique of citizens' juries', *Social Policy and Administration,* 32:3, 226–244.

Pierson, C. (1991), *Beyond the Welfare State,* Cambridge, Polity.

Pierson, P. (1994), *Dismantling the Welfare State? Reagan, Thatcher and the politics of retrenchment*, Cambridge, Cambridge University Press.

Pollak, M. (1990a), 'AIDS policy in France: biomedical leadership and preventive impotence', in Misztal, B. A. and Moss, D. (eds) *Action on AIDS: national policies in comparative perspective*, New York, Greenwood.

Pollak, M. (1990b), 'AIDS in West Germany: coordinating policy in a federal system', in Misztal, B. A. and Moss, D. (eds) *Action on AIDS: national policies in comparative perspective*, New York, Greenwood.

Pomey, M.-P. and Poullier, J.-P. (1997), 'France's health policy conundrum', in Raffell, M. W. (ed.) *Health Care and Reform in Industrialized Countries*, University Park, PA, Pennsylvania State University Press.

Raffell, M. W. (ed.) (1997), *Health Care and Reform in Industrialized Countries*, University Park, PA, Pennsylvania State University Press.

Ranade, W. (1994), *A Future for the NHS? Health care in the 1990s*, Harlow, Longman.

Ranade, W. (1998a), 'Reforming the British National Health Service: all change, no change?', in Ranade, W. (ed.) *Markets and Health Care. A comparative analysis*, Harlow, Longman.

Ranade, W. (1998b), 'Conclusions', in Ranade, W. (ed.) *Markets and Health Care. A comparative analysis*, Harlow, Longman.

Rehnberg, C. (1997), 'Sweden', in Ham, C. (ed.) *Health Care Reform. Learning from international experience*, Buckingham, Open University Press.

Renard, D. (1995), 'The relations between assistance and insurance in the constitution of the French welfare system', in MIRE *Comparing Social Welfare Systems in Europe*, vol 1, Oxford conference France – United Kingdom, Paris, MIRE.

Rimlinger, G. V. (1971), *Welfare policy and Industrialization in Europe, America and Russia*, New York, Wiley.

Robb, J. H. (1986), 'The Italian health services: slow revolution or permanent crisis?', *Social Science and Medicine*, 22:6, 619–627.

Rodwin, V. G. (1981), 'The marriage of National Health Insurance and la Médecine Libérale in France: a costly union', *Milbank Memorial Fund Quarterly: Health and Society*, 59:1, 16–43.

Rose, R. (1996), *What is Europe? A dynamic perspective*, New York, Harper Collins.

Rosewitz, B. and Webber, D. (1990), *Reformversuche und Reformblockaden im deutschen Gesundheitswesen*, Frankfurt, Campus.

Saffer, H. (1991), 'Alcohol advertising bans and alcohol abuse: an international perspective', *Journal of Health Economics*, 10:1, 65–79.

Salmela, R. (1991), 'Health policies and Health for All strategies in the Nordic countries', *Health Policy*, 18:3, 207–218.

Saltman, R. (1998), 'Health reform in Sweden: the road beyond cost containment', in Ranade, W. (ed.) *Markets and Health Care. A comparative analysis*, Harlow, Longman.

Saltman, R. and Figueras, J. (1998), 'Analyzing the evidence on European health care reforms', *Health Affairs*, 17:2, 85–108.

Schieber G. J. and Poullier, J.-P. (1990), 'Overview of international comparisons of health expenditures', in OECD *Health Care Systems in Transition. The search for efficiency*, Paris, OECD.

Schmitter, P. C. (1974), 'Still the century of corporatism?' *Review of Politics*, 36, 85–131.

Schneider, M. (1991), 'Health care cost containment in the Federal Republic of Germany', *Health Care Financing Review*, 12:3, 87–101.

Schneider, M., Dennerlein, R. K.-H., Köse, A. and Scholtes, L. (1992), 'Special issue: Health care in the EC member states', *Health Policy*, 20:1/2, 1–252.

Schülein, J. A. (1983), 'Gesellschaftliche Entwicklung und Prävention', in Wambach, M. M. (ed.) *Der Mensch als Risiko. Zur Logik von Prävention und Früherkennung*, Frankfurt, Suhrkamp.

Schulenburg, J.-M. Graf v d (1992), 'Germany: solidarity at a price', *Journal of Health Politics, Policy and Law*, 17:4, 715–738.

Schulenburg, J.-M. Graf v d (1994), 'Forming and reforming the market for third-party purchasing of health care: a German perspective', *Social Science and Medicine*, 39:10, 1473–1481.

Schwartz, F. W. and Busse, R. (1997), 'Germany', in Ham, C. (ed.) *Health Care Reform. Learning from international experience*, Buckingham, Open University Press.

Scott, S. and Freeman, R. (1995), 'Prevention as a problem of modernity: the example of HIV and AIDS', in Gabe, J. (ed.) *Medicine, Health and Risk. Sociological approaches*, Sociology of Health and Illness Monograph Series, Oxford, Blackwell.

Serner, U. (1980), 'Swedish health legislation: milestones in reorganisation since 1945', in Heidenheimer, A. J. and Elvander, N. with Hultén, C. (eds) *The Shaping of the Swedish Health System*, London, Croom Helm.

Spence, R. (1996), 'Italy', in Wall, A. (ed.) *Health Care Systems in Liberal Democracies*, London, Routledge.

Stacey, M. (1988), *The Sociology of Health and Healing*, London, Routledge.

Stacey, M. (1992), *Regulating British Medicine: the General Medical Council*, Chichester, Wiley.

Starr, P. and Immergut, E. (1987), 'Health care and the boundaries of politics', in Maier, C. S. (ed.) *Changing Boundaries of the Political: essays on the evolving balance between state and society, public and private in Europe*, Cambridge, Cambridge University Press.

Steffen, M. (1992), 'France: social solidarity and scientific expertise', in Kirp, D. and Bayer, R. (eds) *AIDS in the Industrialised Democracies: passions, politics and policies*, New Brunswick, Rutgers University Press.

Steffen, M. (1998), 'Welfare systems and public health management in eastern and western Europe: the response to AIDS', paper presented to 6th annual conference of the Network of Institutions and Schools of Public Administration in Central and Eastern Europe, Prague, 18–20 March.

Steffen, M. (1999), 'The nation's blood and HIV: medicine, justice and the state in France', in Bayer, R. and Feldman, E. (eds) *Blood Feuds: AIDS, blood and the politics of medical disaster*, Oxford, Oxford University Press.

Steudler, F. (1986), 'The state and health in France', *Social Science and Medicine*, 22:2, 211–221.

Stocking, B. (1991), *Factors Affecting the Diffusion of Three Kinds of Innovative Medical Technology in European Community Countries and Sweden*, London, King's Fund Centre.

Stone, J. (1985), *The Search for Social Peace. Reform legislation in France, 1890–1914*, Albany, State University of New York Press.

Strauss, A., Schatzman, L., Ehrlich, D., Bucher, R. and Sabshin., M (1963), 'The hospital and its negotiated order', in Freidson, E. (ed.) *The Hospital in Modern Society*, New York, Macmillan; repr. Salaman, G. and Thompson, K. (eds) (1973), *People and Organisations*, London, Longman/Open University.

Street, J. (1988), 'British government policy on AIDS: learning not to die of ignorance', *Parliamentary Affairs*, 41:4, 490–507.

Street, J. and Weale, A. (1992), 'Britain: policy-making in a hermetically sealed system', in Kirp, D. and Bayer, R. (eds) *AIDS in the Industrialised Democracies: passions, politics and policies*, New Brunswick, Rutgers University Press.

Strong, P. and Berridge, V. (1990), 'No one knew anything: some issues in British AIDS policy', in Aggleton, P., Davies, P. and Hart, G. (eds) *AIDS: Individual, Cultural and Policy Dimensions*, Brighton, Falmer.

Strong, P. and Robinson, J. (1990), *The NHS: under new management*, Milton Keynes, Open University Press.

Sturdy, S. and Cooter, R. (1998), 'Science, scientific management and the transformation of medicine in Britain c. 1870–1950', *History of Science*, 36, 421–466.

Sulkunen, P. (1997), 'Logics of prevention: mundane speech and expert discourse on alcohol policy', in Sulkunen, P., Holmwood, J., Radner, H. and Schulze, G. (eds) *Constructing the New Consumer Society*, Basingstoke, Macmillan.

Swaan, A. de (1990), 'Expansion and limitation of the medical regime', in Swaan, A. de *The Management of Normality. Critical essays in health and welfare*, London, Routledge.

Taylor, R. C. R. (1984), 'State intervention in postwar western European health care: the case of prevention in Britain and Italy', in Bornstein, S., Held, D. and Krieger, J. (eds) *The State in Capitalist Europe*, London, George Allen and Unwin.

Thane, P. (1982), *Foundations of the Welfare State*, Harlow, Longman.

Thompson, A. (1997), 'Customizing the public for health care. What's in a label?', in Kirkpatrick, I. and Martinez Lucio, M. (eds) *The Politics of Quality in the Public Sector. The managament of change*, London, Routledge.

Thompson, G., Frances, J., Levačić, R. and Mitchell, J. (eds) (1991), *Markets, Hierarchies and Networks. The coordination of social life*, London, Sage/Open University Press.

Towers, B. (1992), 'From AIDS to Alzheimer's: policy and politics in setting new health agendas', in Bailey, J. (ed.) *Social Europe*, Harlow, Longman.

Turner, B. S. (1987), *Medical Power and Social Knowledge*, London, Routledge.

van de Ven, W., Schut, F. T. and Rutten, F. F. (1994), 'Forming and re-forming the market for third-party purchasing of health care', *Social Science and Medicine*, 39:10, 1405–1412.

van Doorslaer, E., Wagstaff, A. and others (1992), 'Equity in the delivery of health care: some international comparisons', *Journal of Health Economics*, 11: 389–411.

Vobruba, G. (1983), 'Prävention durch Selbstkontrolle', in Wambach, M. M. (ed.) *Der Mensch als Risiko. Zur Logik von Prävention und Früherkennung*, Frankfurt, Suhrkamp.

Wagstaff, A., van Doorslaer, E. and others (1992), 'Equity in the finance of health care: some international comparisons', *Journal of Health Economics*, 11, 361–387.

Walt, G. (1994), *Health Policy. An introduction to process and power*, London, Zed.

Webber, D. (1988), 'Krankheit, Geld und Politik: zur Geschichte der Gesundheitsreformen in Deutschland', *Leviathan*, 16:2, 156–203.

Webber, D. (1989), 'Zur Geschichte der Gesundheitsreformen in Deutschland – II Norbert Blüms Gesundheitsreformen und die Lobby', *Leviathan*, 17:2, 262–300.

Weber, A. (1990), 'Ordnungspolitische Aspekte europäischer Gesundheitssysteme', *Medizin, Mensch, Gesellschaft*, 15:2, 76–86.

Weeks, J. (1989), 'AIDS, altruism and the New Right', in Carter, E. and Watney, S. (eds) *Taking Liberties. AIDS and cultural politics*, London, Serpent's Tail.

Westert, G. P. (1997), 'State control and the delivery of health care: a preliminary study in eleven European countries', *Environment and Planning C: Government and Policy*, 15, 219–228.

White, J. (1993), 'Market choices', *Health Service Journal*, 8 April, 22–25.

WHO (1978), *Alma Ata Declaration on Primary Health Care*, Geneva, WHO.

WHO (1986), *Ottawa Charter for Health Promotion*, Geneva, WHO.

WHO (1997), *European Health Care Reform. Analysis of current strategies*, ed. Saltman, R. B. and Figueras, J., Copenhagen, WHO Regional Office for Europe.

Widgery, D. (1988), *The National Health: a radical perspective*, London, Hogarth.

Wilding, P. (1967), 'The genesis of the Ministry of Health', *Public Administration*, 45, summer, 149–168.

Wilding, P. (1982), *Professional Power and Social Welfare*, London, Routledge and Kegan Paul.

Williams, S. J. and Calnan, M. (1996), 'The "limits" of medicalization?: modern medicine and the lay populace in "late" modernity', *Social Science and Medicine*, 42:12, 1609–1620.

Wilsford, D. (1987), 'The cohesion and fragmentation of organized medicine in France and the United States', *Journal of Health Politics, Policy and Law*, 12:3, 481–503.

Wilsford, D. (1989), 'Physicians and the state in France', in Freddi, G. and Björkman, J. W. (eds) *Controlling Medical Professionals: the comparative politics of health governance*, London, Sage/ECPR.

Wilsford, D. (1991), *Doctors and the State*, Durham, NC, Duke University Press.

Wilsford, D. (1994), 'Path dependency, or why history makes it difficult but not impossible to reform health care systems in a big way', *Journal of Public Policy*, 14:3, 285–309.

Wilsford, D. (1995), 'States facing interests: struggles over health policy in advanced industrial democracies', *Journal of Health Politics, Policy and Law*, 20:3, 571–613.

Wilsford, D. (1996), 'Caught between history and economics: reforming French health care policy in the 1990s', in Schein, M. and Keeler, J. (eds) *Policymaking in France in the 1990s*, New York, St Martin's Press.

Wysong, J. A. and Abel, T. (1990), 'Universal health insurance and high-risk groups in West Germany: implications for US health policy', *Milbank Quarterly*, 68:4, 527–560.

Zola, I. K. (1972), 'Medicine as an institution of social control', *Sociological Review*, 20:3, 487–504.

Index